W9-CCA-352

SHE'S THE BOSS

THE DISTURBING TRUTH
ABOUT NANCY PELOSI

ROCHELLE SCHWEIZER

SENTINEL

SENTINEL
Published by the Penguin Group
Penguin Group (USA) Inc., 375 Hudson Street,
New York, New York 10014, U.S.A.
Penguin Group (Canada), 90 Eglinton Avenue East, Suite 700,
Toronto, Ontario, Canada M4P 2Y3
(a division of Pearson Penguin Canada Inc.)
Penguin Books Ltd, 80 Strand, London WC2R 0RL, England
Penguin Ireland, 25 St. Stephen's Green, Dublin 2, Ireland
(a division of Penguin Books Ltd)
Penguin Books Australia Ltd, 250 Camberwell Road, Camberwell,
Victoria 3124, Australia
(a division of Pearson Australia Group Pty Ltd)
Penguin Books India Pvt Ltd, 11 Community Centre, Panchsheel Park,
New Delhi—110 017, India
Penguin Group (NZ), 67 Apollo Drive, Rosedale, North Shore 0632,
New Zealand (a division of Pearson New Zealand Ltd)
Penguin Books (South Africa) (Pty) Ltd, 24 Sturdee Avenue,
Rosebank, Johannesburg 2196, South Africa

Penguin Books Ltd, Registered Offices:
80 Strand, London WC2R 0RL, England

First published in 2010 by Sentinel,
a member of Penguin Group (USA) Inc.

10 9 8 7 6 5 4 3 2 1

Copyright © Rochelle Schweizer, 2010
All rights reserved

LIBRARY OF CONGRESS CATALOGING-IN-PUBLICATION DATA

Schweizer, Rochelle, 1961-
She's the boss : the disturbing truth about Nancy Pelosi / Rochelle Schweizer.
    p. cm.
Includes bibliographical references and index.
ISBN 978-1-59523-066-9
1. Pelosi, Nancy, 1940- 2. Women legislators—United States—Biography. 3. Legislators—United States—Biography. 4. United States. Congress. House—Biography. 5. United States. Congress. House—Speakers—Biography. 6. United States—Politics and government—1989- 7. California—Politics and government—1951- 8. Women—Political activity—United States—Biography. I. Title.
E840.8.P37S34 2010
328.73'092—dc22
[B]
                                                                          2010017326

Printed in the United States of America
Set in Janson text
Designed by Victoria Hartman

Without limiting the rights under copyright reserved above, no part of this publication may be reproduced, stored in or introduced into a retrieval system, or transmitted, in any form or by any means (electronic, mechanical, photocopying, recording or otherwise), without the prior written permission of both the copyright owner and the above publisher of this book.

The scanning, uploading, and distribution of this book via the Internet or via any other means without the permission of the publisher is illegal and punishable by law. Please purchase only authorized electronic editions and do not participate in or encourage electronic piracy of copyrightable materials. Your support of the author's rights is appreciated.

To the memory of my mother, Evelyn
Your love and wisdom are deeply missed

CONTENTS

SHE'S THE BOSS

THE TITANIUM QUEEN

I am not giving the gavel away to anyone.[1]

—Nancy Pelosi

What is the first thing you think of when you hear her name?

Nancy Pelosi has pushed aside Hillary Clinton, Madonna, and Gloria Steinem as the most controversial woman in America today. A November 2009 edition of *New York* magazine featured Pelosi's face on the cover with the headline "The Most_____Woman in the United States" and offered the reader the following choices: powerful, reviled, effective, oblivious, sincere, plastic, misunderstood. The article's subtitle captured the dilemma with the question "What is it about Nancy Pelosi?"[2]

Names to describe her abound. Republicans, conservatives and independents have expressed their dislike and frustration, calling her "Queen" or "Czar."[3] Even members of her own party in the Senate who have been burned by her imperiousness have their choice titles: "she who would be queen," "House mother," "madam," "mother superior," and "mother bear with her cubs."[4] Perhaps most bizarrely, Rahm Emanuel, President Obama's White House chief of staff, calls her "mommy."[5] We'll just leave that one alone.

Despite the maternal monikers, there is more than a little Machiavelli in Pelosi. Her typical modus operandi suggests she would rather be feared than loved. To be sure.

Pelosi's influence on Washington is unmistakable. Those who work with her say she is "strategic, shrewd, tenacious, and driven."[6] She is also ruthless. As Politico quoted a Democratic insider, Pelosi "will put a bullet in the head of anyone she needs to. . . . She'll do anything it takes to keep her majority, anything."[7] And while Republicans may have true philosophical disputes with the Speaker, many have a grudging respect for her tenacity, knowing few can fight as she can. *U.S. News & World Report* senior writer Katherine Skiba noted, "One Republican called her arrogant and unafraid to stick a knife in someone's back, then added, admiringly: 'She was interested in one thing—winning—and it worked.'"[8] Even conservatives recognize her muscle and verve. Michael Franc, vice president of government relations at the Heritage Foundation, may vehemently oppose the Speaker on almost all issues, but he recognizes her strength. "She's fundamentally transformed the House of Representatives. This is 'Pelosi's House.'"[9] Capable, yes, but of what? Abilities and talents aside, there is nonetheless a real unease, if not fear, of what Pelosi's House has planned for the country.

Like Hillary Clinton, Pelosi is a lightning rod. For years it was the powerful Clinton who was presumed to lead women to the apex of power and break the marble ceiling. It was Hillary who was going to leave her radical imprint. But not all predictions come true. While Hillary was plotting her path to the presidency, Nancy Pelosi was skillfully moving her political machine by raising and pushing wheelbarrows full of money to candidates around the country. So it took many by surprise when the first woman to be just two heartbeats away from the presidency turned out to be a San Francisco congresswoman. Still, Pelosi had been carrying out her leftist agenda with determination and calling in favors for years before the Clintons even arrived in Washington. When Madam Speaker took the gavel from House minority leader John Boehner in January 2007, it was Nancy Pelosi, not Hillary Clinton, who became the highest-ranking female politician in United States history.

Most people view Pelosi as a granola-liberal San Francisco ideologue. She is all of that, but there is much more. In totality, the true woman is a demanding politico who will dare anyone to challenge her. And when it's time for her to take on one of her causes, she does it with chutzpah. Social critic Camille Paglia recognized Pelosi's political abilities following her victory in getting her health-care reform bill narrowly through her House in November 2009. Paglia said, "Pelosi's hard-won, trench-warfare win sets a new standard for U.S. women politicians and is certainly well beyond anything the posturing but ineffectual Hillary Clinton has ever achieved."[10]

The problem for Pelosi is partly her liberal views. She's reliably left on every issue: abortion, taxes, the environment, gay rights, health care, defense, immigration, education. But even more startling and, in the eyes of her critics, more dangerous than her leftist agenda is the fact that she strategizes and executes like a machine political boss.

So how did a political boss from one of the most left-leaning congressional districts ride a wave to the crest of such power? It is unlikely Pelosi would win any national elections. She is wildly unpopular around the country. A few months before she started pounding the gavel, she told *Newsweek*, "Two-thirds of the public have absolutely no idea who I am. I see that as a strength."[11] But as her profile rose, her favorable ratings dropped. The findings of a WSJ/NBC poll in September 2009 confirmed that only 27 percent of those polled had a "positive" view of Pelosi, while 44 percent viewed her "negatively."[12] Furthermore, an October 2009 poll revealed that she had only a 34 percent approval rating in her home state of California.[13] And astoundingly, the results of a CBS News poll taken before the House voted on the health-care reform bill in March 2010 showed that while more than half of those questioned didn't have an opinion of the Speaker, of those who did, her favorable rating came in at 11 percent, compared with an unfavorable rating of 37 percent.[14] Yet she wields substantial power and has used her position to effect change through policies not representative of mainstream America.

The Speaker is willing to get into the trenches and fight the ugly battles many of her colleagues prefer to avoid. Her leadership skills have been debated. Author and columnist Arianna Huffington said that Pelosi is willing to take up the banner for unpopular causes—"that's being a leader."[15] Representative Tom Cole (R-OK) says, "I admire her political leadership. She's tough-minded, aggressive, knows what she believes in and acts on it. But sometimes she goes too far and isn't bipartisan, and the problems we face will require bipartisanship."[16]

Colleague and friend Charlie Rangel (D-NY) is right on when he describes Pelosi. He claims, "She has the ability like the local priest to listen. So much of it is endurance; the other is an ability to be persuasive. But whatever combination it is, they don't teach that in school."[17]

Pelosi's mastery of the insider game most definitely took place beyond the classroom walls. Indeed, Pelosi possesses the political street smarts of a party boss harkening back to the days of Boss Tweed of Tammany Hall or the Daley machine in Chicago. And that's not surprising, since her father, "Big Tommy" D'Alesandro, Jr., ran his own well-oiled machine. She saw precinct party politics up close where the means to power was deal making, backroom bargains and, when necessary, strong-arm tactics and intimidation. *New York Times* reporter David Firestone writes, "The ability to make merry while reaching for the jugular is an essential characteristic for politicians, and friends say Ms. Pelosi learned it from one of the classic political bosses and characters of an earlier era, Thomas J. D'Alesandro, Jr., a congressman, mayor of Baltimore and doler of favors for northeastern Maryland for 40 years."[18]

During her years in politics, she has often repeated her father's advice: "Throw a punch, take a punch."[19] That, undeniably, mirrors her leadership style. And her boss politics set her apart more than the fact that she's a woman. Representative Tom Reynolds (R-NY) agrees: "It's not that she's the first woman, it's her style. She's a risk taker."[20] For any skillful boss, great risk may lead to great reward.

Alliances are critical to bosses, and after every round of deal making and hand-to-hand politicking, there is one measure of success: the number of votes delivered. Pelosi is willing to build coalitions, no matter how diverse, to round up the votes she needs and to grow her power. Early on, while George W. Bush still occupied the White House, Pelosi focused on building unity within her own caucus and avoided controversial issues such as ending the military policy of "don't ask, don't tell" toward lesbians and gays, impeaching President Bush, and reinstating the draft. Congressional columnist Norman Ornstein says that she was willing to provide protection for the moderates and, surprisingly, took "a lot of heat from the left."[21]

Even after President Obama was in office, the Speaker's attempt to ram through her health-care monstrosity involved expert deal making with moderates over the abortion issue. She appeased them on their point, but shrewdly saved her larger plan. In fact, Pelosi's winner-take-all attitude was obvious when she stuck with legislation that received only one Republican vote. As she put it, "Bipartisanship is a two-way street. A bill can be bipartisan without bipartisan votes. Republicans have left their imprint."[22]

Pelosi also engaged in mind-numbing negotiations to achieve a stunning triumph with her climate change legislation. And when it looked as if she was going to come up short of the votes she needed to get her "flagship issue" passed, she took action. "Everybody out of the office. Just give me the whip list," she ordered her lieutenants. The list reveals how each member is likely to vote. Pelosi descended on the House floor and found those members she needed to get on board. California congressman George Miller, a key Pelosi confidant, likened her movement in the House chamber that day to *Jaws* as he hummed the theme music. A reporter saw her in action and asked Miller, "What is she doing?" Amused, he answered, "She's getting the votes to pass the energy bill."[23]

Political machines operate by patronage, and bosses maintain their power through the largesse they distribute. And Pelosi's muscle to protect her largesse was clear during the health-care debate as she politically outmaneuvered the president. Pelosi and Big Labor strong-armed Obama to concede the "Cadillac tax" on union workers. The president returned to the Capitol and praised Pelosi: "She's smart, she's articulate, she knows her issues. But what people don't understand is, Nancy is tough. She is *tough* [emphasis mine]."[24]

The key to the votes for Pelosi has been all the financial sources she has been able to tap. Her fund-raising prowess has fueled her money tank. Pelosi not only has a favor file stuffed full with donors across the country, but her own backyard includes a deep well. Over the years, San Francisco has filled her campaign treasuries with dollars. Moreover, in recent years, Northern California has emerged as one of *the* places to find money for Democrat candidates. Mark Gorenberg, a venture capitalist who was John Kerry's biggest fund-raiser in 2004, and his friend Nadine North, a headhunter for tech firms, embarked on a mission to help return the House to the Democrats in 2006, knowing there was plenty of money in Silicon Valley to fund candidates across the country.

And they knew whom to go to for a game plan: Nancy Pelosi, "San Francisco's reigning power."[25]

To accomplish her agenda, if necessary, the Speaker lands blows against even those in her own party. Following Jimmy Carter's loss to Ronald Reagan in 1980, she made her displeasure known when Carter conceded the election before her state's polls had closed. Pelosi saw the old guard in the Democratic Party as stale, even lazy. She wanted to awaken them from their stupor. And she was more than willing to do the shaking. She said, "We have been delinquent, or lazy, or not hungry enough."[26] And when she was minority leader, *Washington Post* reporter Lynne Duke said she was not "reluctant to bare her teeth or throw her elbows to enforce party discipline."[27]

Pelosi's insistence on party loyalty is matched by the rigid ideological positions she stakes out on the issues. Strong positions are a politician's protein. But the consequences of the Pelosi agenda and her strong-arm methods have been either ignored or shored up by the media. She claims that Republicans are operating a "criminal enterprise." On the other hand, *National Review* editor Rich Lowry says that the media gives Pelosi kudos for her talents. For example, *The Washington Post* writes that she is a "tough-minded tactician." If Pelosi were a Republican, her steeliness would be perilous. Lowry writes, "The press usually professes to like none of these qualities, and typically dubs someone exhibiting them as 'radical,' 'partisan,' 'obstructionist,' and 'mean-spirited.' "[28]

The pass she receives from the media and other elites is even more complex. Male Speakers such as Newt Gingrich or even Jim Wright would never have gotten away with saying they need a knife on the table (see chapter 6). And then add to the dynamic her liberalism. Margaret Thatcher was a tough lady—the Iron Lady. The media, however, portrays Pelosi as a tough grandmother. But those who have crossed her know better. If Margaret Thatcher is the Iron Lady, Nancy Pelosi is the Titanium Queen.

She said, "Listen, I go on the floor of the House every day and deal with people who don't want to give health care to poor little children in America. We're trying to get a job done. This is a giant kaleidoscope. One day you and I are on the same side. The next day it's the two of us against you."[29]

Just ask former congressman and Pelosi colleague Billy Tauzin what it's like to be "you." In 2004, the Pharmaceutical Manufacturers of America began courting the Louisiana congressman to take over as head of the trade association. Tauzin, formerly a Democrat but now a Republican, was sharply attacked by Democrats for having supported the Medicare prescription drug bill. Tauzin, a longtime friend of Pelosi's, requested a meeting with her to offer evidence that the negotiations between his lawyers and the trade association had not started until *after* the Medicare bill had passed. They never had that meeting but instead spoke briefly on the House floor. Tauzin's recollection is that Pelosi then told him, "I know it's not true." He was relieved, but that afternoon Pelosi delivered a harsh speech in which she accused him of making a secret deal with the pharmaceutical companies. Tauzin was stunned and vowed, "I could never trust Nancy Pelosi again in my life."[30]

Political bosses are generous with their friends at the expense of the government coffers, and toward their opponents they impose stern discipline. Boss Tweed solidified his power in New York in the 1800s through the election and appointment of his friends ("the Tweed Ring"). He was elected to the U.S. House of Representatives in 1852, and by 1860 he controlled all the Democratic nominations in both New York City and the state, and would for the next ten years. The estimated cost of his plunder may have been as high as $200 million.[31] Pelosi has elevated this political boss model to the national level with her sweeping legislation, earmarks, and perks designed with benefits and rewards for not only herself but also her allies.

To her colleagues, Nancy Pelosi embodies political tenacity. Her party hasn't had a leader who has aggressively pursued such power since the other Clinton, husband Bill, was at the helm.[32] Both the Speaker's allies and her opponents revere her mettle, and it is easy to compare her to giants like Tip O'Neill and Sam Rayburn. According to Politico reporters John Bresnahan and Jonathan Allen, "Pelosi is inarguably one of the strongest speakers in modern history—an authoritarian figure in an era of centralized power in the House."[33] She has legislated a government takeover of at least one-sixth of the economy, challenged the Catholic Church on abortion, circumvented the White House to meet with a Mideast dictator, and claimed that her liberal agenda is part of a holy calling.

Pelosi may have dazzled outsiders when she delivered her acceptance speech in 2007, calling for unity in Washington. Having just been elected Speaker of the House, she said, "I accept this gavel in the spirit of partnership, not partisanship, and I look forward to working with you, Mr. Boehner, and the Republicans in the Congress on behalf of the American people."[34] But Mr. Boehner and his colleagues, who were acquainted with her political DNA, knew better than to fall for her ruse. Instead, they prepared themselves for the limited partnership it would be.

Once installed in the Speaker's chair, Pelosi proceeded with startling speed. In less than 100 legislative hours, she shoved six major bills through her House and even took over some of her opponents' territory—traditionally Republican office space she wanted for herself.[35] And she put everyone on notice: "Democrats are in power now. It's a different world. Things will move faster now."[36]

This is a story that tells how Speaker Nancy Pelosi is steeped in boss politics, and has grafted those politics to her agenda for the country. Representative Edward Markey (D-MA) says of Pelosi, "She's San Francisco on the outside, and Baltimore inside." And while he agrees that she's a "liberal," she operates like a "pragmatist."[37]

It was the late Pennsylvania Democrat Jack Murtha who said about his friend Nancy Pelosi, "Don't think she's from San Francisco. She's from Baltimore."[38]

1

BIG TOMMY

I don't know [whom I'm running against], but it's some
no-good son of a b——.

That's all I can tell you.

—Thomas "Big Tommy" D'Alesandro, Jr.[1]

In 1940, Nancy D'Alesandro was born into a tough, gritty, unforgiving political town. Baltimore was a city that proved to be the perfect breeding ground for learning the brass-knuckled political tactics for which the Boss would later become well known.

Back then, Baltimore was a major seaport and had served as a hub for world trade since the 1700s. At one time it was the second-busiest U.S. harbor for immigrants. Irish, Germans, Poles, Greeks, Jews and Italians had built the city's neighborhoods. Shipbuilding, steelmaking and railways leaned on the influx of settlers, as did the many packing plants and canneries. Swallowed up by the rank odors of industry, Baltimore was primed for those who could marshal power by rallying the struggling immigrants longing to connect to the world beyond their neighborhoods with promises and lies they could believe in. Learning how to exploit immigrants and leverage disparate and competing ethnic fashions would later prove useful lessons for Nancy Pelosi. In those days the Democratic Party dominated, fused together by ethnic alliances and directed by the political bosses. And the bosses reigned with patronage for the public and graft for themselves, personally pocketing the spoils.

In 1926, H. L. Mencken, the "Sage of Baltimore," described the place where he would spend his entire life as an "ancient, solid town" with the "impalpable, indefinable, irresistible quality of charm."[2] Baltimore was a corrupt political town, but compared with its neighbors to the north, like Philadelphia and New York, it was considered a little more "genteel."[3]

This bustling, resilient community groomed a family that muscled its way onto the political stage. Indeed, Nancy D'Alesandro Pelosi is a member of a political dynasty. To be sure, the D'Alesandro family may not have had the influence or the name recognition of the Roosevelts, Kennedys, or Bushes, but they became a powerful Italian American family in Maryland politics.[4]

To understand Nancy Pelosi, you need to spend less time looking in sophisticated Napa Valley and, instead, examine the world of Baltimore's boss politics. Pelosi, perhaps more than any other modern Speaker of the House, is the supreme embodiment of a classic political boss. Sixty years before she became Madam Speaker, her father, Thomas D'Alesandro, Jr., had proved that he was not only a man of influence but also the complete politician. Over time, more than just his local Baltimore constituency came to know Thomas D'Alesandro. As he clawed and grappled his way up the power ladder, he forged strong and personal bonds with leaders whose power bases extended far beyond Baltimore's orbit. Eventually, presidents Franklin D. Roosevelt, Harry S. Truman and John F. Kennedy came to call him "Tommy."

Baltimore's ward heeler gave the appearance of a ruthless boss— wearing a ring on his pinkie finger and donning white shoes.[5] And Tommy D'Alesandro fit the mold perfectly. Longtime Maryland political observer Blair Lee colorfully described D'Alesandro: "Tommy the Elder [as he was called, while his son Thomas III, born in 1929, was Tommy the Younger] was the real thing, with his thin mustache, pinkie ring and silk tie. He was an authentic city ward heeler."[6]

The city's political machine was mostly immersed in white-collar crime. And while D'Alesandro may have rationalized his actions by claiming that he had the good of the community at heart, corruption was usually just one beat away. Exploiting racial rivalries, giving sweetheart deals to friends and associates through his ironclad alliance with labor unions, even turning a blind eye to a scandal involving his own wife inappropriately receiving thousands of dollars from an ally who was later found guilty of fraud, conspiracy and conspiracy to obstruct justice—these were all standard operating procedures for Tommy D'Alesandro. Even by Baltimore's smarmy political standards, Big Tommy's brand of ethical malfeasance was eye-popping.

As journalist Mark Bowden describes the Maryland political boss, "Even at the height of local bossism, the graft and patronage and outrageous public lies were perpetuated in a spirit of friendship and party (Democratic) solidarity."[7]

Baltimore native Matthew Crenson, a retired Johns Hopkins University urban politics professor who grew up in the city and attended City College (high school) in the early 1960s, described it in a similar way: "Nobody got killed, nobody's knees got smashed." The transactions were completed in a spirit of mutual interest.[8] According to Peter Marudas, who saw things up close, having served as chief of staff to two Baltimore mayors, "The organizations serviced the people, and the people supported them." The city was divided into six council districts, and each district served as a base of operation for a boss. To attain and consolidate his power, the boss had to make use of the fine art of coalition building, uniting all the competing interests and diverse ethnic groups from within the precincts.[9] Despite the many arguments that Baltimore's bossism was tamer, the operatives in this Maryland city could be ruthless, raiding the electorate for their votes and handing the plunder over to those who had worked their way into the machine. It had plenty of its own stories of payoffs and scandals.

Although there was never any direct evidence that Big Tommy was working directly with the Mob, that did not prevent speculation. As Lee Bernstein puts it in his book *The Greatest Menace: Organized Crime in Cold War America*, "These postwar gangsters were in fact the ultimate organization men. Racketeering, drug smuggling, prostitution, gambling, and the other crimes targeted by police and investigative agencies were transformed from the work of 'mobs' to 'organized' crime. Among the most visible targets of suspicion were Frank Costello, Johnny Dio, Tony Provenzano, Jimmy Hoffa, Tommy D'Alesandro, Jr., William O'Dwyer, and countless others."[10]

Until 1928, the Baltimore political machine was run by John S. "Frank" Kelly and John J. "Sonny" Mahon, both Irish Catholic bosses. And like their machines, both men were incredibly fat. It was understood that these two would do anything to win. Mahon's motto: "Politics is my business, and I make it pay. I would be a fool not to."

Both Kelly and Mahon muscled their way into their perches of power. As Bowden put it, Kelly "started his career collecting garbage and grew rich collecting graft." He ran his operation out of his Baltimore row house basement. He gave Christmas baskets expecting votes in return, and he had his boys ready to deal with any black who tried to vote in his district on Election Day. His rival, Mahon, literally beat his way into the machine, using his fists on a ward leader. He was known as a dishonest pinochle player. A Baltimore pol who played with Mahon at the Rennert Hotel, which was razed in 1941, once recalled, "[Mahon] usually won, because he cheated. I caught him once, pulling an ace out of his vest pocket."[11]

It was around the time of these two bosses' deaths that Tommy D'Alesandro, Jr., or "Big Tommy," entered this rough political world. There were a few new bosses trying to strengthen their base and reincarnate the Kelly and Mahon machines, but none ever achieved that level of power. The party machine bosses were now merely "bosslets" working from their districts or wards, lieutenants left over from the Kelly-Mahon years. Power in Baltimore rested on the ethnic makeup of the neighborhoods. The more homogenous the district, the more powerful the boss.[12] Tommy's base would become East Baltimore's Little Italy, a neighborhood at the eastern edge of the Inner Harbor that comprised about 12 square blocks. The early residents were largely immigrants from Genoa who had left Italy with dreams of finding gold in California. They moved into hostelries along the bustling waterfront, and many traded their hopes of gold for jobs as laborers in Baltimore. The next wave of Italian immigrants was from central Italy[13] and included D'Alesandro's father.

· Thomas Ludwig John D'Alesandro, Jr., was born in Baltimore's Little Italy in 1903, the fourth of 13 children. His father, Thomas D'Alesandro, Sr., "Tomaso," was from the mountains of Abruzzi, Italy. He was a hard worker, digging a railroad tunnel, laboring in both a munitions plant and a rock quarry, and starting up a little grocery store that failed under the burden of customers purchasing on credit.[14]

Tommy was born with political instincts. When he was only eight years old he served as an altar boy at St. Leo's Catholic Church, the heartbeat of Little Italy. It was around this time that he discovered a world beyond Little Italy. The Jewish community around Lombard Street was a few blocks away. He hired himself out as a Shabbos goy—a Sabbath gentile—performing simple tasks for Orthodox Jews on the Sabbath.[15] As a young man, he showed a penchant for reaching out and forging alliances. And his early contacts in and around Little Italy were the power base that would later expand his political reach and control.

Tommy never finished the eighth grade. The story goes that for almost eight years he was a student at St. Leo's Parochial School, the same school all of Nancy's brothers would one day attend. While under the schooling of Sister Pauline, he won a spelling bee in the eighth grade. When a boy saw him wearing his prize medal of the Blessed Virgin, he called Tommy a "sissy." Tommy lobbed a rock at the boy and cracked open his head. Sister Pauline ordered Tommy to bring his father to school the next day, but he was too afraid to tell his parents what had happened. Instead, the next morning he told her his father was sick with pleurisy. When Sister Pauline found out that he had lied to her, he promptly left St. Leo's. There were only two weeks of school left.[16]

Years later, after becoming a member of the U.S. Congress in 1939, the nuns at St. Leo's recanted of their stern discipline of young Tommy. Knowing the lofty standards the nuns had, Big Tommy found it charming that, in their eyes, his success commanded their respect. He had made a mark outside Little Italy, and they were proud of him. They planned a special graduation ceremony and gave him "his full academic honors."[17]

Tommy's early departure from St. Leo's didn't deter him. He faked his age to get ahead, and before he was fourteen years old, he secured a position with Harry T. Poor Insurance Agency, collecting dues. Later, he sold policies, the perfect training ground for the debonair, gregarious young man from Little Italy. According to D'Alesandro's eldest son, Thomas III, or "Little Tommy," "My father was a dapper man, a very attractive, handsome man. He was a great ballroom-style dancer. Won some tournaments. In those days there were very few people in Little Italy who traveled out of Little Italy. With the dancing and the insurance business, he was an attractive character." A polka-dot bow tie was his lucky charm,[18] and every person he came into contact with was a vital future supporter.

One of the neighborhoods D'Alesandro sold insurance policies in was Highlandtown. "My father was outside the Italian community early," Little Tommy said. "He broadened his horizon. He went to Highlandtown and met all the Polish people and the Czechs and the Lithuanians. He was one of the first ambassadors. He went door to door with the insurance and picked up a nickel here, a penny there. That's how they paid in those days. And that's how he built up his political base." Like Tommy, the residents of Highlandtown saw politics as a means to opportunities beyond their ethnic enclave. This Polish community groomed another female Baltimore political trailblazer, Senator Barbara Mikulski. Her grandparents owned a bakery in the neighborhood.[19]

Tommy liked being where the action was, a trait his daughter, Nancy, would one day emulate. Many of the children who grew up in Little Italy viewed the church as a place of power and authority. For many of the boys, including Tommy, the priesthood was their ambition.[20] Even his daughter, Nancy, saw it as a possible calling. "I didn't think I wanted to be a nun," Pelosi said. "But I thought I might want to be a priest. There seemed to be a little more power there, a little more discretion over what was going on in the parish."[21] But for Pelosi, the authority of the priesthood would be feeble compared with the power she would build up in a political life. Undaunted, she would one day even dare to challenge the Church's teachings on issues like abortion and gay rights.

Big Tommy was ambitious, and instead of following the priestly path, he enrolled in some classes at Baltimore's Calvert Business College. It was during this period that he discovered his true calling. Tommy liked spending his time at the Third Ward Democratic headquarters, and before long he was working for the party. He wasn't old enough to vote, but he could earn some stripes as a precinct runner. Thus began the D'Alesandro affair with the party, a union that would benefit the family and the Democratic Party for generations.

Tommy's gusto eventually caught the attention of a local sheriff at a church carnival who was eager to size up Tommy's "politico potential." The sheriff took him to meet a few of the bosses. One of them was Willie Curran,[22] who would serve two years as attorney general. Curran was Kelly's number two man, and although he inherited Kelly's machine, he never equaled his power.[23] Still, he was now one of the city's biggest players, and over the years Tommy would have his backing.

The bosses told young D'Alesandro to secure 500 signatures if he wanted to run for office. For Big Tommy that was nothing. That was how the game was played. Referring to the bosses as "entrenched politicos," Little Tommy said that they wouldn't care if his father secured 5,000 names. So when Big Tommy returned with his 500 signatures, the bosses told him that he didn't need their help.[24] And he didn't. It was 1926, and he won a seat as a member of the Maryland House of Delegates at age 22. It was the first of 23 consecutive election triumphs.

Little Tommy once said of his father's endless politicking, "My father loved every minute of it. He could walk into a funeral parlor and turn it into a rally. I can't follow that."[25] Maybe young Tommy couldn't be lured by political clout, but his little sister Nancy would follow in their father's footsteps. In the DNA lottery, Nancy clearly got the lion's share of D'Alesandro's charm, toughness and zest for political life.

Former Maryland attorney general Joseph Curran, Jr., a member of the Curran political dynasty, who also served as lieutenant governor, recalled, "The old man [Big Tommy] was a political master. He was old-school, grew up in the neighborhoods, was active in the community and he knew how to get people to like him." Curran claims that the "D'Alesandro organization" backed him when he first ran for a seat in the Maryland House of Delegates in 1958.[26]

There are accounts of Tommy's early involvement in the community's affairs. One was Prohibition—an obstacle in the world of finance and patronage. He was one of 50 young Baltimore men who formed the local branch of the Crusaders, an anti-Prohibition organization. Some of the other prominent Crusaders included Daniel Willard, Jr., son of the president of the Baltimore & Ohio Railroad, and Eli Frank, Jr., son of Associate Judge Eli Frank of the Supreme bench of Baltimore City. D'Alesandro is listed as a member of the House of Delegates. Edgar Allan Poe, Jr., chairman of the executive committee of the Baltimore branch, issued a statement thumbing the men's noses at the law: "The leaders declare that they believe the prohibition laws are vicious in effect and that they refuse to abide by them."[27]

Tommy left Baltimore for New York in 1933 on an appointment as general deputy collector in the Internal Revenue Service. It's not clear whether it was a position that he somehow finagled or a subversive move by his opponents to keep him away from Baltimore politics. But by 1935 he was back in the city he loved and had won a seat on the city council.

While Tommy was working for the IRS in New York, his rival from Little Italy, Maryland congressman Vincent L. Palmisano, from the Third District, was making it known to federal officials that one of their employees was engaging in political activity. With his fondness for deal making, the political sidelines were no place for young D'Alesandro. So he left New York and returned to Baltimore, where a few years later he would take his rival on. Little Tommy said, "[Palmisano] always saw my father as an irritant. Didn't like his style."[28]

In 1938, Tommy challenged Palmisano for his Third Congressional District seat in the U.S. House of Representatives. Palmisano had broken new ground as one of the first Italian Americans to be elected to the U.S. Congress. But there was both political and personal animosity between the two. D'Alesandro was for the New Deal and a Roosevelt man. Palmisano was not. And although the two were neighbors, Palmisano was not an early strong supporter of Tommy. But what was most telling about their relationship was that Palmisano didn't pay a visit to the D'Alesandro home when one of Tommy's boys lay dying of pneumonia.[29]

The Democratic primary race between the two rivals brought out Baltimore's big players. Howard W. Jackson, a former Mahon lieutenant who had been involved in his own shady business deals, was at the time the mayor. He sold insurance, and within a year of his first election, in 1923, it was disclosed that he had given his own firm a prize: one third of the city's $12 million fire insurance contract.[30] "Palmisano represented the political forces of Howard W. Jackson," according to historian Gilbert Sandler. "D'Alesandro was a lieutenant with the troops led by the famous Willie Curran. Palmisano versus D'Alesandro, both from Little Italy: it was internecine war, Italian political theater. The community licked its chops."[31]

When Big Tommy saw the printed ballots days before the election, he cried foul, saying the ballots were "unfair." His name was in fine print, while his opponents were in bold. The election board tried to explain that his name was 40 characters long, and it would not fit in its space on the ballot if it was in standard type. "But character counting was not to be the real problem of the campaign, vote counting was—in one of the most hotly contested and disputed elections in the history of the state," said Sandler.

Tommy recalled, "It was wild. I went house to house. Whenever I saw a Palmisano sign in one of the windows, I went inside and put a D'Alesandro sign in the other."

The election was a nail-biter. Tommy's sister, Jessica Granese, remembered, "He sent me into the church. He told me to pray to St. Anthony."[32] Years later, Tommy's daughter, Nancy, would ask people to pray to Saint Joseph, the Worker, for the benefits the American workers would reap if her health-care takeover became a reality.[33]

The Baltimore Sun's initial reports declared D'Alesandro the "unofficial winner" by just 48 votes. It was close, and the lead went back and forth. Big Tommy's hopeful supporters finally hoisted him on their shoulders and took a celebratory walk through the streets of Baltimore, from the downtown Emerson Hotel (the site of boss shenanigans) all the way to Little Italy. But their festivities were premature. By morning Palmisano was in the lead by one vote. Three days later the official canvass gave Palmisano a seven-vote advantage. Big Tommy, however, was not going to lose and, according to Sandler, "filed a petition for a recount." Surprisingly, within a few days the canvass nominated D'Alesandro. He won by 58 votes and withdrew his demand for a recount.[34] If the outcome is close, there is always a way to find more votes.

Cleverly, Tommy distanced himself to some extent from the old district bosses and ran a pro-labor, pro–New Deal campaign.[35] The general election was a much easier path. The Third Congressional District was behind the Roosevelt, pro-labor candidate. D'Alesandro won by 6,200 votes.

If Tommy wrote the book on how to apply maximum torque to political arm-twisting for votes during close elections, his daughter, the

Boss, is working on the second edition. Just as recently as April 2009, in a close battle in New York's 20th Congressional District between Democrat Scott Murphy and Republican Jim Tedisco, Pelosi and her gang of legal snipers were unleashed to affect the election's outcome. Former New York City mayor Rudy Giuliani wrote in a fund-raising letter: "Nancy Pelosi and the D.C. Democrats have sent in a team of attorneys to challenge Republican absentee ballots. They will not rest until the election results show a victory for Jim's Democrat opponent. Their plan is to win at all costs!"[36] Democrat Murphy prevailed. It is one of many examples of how Nancy Pelosi has applied tactics and strategies employed by her father. Big Tommy would have been proud.

Early bosses like Tommy also understood which key would open the door to their political power: making sure their people voted and others did not. Their machine operated on a simple pragmatic premise: in a democracy, most people really don't care about government. And what was the best way to motivate someone? Make it worth his or her time—promise a reward. In the end, though, the bosses knew who would receive the biggest prizes.[37] And getting others to vote was something Big Tommy understood well. Speaker Pelosi recalled hearing a conversation between her father and his political lieutenants. He needed 100,000 votes for a mayoral election, and they had to have a plan to get them. "We need this many from this neighborhood. This many from this neighborhood. How do we get them?"[38] According to Pelosi: "the most important D'Alesandro rule of all: Count Your Votes."[39]

Once, Big Tommy and one of his confidants, John Pica, were driving through Little Italy on Election Day when they heard the St. Leo's bells ringing. That meant one thing: someone was being buried. Tommy panicked. What if it was a supporter? Pica reassured him, saying, "Don't worry. He'll vote."[40]

Stories of Congressman D'Alesandro's legislative career in Washington are many. In the May 14, 1942, edition of *The New York Times*, it was reported that Big Tommy was one of the members of Congress who took the press to task for their criticism of the wholesale allotment of X-ration cards to senators and representatives during World War II; the cards entitled members of Congress to unlimited quantities of gasoline. When the *Times* questioned this practice, some members construed the coverage as a "part of a campaign to destroy and discredit all representative government." Representative D'Alesandro of Maryland agreed that the newspaper had created an "erroneous impression" and should seek to rectify the mistake.

One of D'Alesandro's accomplishments was heading up a district subcommittee that investigated the rampant squalor in the nation's capitol—"of slum housing, social diseases, tuberculosis, and other evils." On June 27, 1943, *The New York Times* published the committee's findings. "Congested Washington is dirty and vice-ridden and faces the danger of disastrous epidemics unless it is cleaned up."

After eight years in Washington, however, Tommy was itching to get back to his city and to the job he really wanted.[41] It would be easier to dole out the patronage to friends and neighbors and reap the rewards if he were in Baltimore. And even though he held a coveted seat on the Appropriations Committee, where he had a key vote on spending matters, he was ready to return home, where, as a mayor in one of the largest cities in postwar America, he could have some real power. Big Tommy resigned from Congress on May 16, 1947, to begin his reign of Baltimore.

One of the city's most influential bosses, who became a key D'Alesandro ally, was James H. "Jack" Pollack. Dan Gifford, who has won an Emmy for Outstanding Investigative Reporting, got to know several of the political bosses soon after moving to Baltimore in the early 1960s, through a friend who'd helped him even the odds in a neighborhood street fight in which Gifford was outnumbered and being tested as the new kid on the block. As he told me in an interview, his friend, Greg Binicki, needed help delivering the envelopes he collected at union headquarters and elsewhere to the designated recipients across the city. The volume of envelopes that were to be delivered ASAP was so great that Binicki needed some help. Jack Pollack was one of the Baltimore powers Gifford remembered. "He had his fiefdom in the city's heavily Jewish Northwest 4th District," he said. Pollack was an ex-boxer with an imposing physical presence. One day Gifford, who at the time was in high school, was goofing around with Pollack when Pollack took the opportunity to show Gifford some of his moves. As he told me, "Pollack had some real power punches, and he was someone I didn't want to have to tangle with."

Like D'Alesandro, Pollack had a grade school education, but he was "smart" and "dapper," wearing rimless glasses. He'd been a bootlegger during Prohibition, netting a small fortune. During his early years he'd been arrested on charges for a wide range of criminal activity, from assault to murder. He somehow always avoided conviction for a serious crime. Journalist Mark Bowden wrote, "Criminal records from his youth mysteriously disappeared from city courthouse files soon after Pollack controlled patronage there."[42]

"On Election Day it was Pollack who was handing out a lot of cash on the streets," Gifford recalled, "and he spent the time between elections accumulating cash in shoe boxes, safe deposit boxes and God knows where else. The whole idea was to hold on to power. The bosses may have had some good intentions for the community, but the bottom line was absolute, total control and power. What I saw was a political machine."

Pollack was well known for his system of bribery and payoffs. With an almost impenetrable network, he had his hands on the controls. He taught many distinguished officials how to pull strings. One of those who worked with Pollack was Deputy Sheriff Sam Greenberg. He learned that part of Pollack's strength came from giving people the perception he was getting things done. When one man's court appearance didn't turn out the way he had hoped, he blamed Pollack for not taking care of him. Greenberg later went on to own businesses on the Block, Baltimore's X-rated zone close to the waterfront.[43]

When it was time to run for mayor, D'Alesandro joined forces with Pollack. Together they would forge a long, mutually beneficial relationship. According to Bowden, "Pollack was the manipulator, and D'Alesandro was the vote-getter." Tommy served as mayor from 1947 to 1959, and the white working class thrived during his three terms. Perhaps symbolic of Tommy's growing power and prestige was the fact that he gained 100 pounds while in office.[44]

It didn't take long for the new mayor to attain command of the levers of authority. Soon after he took office, Tommy sealed the deal at Baltimore's historic Pimlico Race Course. The home of the Preakness Stakes opened its doors in 1870 and is the country's second-oldest racetrack. The anti-gambling movement began in 1910, and besides Kentucky,

Maryland was the only other state to keep its tracks open.[45] It was at this historic site that Tommy completed an essential transaction. The mayor struck the mother lode. He persuaded Governor William Preston Lane to give him and Pollack control of patronage for all state government jobs in Baltimore. D'Alesandro recalled running into his old buddy Willie Curran on his way out of Pimlico. The news had traveled fast. Curran already knew about the transaction. "I guess that means you're their boss now, Tommy," Curran said.[46]

When D'Alesandro claimed victory in his first mayoral race, in May 1947, there was a jubilant celebration in Little Italy "with confetti, honking car horns, and people screaming from the rooftops." Big Tommy was a champion of the unions, and now it was payback time. One union leader said that it was labor's turn to cast their ballot for Tommy, since he always sided with labor.[47]

From the Civil War through the 1920s, the needle trades—production of stitched-together items like umbrellas, luggage, clothes and boots—constituted Baltimore's largest employment base. Immigrant tailors started the garment trade, and German Jews were some of the earliest clothes makers. Eventually there was a garment district west of downtown Baltimore. An impeccable dresser, Tommy was fortunate enough to live in a city where the famed menswear was considered second only to New York City's.[48] But by the 1940s Bethlehem Steel was Baltimore's largest employer,[49] and a significant portion of Baltimore's working class resided in the Third Congressional District. Big Tommy D'Alesandro was their defender.

An important pillar of power for political bosses was organized labor. Bosses struck alliances with labor leaders to benefit themselves. And Big Labor was motivated to serve the bosses to reap greater rewards, such as favorable contractual concessions and political assistance in navigating through the wiles of city and state governmental restrictions and regulations involving labor. The 1940s wartime recruitment triggered a surge in the number of union laborers. Along with the New Deal programs came a working class that backed Roosevelt's agenda. The challenge for labor's muscle was to make sure these workers had the chance to vote. Anticipating the disruption these votes would cause, the Maryland legislature attempted to keep thousands of war workers out of the process by passing a law requiring voter registration a year in advance of voting. The Congress of Industrial Organizations (CIO), however, fought the attempt, and in July 1943 the CIO Political Action Committee was established for the purpose of supporting FDR's 1944 campaign. The CIO-PAC was considered most responsible for organized labor's entry into liberal politics. Soon arms of the PAC were springing up in Maryland's congressional districts, starting with the Third. And meeting with labor's champion, Congressman D'Alesandro, was at the top of the committee's list.[50]

Big Labor became an essential component of Big Tommy's machine. He understood that getting labor support really meant getting the blessing of labor bosses who would deliver the labor vote. It was a lesson not lost on the Boss. Today Pelosi counts the leadership of the AFL-CIO as one of her most important political allies. No one in the business world gives more money to Pelosi than organized labor. In fact, she receives more than the average Democrat from labor. According to data analysis from the Center for Responsive Politics, almost one third of all donations made to her campaign fund since 2001 have been from labor.[51] No one would believe Pelosi has much in common with the average member of a union. She learned from her father to strike alliances with labor bosses in order to count on the support of unions.

Boss politics is not about ideology, but about protecting and strengthening the turf. D'Alesandro embraced Roosevelt's agenda more because of the practicality of the New Deal. It toughened his control over his electorate. During Big Tommy's reign, blue-collar workers reached the pinnacle of their success. And in a place like Baltimore, the real city power was entrusted to the local and district organizations. The source of strength for these organizations existed in the blue-collar political clubs that were formed within the city's districts. "Bosses" George Hofferbert and Thomas D'Alesandro, from southeast Baltimore, were in command of the First District's Highland Clipper Club. Their organization was undeniably one of the most influential—it owned the First District's council seat from 1947 to 1971.

The clubs were most active during elections, and the demands they placed on the politicians could be intense. For example, one night before the 1950 primary, Governor Franklin Lane stopped at seven clubs.

Tommy made appearances, too. *The Baltimore Sun* described his evening in Curtis Bay, southwest of Baltimore's Brooklyn neighborhood. Mayor D'Alesandro became hoarse rallying men dressed in "sweaters and jackets and working clothes" at the Polish American Hall. Before the night was over, Big Tommy was back in southeast Baltimore, singing in a hall behind a bar for the Lithuanian Democratic Club while waiting for Democratic governor Lane to show up.[52]

Longtime politician Joseph Curran, Jr., a recipient himself of 45 years' worth of votes from Little Italy, remembers from his own rich experience in Baltimore how politics intersected with the parish. The two moving parts in the neighborhood were St. Leo's Parish and the Democratic Party, and sometimes it was hard to tell which was which. "The large events in communities were usually church-sponsored or Democratic Club–sponsored," said Curran. "If you went to a bull roast or an oyster roast or a crab feast it had to be at the church or at the Democratic Club."[53]

In a metaphorical sense, Gifford said, Baltimore's coalitions could be likened to a pyramid scheme. "It was an unusual political alliance that you had there," he explained to me. "It was almost like revolving chairs. Somebody got into office, and while they were at the top they got all benefits of the power. When their time was up, they moved over, and the next person moved up for his turn. Everyone got along in public, even though there were some tough battles behind the scenes."

While there were other, regular social events like the roasts to keep the constituents loyal, the bosses and politicians completed most of their deal making and distributing of largesse at local bars and restaurants.[54] A few doors from Big Tommy's house was a landmark that was not only at the geographic center of Little Italy[55] but also a hub of political transactions beginning in the mid-1950s: Sabatino's restaurant. Sabatino's was one of Gifford's drop points, and the recipient was Big Tommy. Although Tommy was out of the mayoral office by that time, Gifford found him as a person to be quite engaging, old-school and genuinely interested in the good of the community. "Big Tommy certainly had a lot of views that if expressed publicly would be very, very politically incorrect. He and his kind were different from many Democrat politicians today, they were blue-collar, not accumulating money in Swiss bank accounts. Even if he had, he wasn't the type that you would find in Vail hanging out with John Kerry."

But to maintain his control, D'Alesandro employed a politically moral dichotomy. Gifford said, "He had a big heart, but he was a corrupt politician, involved in big-city politics. He took alleged cash payoffs with one hand while keeping organized crime and street criminals under tight control with the other." And Gifford claims that he never opened any of the envelopes. "If you put me on the witness stand and ask, 'Did you deliver money to Tommy D'Alesandro or anybody else?' I don't know. I delivered envelopes. You can certainly connect the dots. The people in the police department got them, and some over in the courthouse and in City Hall. And they all wanted them lickity split."

According to author Michael Olesker, "Politics and law mixed with the culture of the street here [Sabatino's]." It was a place where bookmakers, judges and governors dined on a menu favorite, the Bookmaker's Salad. Ted Kennedy and Frank Sinatra were guests, and a Baltimore native by the name of Spiro Agnew frequented Sabatino's. It was the place he chose to dine the first evening after his resignation.[56]

And the patronage wasn't always about high civic matters. Sociologist Herbert Gans argued that "the image of the working-class politician as a beloved neighborhood figure is largely fiction." As long as the deals served the working person's interest, the sleaziness of the system was tolerated, if not completely trusted. "Politics was a big fat party all the time with a whole lot of bull, promising you this and promising you that," said one South Baltimore resident.[57]

A well-known lawyer who himself was involved in Baltimore politics during those years recalls how the game was played: "During D'Alesandro's administration every aspect of city government was under Pollack's influence. If you had to do business with the city of any kind, whether to open a bar or sign a contract, you first had to do business with Pollack. The odd thing was, I don't think Old Tommy had any direct hand in the graft. He seemed content to be mayor, and left the profit to Pollack."[58] Still, it is obvious that the control, perks and prestige were enjoyed by D'Alesandro.

Near the end of D'Alesandro's second term as mayor, however, stories of scandal and payoffs tarnished the surface of his mythical, celebrated standing. In the summer of 1953, Big Tommy and some members of his family, including daughter Nancy, traveled to Europe on a junket where he represented the U.S. Conference of Mayors. Immediately upon his return to the States, D'Alesandro was confronted with the news that his second-oldest son, Franklin Delano Roosevelt "Roosey" D'Alesandro, born on the day FDR was sworn into office in 1933, had been arrested on charges of statutory rape. Nancy Pelosi's brother and his cohorts had allegedly kept two young girls in an apartment for a week.[59]

Near the end of the year, young Roosey had more problems. A December 12, 1953, *New York Times* story detailed the previous charge and reported on a new one. Earlier in the year, the "20-year-old son of Mayor Thomas D'Alesandro was charged with more than a dozen other youths of morals charges involving two girls, ages 11 and 13." Surprisingly, Pelosi's brother was the only one acquitted following his testimony. He claimed that the first time he had ever seen the girls was at the trial. However, now there was a new charge of perjury. According to the *Times*, "A Baltimore city grand jury recommended today that Franklin D. Roosevelt D'Alesandro, son of Baltimore's Mayor, be prosecuted for lying during his recent rape trial. . . . The grand jury presentment said his testimony was 'willfully and corruptly false.'"

Another person's name that surfaced in the article was none other than James Pollack. The grand jury was also recommending that an indictment be brought against him. The reason: obstruction of justice.[60]

In the end, the young D'Alesandro emerged from the scandal unscathed. All charges were dismissed.[61] Pollack may have saved Roosey, but the scandal put a stain on Big Tommy's mayoral standing.

That same year, there was another revelation—one that got even closer to the operation of D'Alesandro's machine. Business dealings were catching up with Tommy's friend and big-time contractor Dominic Piracci. Piracci was found guilty of fraud, conspiracy and conspiracy to obstruct justice. He had finagled a deal that secured him most of Baltimore's garage-building contracts. Not only was he D'Alesandro's friend, he and Tommy had become family when Tommy III married Piracci's daughter, Margie, in 1952. Unfortunately for D'Alesandro, the Piracci scandal next snared an even closer family member: his wife, "Big Nancy." First, it was revealed that Piracci had removed some key names from his ledgers. And Nancy D'Alesandro was one of the names that had disappeared. During Piracci's trial, Pelosi's mother admitted that she had received payments in the amount of $11,130.78 from the contractor. Her explanation for the payments: one was a $1,500 wedding gift to their children, and the remainder of the money she borrowed to pay her debts from previous business ventures, including a skin-softener endeavor called Velvex.[62]

Big Tommy's response to the scandals was just to dismiss them. "No one is infallible. I haven't done everything right," D'Alesandro told the press. Sympathetic biographers, such as Vincent Bzdek, have papered over the scandals: "History has shrugged off the chapter as well: D'Alesandro and his three storied terms remain legendary in Baltimore. The scandals didn't even warrant a mention in the Baltimore media when Nancy ascended to office."[63] While history has pardoned Tommy and polished his image to that of a benevolent public servant, leaving his legacy at that underestimates the real background and perspective of Nancy Pelosi. There is no doubt that if similar scandals were a part of the history of the legendary Bush dynasty, or any other Republican candidate, they would not only warrant mention but would be subject to headlines, unending discussions by pundits, and reporters whose sole occupation would be to investigate further to discredit and destroy the career of the candidate because of crimes committed by a family member years ago.

Following the scandals, Big Tommy suffered a nervous collapse, and for more than four months he was a patient in Baltimore's Bon Secours Hospital. It seemed that maybe his political career was also going to cave in. While preparing to seek his third term, other Democrats perceived that the mayor was vulnerable. Six candidates saw a possible opening and filed against him in the primary. What was most telling about his standing was that only one Democratic district boss remained in his camp. But it still wasn't the end for Tommy. He carried all 28 city wards, received 80,370 votes and earned his 21st consecutive victory.[64] His win in the general election for mayor that year, however, would be his last major triumph.

Midway during Mayor D'Alesandro's reign in the 1950s, emerging modern America began to dismantle the tenets of the Old World political operations. The ethnic-neighborhood strongholds began to crumble as poor blacks moved into cities looking for the new jobs created by the demands of the war. Racial tensions festered while young white families found a haven in suburbia. Naturally, this put a huge snag in the cog of the smooth-running Baltimore political machine. During most of the 1900s, black voters represented a direct threat to the white political bosses. Early on, Kelly and Mahon recognized the challenge the demographic changes might create for their machine. So they resorted to "Ku Kluxian tactics" designed to make certain that blacks didn't vote. One strategy used during the 1930s and 1940s was exceptionally crooked. White bosses paid the "so-called black political leaders" to provide sandwiches and free booze at picnics on Election Day to keep blacks from going to the polls.[65]

Coinciding with the social unrest of the early 1950s was the rotting of the Baltimore Inner Harbor. Taverns, brothels and other questionable establishments started crowding the waterfront's landscape. "It was understood that people wanted prostitutes, wanted to gamble, take drugs. So the area near the waterfront, known as The Block, was the place where these activities were allowed to flourish," says Dan Gifford. "They did have their limits; it was strictly for consenting adults. Of course the bosses took their cut. Everybody paid their dues and were then left alone."

While the political bosses quietly benefited from these new enterprises, they loudly blamed the banks and other local businesses for allowing the Inner Harbor to go to pot. At a Chamber of Commerce convention in Pittsburgh, Big Tommy took a jab at Baltimore's businessmen, further implicating them in his city's decline. Mayor D'Alesandro contrasted the Mellons' rebuilding efforts in Pittsburgh with the works of his own local business leaders: "Pittsburgh had its Mellons. And Baltimore has its watermelons." Soon after the convention, the Greater Baltimore Committee (GBC) was created to undertake the city's renewal endeavor. Undoubtedly, Pollack was waiting eagerly for all the new building contracts. He and the mayor collaborated to push legislation that gave Big Tommy the power to conveniently condemn almost 30 acres of prime downtown real estate to make room.[66] Big Tommy was always planning ahead and on the lookout for his next power grab.

By the time D'Alesandro was in his third mayoral term, the machine began to go kaput. The social unrest of the late 1950s threatened his power base. Tommy was a pragmatist. It was time to make a move. So in 1957, while still mayor, he threw his hat into the race for governor. But by early 1958 he'd agreed to quit that race and instead make a run for a U.S. Senate seat. The Maryland Democratic party was "split by intra-party factions," and hadn't won a key statewide election since 1946. D'Alesandro agreed to run for the U.S. Senate at a conference of state party leaders in Annapolis.[67]

Big Tommy no longer had enough muscle. Although he won the primary, he suffered his first-ever election loss in the Senate race in the fall of 1958. Republican candidate J. Glenn Beall defeated him. What was most telling about his loss, *The New York Times* observed, was that the "other Democrats were enjoying a landslide in the state."

D'Alesandro's campaign for a fourth term was also doomed. Tommy was now in his fifties, and the young Democratic challenger was a former FBI agent, J. Harold Grady. Mark Bowden called it "a race between the dinosaurs and the dynamos." Even though Grady ran a campaign portraying himself as the young outsider, it was nothing more than a "new bossism"—just a little more sophisticated.[68] On March 4, 1959, *The New York Times* reported the outcome of Tommy's bid for a fourth term. "J. Harold Grady, who waged a 'good government' campaign, scored a smashing victory today over Mayor Thomas D'Alesandro in the Democratic primary election." The final vote of the unofficial returns from all the precincts: Grady 103,358 votes to D'Alesandro's 70,341 votes. The "well-entrenched D'Alesandro machine" had been brought down. It was the first time he'd lost a primary election.[69]

Big Tommy's campaign suffered the misfortunes of ill-timed patronage. Governor J. Millard Tawes, who owed some of his election fortunes to the Baltimore machine, had made a couple of key political appointments too close to Election Day. And it was clear to voters who had really made the choices. Pollack's son-in-law had been nominated to be in charge of the traffic court, and the nominee for chairman of the city elections board was none other than Little Tommy. The voters weren't up for any more Pollack/D'Alesandro deal making.[70]

According to the *Times*, "Mr. Grady had attacked the D'Alesandro administration as being bossed by James H. Pollack, a district political leader. [Grady] charged that patronage spread through the mayor's office has been typical of the administration's wasteful spending in many city departments."[71]

Big Tommy, however, just ignored critics who questioned how he handled lucrative contracts. Upon returning from his ten-week junket to Europe in 1953, where he also attended a conference of the International Union of Cities in Vienna, he was not only dealing with the charges against his son but also facing criticism about the way in which the city awarded parking garage contracts. The mayor was always big on words: "If anything is wrong, we will right it."[72] He responded to Grady's attacks in 1959 by heralding his mayoral years as ones of public improvement.

There was still some patronage left for D'Alesandro in the years after he was booted out of elective office. On February 18, 1961, *The New York Times* reported that President Kennedy had tentatively selected Thomas D'Alesandro, Jr., as head of the Urban Renewal Administration. The story went on to report that, according to reliable sources, Dr. Robert C. Weaver, whom D'Alesandro would serve under, "strongly opposed Mr. D'Alesandro's appointment, but has been under heavy pressure from the White House and John M. Bailey, Democratic National Committee chairman, to give his assent." There was further opposition to Big Tommy's appointment from civic groups concerned with urban renewal, claiming he was not qualified for the $20,000-a-year appointment. The story said that both the president and Mr. Bailey felt a "strong political obligation to Mr. D'Alesandro" for his early support of Kennedy.[73]

Less than a decade after his final defeat, Big Tommy passed the political baton to his eldest son. Thomas III captured City Hall when he was elected mayor of Baltimore in 1967. Just two years later, however, Dominic Piracci's name surfaced again. This time the charges involved bribery and illegal payments. The first case incriminated thirty-three-year-old Joseph P. Doherty, a Post Office Department official in the Kennedy and Johnson administrations. According to the May 29, 1969, edition of *The New York Times*, "Mr. Doherty allegedly took a total of $3,000 from Dominic Piracci, Sr., the father-in-law of Mayor Thomas J. D'Alesandro 3d, to influence bids on behalf of the Piracci Construction Company."

The report says that on March 15, 1968, in exchange for his "influence with Post Office officials in Washington," Doherty agreed to accept a $20,000 payoff and a public relations position with Piracci's company.[74]

The next day, on May 30, 1969, the *Times* reported that a special United States District Court grand jury had indicted Doherty "on charges of corruptly soliciting $20,000 from Piracci for using his influence on the contractor's bid for a new Post Office in Baltimore."[75]

Piracci escaped indictment in the Doherty case, but was mentioned in the May 30 piece for other criminal wrongdoing that was tied to payment for construction work thrown his way at the Social Security Administration's national headquarters. Dominic A. Piracci was fined $5,000 and sentenced to federal prison for 183 days for paying $5,000 to a labor leader.[76]

In August of that year, the *Times* reported that Piracci had pleaded no contest to a charge that he'd bribed Guido Iozzi, a corrupt Baltimore labor leader, with a $20,000 payoff in a government construction project.[77]

Little Tommy just wasn't up to playing the old game. He projected himself as a candidate who was distinctly different from his father, one who was "concerned and articulate about big public issues instead of [being] a provincial political leader." But he couldn't completely sever his ties to the past. The bosses had seen some of their power weaken with the introduction of civil service jobs, based on scores and merit. But they still had some influence in Annapolis, and the city's non–civil service positions were under their command.[78]

Tommy III did break traditional boundaries when he left the confines of Little Italy for the beckoning new neighborhoods. He maintained some ties by attending Mass at St. Leo's and making visits to his parents, but the church, the party and the community were no longer as interconnected. More important, however, he just didn't possess the same zeal that his father and, later, his sister, Nancy, would have for the political game. And young Nancy learned many valuable lessons about how to play the game successfully living in Big Tommy D'Alesandro's house. According to journalist Mark Barabak, Pelosi "trained literally at the knee of a master—her father."[79]

2

BASIC TRAINING

Some predictions come true. In celebration of Nancy Patricia D'Alesandro's birth, a Baltimore newspaper headline declared: "D'Alesandro Will Find New Boss in First Daughter." The story went on to make another speculation: "This little lady will soon be a 'Queen' in her own right."[1]

"Little Nancy" was born on March 26, 1940, just a little more than a year after Big Tommy had been sworn in as a member of the 76th Congress. In fact, even as she was entering the world, her father was on the House floor doing what he did best: collecting votes. This time it was for the FDR-supported National Youth Administration bill, which would offer job training to kids. He received a message, however, that it was time for his wife to give birth to their seventh child, and that he needed to hurry back to Baltimore. But he didn't want to miss out on the House vote. Fortunately, D'Alesandro found a colleague who would help him: he would not vote for FDR's job initiative if the other gentleman would agree not to vote against it, thereby ensuring his absence wouldn't affect the bill's outcome.[2] Now he could rush back to Baltimore to welcome his infant daughter—the girl who would grow up to become one of the most effective political bosses to work under the Capitol dome.

Big Tommy D'Alesandro, at his core, was a political operative—or, more accurately, a political boss. Power came from taking care of friends and donors with taxpayer money, and by shutting out political opponents from government largesse. As a political boss, every opportunity had to be seized, and in every opportunity was personal gain. And his young daughter would learn the same brutal art of using political power to leverage personal advancement.

Self-promotion was a given. Back in 1938, Tommy was in the midst of his first run for the U.S. Congress. When he received word that FDR was visiting Maryland's Eastern Shore, he saw much more in the visit: he instinctively considered it a chance to be photographed with the popular leader. The entire family made the trip, and according to eldest son Tommy III, or Little Tommy, "My father went over to meet him at his car, and I walked behind him." But none of the photographers took any interest in D'Alesandro. In author Michael Olesker's words, "In [Tommy's] mind, he was reaching not only for the president's hand, but a piece of the political pie, a bridge between the immigrant risen from the working class and the president descended from the upper crust. And nobody was watching." This chance could not be lost. So Big Tommy swung into action. He noticed a little girl with a box camera and asked her to take a picture of him as he grabbed hold of FDR's hand. "Glad to meet you, Mr. President." At first the young girl was not sure what to do, so D'Alesandro persisted: "Snap the picture, snap the picture." After she had finally taken the photograph, he offered the girl $20 for the camera and dropped the film at *The Baltimore Sun*.[3]

It wouldn't be long, though, before FDR would know who D'Alesandro was. Big Tommy was elected to Congress that year, and just 12 months later he finally gained entrée to the highest levels of political power when he got his "first private talk with Mr. Roosevelt" at the White House. There had been reports that Big Tommy hadn't received much patronage during his first year in office. So after their 17-minute meeting, he was asked if they had discussed patronage. "Now! Now! Why ask me? Ask the President," he responded. Undoubtedly he was pleased when FDR not only called him "Tommy" but also offered him a cigarette.[4]

Nancy was named for her mother, Annunciata (who was also called Nancy). Her mother was given that name because she was born on

March 25, the Feast of the Annunciation.[5] Although Nancy's mother was born in Italy, she and Big Tommy both grew up on Little Italy's Albemarle Street. The dark-eyed, attractive 19-year-old caught the young politician's attention one Sunday morning while leaving St. Leo's Church. He was six years older, and when they married he was already immersed in a political life. Right from the beginning, politics and family mixed. The wedding was a big celebration, by some accounts the biggest Little Italy had ever seen. Baltimore writer and historian Gilbert Sandler wrote about what became known as "Tommy's Wedding Day": "From the light of early dawn to long after midnight all of Little Italy became a carnival, with dancing in the streets, singing on the steps, and what a newspaper report called a 'long distance contest in eating.'"[6] Many of the partygoers were contacts Tommy had made from around the state.[7]

Events defined March 1940. The Japanese hadn't attacked Pearl Harbor yet, but Hitler was storming Europe. Disney released *Pinocchio*, children loved Elmer Fudd and Woody Woodpecker, and McDonald's arrived on the American scene.[8] That year there was only one female senator and eight female members of the House.[9]

Fortunately, Little Nancy had just been born into enviable circumstances for a future political boss. Politics truly was in her genes. Her home would provide the best basic training available for someone who decades later would command her own political operation. While there is a prevailing assumption that Speaker Pelosi is just a granola-type politician who represents San Francisco values, that notion misses the core of who she is. While she may embrace leftist values, the "Left Coast" label belies her true political nature. Pelosi biographer Vincent Bzdek captures well what motivates her politically: "Her particular strain of liberalism is probably rooted more deeply in the East Coast ward-boss politics her father practiced for more than 22 uninterrupted years on the streets of Little Italy."[10] Indeed, understanding Nancy Pelosi requires going beyond ideology. What separates Pelosi from other national leaders is that she understands and utilizes a powerful and intimidating political machine.

According to Gilbert Sandler, "She got her understanding of precinct politics from her father's world, watching big city political organizations at work."[11] It was a place where the strength of your power was based on what you got done and what you had to give. And to get things done you needed to build coalitions between diverse, strong groups. You had to persuade the Poles and the Italians and the Germans and the Irish and the Jews to work together. For Big Tommy, it wasn't about ideas; it was about cutting deals. Acting pragmatically accomplishes more than thinking ideologically.[12] And the lesson was not lost on Speaker Pelosi. She runs the House as her father ran Baltimore. It is her laboratory for precinct politics. Like her father, the Boss is undaunted by tests of leadership and is a master at building coalitions. Once the alliance has been created and the deal has been cut, House members know what is expected. Pelosi demands loyalty. Those who fall in line are rewarded, and those who don't receive her discipline.

Politics was the D'Alesandro family business. Tommy was only eight years old when he was introduced to the profession that his family would dominate. The 1912 Democratic National Convention was held at the Fifth Regiment Armory in Baltimore, and New Jersey's Governor Woodrow Wilson would emerge as the party's nominee. Tommy's mother must have had some curiosity about politics herself, since she made the effort to venture outside of Little Italy to attend the event with her young son.[13] For Tommy, it was just the first of several conventions. He would serve as a delegate to every Democratic National Convention from 1944 to 1968.

Tommy was the tireless, complete politician. He never left anything to chance—every detail was worthy of consideration. For example, when a supporter's son or daughter reached the magical age of twenty-one, he made certain he or she was registered to vote. He knocked on doors and carefully studied the precinct lists.[14] Fifty years later, Nancy, as her father had done, would visit neighborhood after neighborhood during her campaign for the U.S. Congress. Instead of the streets of Baltimore, however, she would walk the streets of San Francisco. And like her father, she took nothing for granted. According to close friend Anna Eshoo, a congresswoman from California's 14th District, the birthplace of Silicon Valley, "She knows that words matter. Once you put feet on them, these words walk into people's lives. There's a reality to it; she can more than hold her own—she's a master of detail."[15]

Tommy's home served as the headquarters for his well-oiled machine, and his children each had a role to play. It is well known that he kept copies of the *Congressional Record* under his daughter's bed. The D'Alesandro home almost always looked like official campaign headquarters and included hanging portraits of FDR and Truman. In the living room, brochures, placards and bumper stickers were everywhere. The only times the campaign paraphernalia was not visible were Easter and Christmas—"when the church took priority over politics."[16]

"Our whole lives were politics," Pelosi said in an interview during her first race for Congress, in 1987. "If you entered the house, it was always campaign time, and if you went into the living room, it was always constituent time."[17]

Politics in the early decades of the 1900s was more personal than it is today. The patronage provided a way for immigrants, especially their sons and daughters, to carve out their place in big, bustling cities. According to historian Sandler, "There weren't a lot of vertical lines open to those kids, and the ward was where you got jobs. They would get you jobs. And whole political machines were born out of these jobs. A job driving a car for city hall. A job picking up trash. Jobs were everything." Sandler contends that Big Tommy "was the king of it. It's just the way things were. It's not pejorative at all. These kids, you don't think they went off to Yale, do ya?"[18]

In her book *Know Your Power*, Pelosi claims that through her parents' example of public service she and her brothers learned to be "compassionate" and aware that the world outside their home was full of people needing their assistance. Pelosi wrote, "Helping others was part of daily life in the D'Alesandro household. People knew that this was where Congressman D'Alesandro lived, and would line up at our door, looking for help."[19]

But the help was not without strings. At the heart of Tommy's machine was his favor file. According to reporter Joe Feuerherd, "Favors could be called in and patronage flowed." It was an ongoing pursuit. Big Tommy taught Nancy that in exchange for fixing a problem you could get a vote. The family believed they were serving others. And brothers Hector and Joey even found positions at the courthouse.[20]

Nancy learned from her father, according to biographer Bzdek, that "elections were about taking care of people, that pragmatism trumped ideology, and that service came before ego. You scratch my back, I'll scratch yours, but be sure to keep track of each and every scratch."[21] Everyone in the family was well trained.

This is how the favor file worked. One of the first things you would encounter when you entered the D'Alesandro home was a yellow legal pad. The front door was figuratively a revolving door for constituents, and the front-room desk was used for business. This was the place to come to get things taken care of, whether it was a cracked sidewalk, a pothole, a permit, a job, a hospital room, a way out of jail or even a cannelloni dinner. Copious details were written on the legal pad, including, most important, names and numbers. Next, the information was typed onto an index card and filed. Pelosi Biographer Marc Sandalow says, "Other households had a recipe file. The D'Alesandros had a favor file."[22]

According to Thomas III, "We built up our organization with favors. It was a chore that we all did, and it wasn't really a chore. We took it for granted, and we did it."[23] Tommy added, "Just something we had to do for Daddy. We'd fill in those yellow sheets of paper from eight or nine in the morning until eight or nine at night."[24]

The favors, however, were always called in at election time. "We'd call people up and say, 'Mrs. So-and-So, we did this favor for you, and now my father is running for reelection. We'd like to borrow your car to get people out to vote' or 'you can come lick stamps' or 'you can organize a coffee klatch,'" Little Tommy recalled.[25] The transaction would be complete after the constituent carried out his or her end of the bargain.

All the children had their turn at the desk. It was Nancy, however, who became exceptionally good at working the favor file, and over time her brothers' services were no longer needed. By the time she was 13, the desk was solely her responsibility. Her mother, like many political wives, became the gatekeeper for all the favors. As Little Tommy explained, "We had our instructions—get as much detail as we could." Little Nancy would first gather the requests and then deliver them to Big Nancy. The favor file and "constituent service desk" were two things Speaker Pelosi would not forget.[26]

Speaker Pelosi claims she knew how to get things done at an early age. "Even when I was a little girl, I, too, could tell someone whom to call to get on welfare, get into City Hospital, or be accepted in the projects." Even though she wasn't allowed to greet strangers at the door, she spoke to people on the telephone. She had been trained by her mother in just how to answer the requests.[27]

Symbolically, the constituent desk would prove to be invaluable for the future Speaker's ascendancy. And today, although much more sophisticated, she has her own favor file. The file contains a list of almost 30,000 "loyal" donors, stored in the headquarters of the Democratic Congressional Committee. She manages the file personally, delivers birthday greetings, and makes telephone calls to her supporters.[28] Loyalty is at a premium and provides the glue that holds her machine together.

Pelosi has been quoted as saying about her upbringing, "We didn't know any other life. We were proud of the Democratic Party and the fact that it was for the people. That's my DNA."[29] The fact that "the people" were not just her constituency but also friends, associates, financial supporters and cronies seems to be ignored in Pelosi's account. And the fact that she has replaced her working-class cloth coat with Chanel handbags escapes her comments as well.

Pelosi was a keen observer of politics as a child. She recalls a conversation between her father and eldest brother, Tommy, in the early hours on Election Day the first time her father ran for mayor of Baltimore. Little Tommy asked his father how he thought they were going to do, and Big Tommy answered, "Let's go to the roof." It was from there they could get a good view of central election headquarters. The keys were organization and turnout. If the workers who were responsible for getting out the vote were arriving at 5:00 A.M., then the campaign would be successful. When Big Tommy and his son reached their roof, they saw what they had hoped to find: "headlights coming from every direction, converging on election headquarters." D'Alesandro accurately predicted the winning outcome: "I think we are going to give them a good run."

As Pelosi writes in *Know Your Power*, "You have to know how to count the votes—to anticipate how many people will vote for you. And in order to turn out those votes, you have to be organized on every level."[30] There is no doubt that she is organized for every battle. And both Pelosi's friends and her enemies admit that above all else she knows how to count votes.[31]

Early on, Little Nancy would have to learn to make her way through the world of "boys." While growing up, she contended with five older brothers. (A sixth brother died of pneumonia before she was born.) And when their proud father told them that this time they would be welcoming an eight-and-a-half-pound baby girl home, they were unanimous in their judgment: "We don't want any girls around here."[32] It was a scenario the future Speaker would become used to. She credits growing up with five brothers as the reason she "learned to assert my independence early." Pelosi adds, "I'm not saying I was particularly rebellious, but with all of those older brothers, I did have to find ways to hold my own."[33] And of the six D'Alesandro children, Nancy would be the one to break the confines of Little Italy and move away from Baltimore.

Big Nancy had an independent streak as well. Like her daughter, she graduated from the Institute of Notre Dame, an all-girls Catholic school still located in Baltimore. It was the 1920s, and, following graduation, she broke ground by securing a position as Baltimore's first female auctioneer. According to some accounts, she had to sneak out of the house, not wanting to tell her parents that her job was really a man's job. When they did find out, they didn't like the idea—that was just not a woman's territory. Eventually the company thought Big Nancy was ready to take her talents to New York. To that her family said no.[34] Instead, she married Tommy and stayed in Little Italy. For her only daughter, however, she would have different plans. A family friend recalled a story told by one of Pelosi's brothers at their mother's funeral. When Big Tommy declared that his only daughter would leave Baltimore for Trinity College in Washington, D.C., over his "dead body," his wife assured him, "That could be arranged."[35]

Pelosi admits her mother's thinking was ahead of her time. "The truth is that my father and the times held her back." For a while Big Nancy attended law school but was forced to give that up when three of her sons came down with whooping cough. She knew how to choose investments. Big Tommy, however, would not "sign off on them." She received a patent on the first gadget that softened skin by applying steam to the face, which, according to Pelosi, "she called Velvex—Beauty by Vapor. It was her brainchild, and she had customers throughout the United States, but Daddy wanted her close to home."[36] Unfortunately, some of the expenses that she incurred in her Velvex endeavor may have gotten her caught up in the Piracci trial.

Today Speaker Pelosi is a formidable leader because she possesses the strongest abilities of both parents. She started out wanting to be like her mother, and she admired Big Nancy. "She was the one. She's the star. Absolutely. If she lived in another era, God knows what she would have done . . . in anything—business, politics, the academic world, whatever," Pelosi said about her mother.[37]

According to Tommy III, "My mother was really the politician in the family, and Nancy was the apple of her eye. She takes after her. She's tough."[38]

Another brother, Nick D'Alesandro, who still occupies his parents' home in Little Italy, added, "Nancy was a carbon copy of my mother. My mother tutored her, and they were confidantes and close friends."[39]

Soon after her marriage to Tommy, Big Nancy got involved in his political world. Her basement became the headquarters for the local Democratic Women's Club, and she was its leader. It could be said that Nancy's mother was the ultimate modern-day multitasker. Years later, Pelosi would emulate her mother when she juggled her mothering duties with her obligations to the California Democratic Party. In her mother she had an incredible model of what it could look like. Big Nancy raised her children, cooked, strategized, stuffed envelopes, organized, and raised money. She tended to her family and home, but she was the one, not Tommy, who had the real political instincts. She instructed him on how to run the precincts and determined whom he could trust.[40] In the end, it all contributed to Big Tommy's winning the political game.

Pelosi herself recalled the strengths of her mother. "My mother was a boss. She wasn't one of the boys, but she was a boss."[41]

The women of Little Italy were mobilized, and were effective. And Little Nancy saw them in action. They essentially accomplished what today would be considered all the essentials of a well-managed campaign: they raised money, organized rallies, got the vote out, sponsored events to maintain voter loyalty and worked the phones. Journalist Johanna Neuman says that it was Pelosi's mom who was the "real grass-roots organizer."[42]

Little Tommy agreed that their home's cellar was where the brain trust was located, "That's where the power was, down in that cellar, all those sweet women, about a hundred of 'em who turned into the most vicious people you'd ever see in your life in a political campaign. I mean, they would go out and tear wild dogs apart. It wasn't a ladies group, it was like a pack of wild animals. They controlled precincts. They worked year 'round. They went out with vengeance from that cellar."[43]

Vince Culotta, owner of Sabatino's restaurant, said of Big Nancy, "She was a wheeler-dealer, she knew where all the bones were buried."[44]

Tommy III recalled memories of his mother. "When she met my father, she didn't know anything about politics, but she wound up knowing more than him. They weren't afraid of my father, but they were terrified of my mother." There is an account that suggests just how formidable she was. A precinct worker from the opposition got caught doing the wrong thing at the wrong time in the wrong place. According to Michael Olesker's account, when Big Nancy saw the worker ripping up some D'Alesandro Election Day ballots, she made certain the act did not go unpunished. She slugged the guy hard enough that the police had to be summoned.[45]

People in the neighborhood understood that Annunciata D'Alesandro was not someone to mess with. "Cross [my mother]? You're dead in the water," said her son Tommy. "She'd get you. With my mother, there was no forgiving."[46] Nor were the offenses forgotten.

During the years Big Tommy was in Congress there was a young Congressman from Texas by the name of Lyndon Johnson. One of D'Alesandro's aides was John Pica, Tommy's neighbor from Little Italy. Whenever Pica had any interactions with the Texan, Johnson poked fun at their Italian names, referring to either him or Tommy as "Tony." Pica told Tommy, "He keeps calling us 'Tony.' Everything's 'Tony.'"

Well, Big Nancy didn't let the offense pass. During Johnson's presidential campaign appearance at Baltimore's Fifth Regiment Armory in the 1960s, she finally had her chance to meet the Texan. She greeted him saying, "My husband's name is Thomas John D'Alesandro. It is not Tony." John Pica witnessed the exchange: "Johnson's ears started flapping. His eyeglasses got bent out of shape. They had to take him into a lounge and get his composure back."[47] Big Nancy had a way of doing that. Tommy might forget grievances, but his wife did not.

Like her mother, the Speaker possesses a great deal of inner strength. But for political purposes she conceals her emotions. Journalist Ellen Gamerman wrote, "Pelosi has distilled her mother's steely will into cool-headed pragmatism—qualities that fueled her rise in Congress."[48]

Clearly Big Tommy also shaped his daughter, and the skills that he passed on to her became sharper as she used them to go after bigger prizes. Her mother had insider sensibilities and could play the tough political enforcer, but it was her father who was passionate about the family's profession. Little Tommy recognizes that although his father was the "consummate politician," compared with his mother, he had the softer side.[49] Something Speaker Pelosi remembers her father always telling her was "Keep the friendship in your voice."[50] But for Pelosi the friendship lasts only if the troops fall in line.

Like his wife and daughter, D'Alesandro would at times refuse to be controlled by the expectations of others. Although he almost "idolized" FDR, he threw his support behind a group that openly defied the president in the 1940s. He was one of the congressmen who supported the Bergson Group, a Jewish political action committee that disagreed with FDR on his administration's policy relating to rescuing the Jews during the war. FDR believed that first the war had to be won. The Bergson Group thought otherwise. There were ways to save Jews from Hitler even during the war. D'Alesandro was one of many prominent citizens who helped the group achieve its goal. After receiving considerable pressure from Congress, FDR created the War Refugee Board in early 1944. Possibly more than 200,000 Jews escaped the Holocaust because of the board's efforts.[51]

Still, Little Nancy learned from her father that the party must come before any disagreements, since Democrats do a better job taking care of the people. As Sandalow put it, "D'Alesandro was an unwavering partisan who implored his fellow Democrats to patch up their differences in order to advance the party, much as his daughter would do in Congress 50 years later." This has been one of Pelosi's most effective weapons.

D'Alesandro was also a pro at bait-and-switch tactics. He claimed, "Republicans always play the same game. They are for big business and money interests." From whom else have we repeatedly heard those exact words? Big Tommy argued, though, that if he had to choose whom to run against, he would pick either a banker or a businessman. The reason: "They were easily intimidated." In Sandalow's book *Madam Speaker*, Tommy is quoted as saying he could "hit them in the solar plexus." The wives and mothers of the other candidates warned that he was trouble. "Stay away from the Italian boy. He's too rough. You stay away from him."[52]

Big Tommy, however, was always charming and extremely skillful at playing the partisan game. It was a game his daughter not only learned from him but, over time, became much better at than he ever was. Class warfare has been one of the big guns in the Democrats' arsenal for years, and it was a weapon Tommy used. Still, he had no problem filling his pockets with money from the classes he claimed to be protecting. For example, in November 1951, the *Afro-American* newspaper reported that the mayor had received a $5,000 pay raise. And it didn't end there. The director of public works got a $3,000 raise, and both the city solicitor and city comptroller pocketed $5,000. At the same time, the city workers who, according to the article, "work in sun, rain, snow, sleet, slush, and heat" were threatening a strike. The city offered to raise their wages from $1.10 an hour to $1.18. The workers felt that in light of the mayor's raise, they should receive at least 50 cents per hour more.[53]

In the June 18, 1939, edition of *The Baltimore Sun*, Big Tommy was described as a politician "full of fire and animation." When he couldn't deliver what he had promised, he went on the attack. Tommy was having a tough time finding employment for those he had promised jobs to. He told a *Sun* reporter who interviewed him at his home in Little Italy, "And all the time my political foes are out undermining, asking people why they aren't getting jobs. They say: 'You worked for Tommy, didn't you? Why don't he give you a job?' It's awful."

During the interview, a workman on a project at a state institution came to see Tommy. He was a stonemason who'd just found out he was going to be laid off. During his conversation with Tommy, it became obvious to the reporter that the man spoke little English. Tommy's response: "I have to talk in several languages somehow or other. This is a cosmopolitan district." The worker left Big Tommy's home with assurances that Tommy would do what he could for him. D'Alesandro said, "With all the requests for favors, a congressman has to make new friends every day to make up for the people he can't satisfy."[54]

It is expensive to keep political operations working well, so just like

Pelosi and other Democratic leaders today, the bosses were always on the lookout for more money. D'Alesandro masterfully found creative ways to slap on new taxes. Most famous was his Ad Tax, which even received mention in his *New York Times* obituary. A story highlighting the tax was featured in the January 18, 1958, edition of *The Nation*. According to author and a former *Life* editor David Cort, "It all began when Baltimore's Mayor Thomas D'Alesandro, Jr., who has firm command of his all-Democratic City Council, looked about for some new taxes to balance his city budget at a moment when he was also campaigning for the Democratic nomination for governor of Maryland. D'Alesandro is experienced, imaginative, and also impulsive."

The mayor suddenly had a revelation for a new tax: hit advertising. Of course, at the time the mediums were television, radio, newspapers and other periodicals. Big Tommy decided these mediums should charge the advertisers another 7½ percent, add 2 percent more of their own money, and then hand it all over to the city. The business community's response was clear: "Immoral!" Cort wrote, "Immediately, a thrill of sheer agony shot through the Baltimore business community." A *Baltimore Sun* editorial claimed that Big Tommy was becoming increasingly "more and more anti-Baltimore-business." The mayor's response: "Crybaby nonsense," unless the paper was saying that "I am more interested in the average Baltimorean . . . than in adding to the already swollen profits of big business, of which the Sun-papers are a most prosperous part."[55] In reality, these mediums were producing money, and Tommy's machine had to find out how to collect some of it.

The outcry to the tax was expressed in publications of the day: "dangerous and stupid," "foolish," "utterly and completely ridiculous," "utmost danger to the whole economy," "direct violation of the freedom of the press guaranteed by the United States Constitution." A six-hour public hearing was held to debate the tax. D'Alesandro didn't attend the hearing. And although he reduced the advertisers' rate to 4 percent, his city council approved the tax. Not surprisingly, other city governments latched on to the idea of an advertising tax. Cities like St. Louis and Kansas City toyed with the idea. An unconfirmed rumor was even floating around that the San Francisco City Council had contacted Baltimore to get more facts about the mayor's tax scheme.[56]

Tommy heralded his time in power as one that was hugely beneficial for the citizens. In some ways he was a modern-day Boss Tweed, targeting community projects he would be remembered for. And for all the building and spending that went on from 1947 until D'Alesandro was voted out of office in 1959, an enormous amount of money was needed. He broke ground or laid cornerstones for more than 50 Baltimore public schools. Public pools, recreation facilities, hospital additions, and firehouses sprang up. He also broke ground for the addition of two new wings to the Baltimore Museum of Art, elevating it to premier status. And Big Tommy made sure that the airport his predecessor, Theodore McKeldin, had commenced plans for was built. On June 24, 1950, he got President Truman to fly in with him to Friendship International Airport for the opening day ceremony.[57] It was a big trip for him, since he was afraid to fly. In contrast, Pelosi estimated that she had logged approximately 800 round-trip flights between San Francisco and Washington during her first 20 years in Congress.[58]

Then there were the 21,947 new streetlights installed and 1,400 miles of new streets built.[59] According to *The New York Times*, "He tried out the harbor's new radar-control system in 1949 using the ship-to-shore equipment of his own 46-foot cruiser in rain and fog. He snipped the ribbon for a new heliport in 1958, helped establish the Maryland Port Authority in 1956 and saw the opening of the harbor tunnel in 1957."[60]

The crowning achievement for Big Tommy, however, was bringing the Orioles to Baltimore. The city had not had a major league baseball club since the year before Tommy was born. But in September 1953, "after a year of dogged effort and two rejections by the American League," he succeeded in his efforts to get the St. Louis Browns moved to Baltimore. The day of the parade for the new Orioles, in April 1954, Tommy was still in Bon Secours Hospital following his nervous collapse after the scandals involving his son, wife, and friend Dominic Piracci. Yet he made sure the Baltimore electorate didn't forget that it was his triumph. Along with the Orioles' home-game schedule, his campaign posters for his next mayoral run read, "50 Years of Progress in Eight Years."[61] When his first attempt to bring the Orioles to his city had failed, he denounced the owners as "greedy," a charge that future generations of his family would use often against those who resisted their agenda. He also threatened a couple of the owners, including Clark Griffith of the Senators and Connie Mack of the Athletics, saying that "if it comes to war, the city is ready to fight."[62]

One of Big Tommy's public improvements was a $25,000 renovation of his office in the late 1950s, with the bill going straight to the taxpayer. *The Baltimore Sun* assigned a reporter by the name of Frank Somerville to City Hall to question the mayor about the upgrades. "Mr. Mayor," Somerville said, "my desk wants me to ask you why you are spending so much money on your office." As D'Alesandro bent over, he put his ear to his desk and responded, "My desk tells your desk to [expletive]!" Tommy was well known for his contempt of the establishment, often "thumbing his nose" at them.[63]

Like many big-city Democrats at the time, D'Alesandro believed that the nanny state was a good thing. It was there to take care of people.[64] But for most of those who were elected in urban areas, helping people meant enslaving the electorate for the sake of winning power and spoils. Even during his years in Washington, Big Tommy doled out as much of the people's money as he could. Spending money was the name of the game for the ambitious New Dealer from Baltimore, whether it was for public works, youth programs or jobs. After only one month in office as a U.S. congressman, he was on the House floor persuading members to fund a veterans hospital in his district.[65] Tommy was successful early on in Washington, securing a seat on the Appropriations Committee, where bills tagged for spending originate. He was also appointed as chair of the District of Columbia Committee and in that role unofficially became "mayor of DC." It wasn't until the 1970s that the District of Columbia set up its own government. So until then the committee chair presided over the District.[66]

Years later, after his daughter won her first campaign for California's Fifth Congressional District seat (after her third term it would become the Eighth), Tommy reminded Nancy that he didn't need a ticket to the House floor for her swearing-in ceremony, since he had himself once been a member of Congress.[67] When he arrived, on June 9, 1987, a few months before his death, he didn't miss the opportunity to request one final favor. This time it was for his daughter. At Nancy's ceremony, Tommy told Speaker Jim Wright (D-TX), as he rolled by him in his wheelchair, "She ought to be on Appropriations."[68] It took her only a little more than three years to get a seat at that coveted table, asserting, "It was my privilege to serve on the Appropriations Committee, and to learn from a master, our Chairman, David Obey."[69]

With his success, Tommy never compromised his Italian heritage. He never moved out of Little Italy. "I'm a paisano," the mayor once said. "These are my people. This is where I belong."[70] But he was also a patriot. During World War II, he made it clear that even though his father had come from Italy, the United States was the country that had his supreme allegiance. Tommy spoke for Italian Americans when he delivered a shortwave radio message that was broadcast to Italy through the Office of War Information. "Mussolini is just one individual. Fascism has brought nothing but destruction to the Italian nation. You are fighting for a lost cause. For the honor of Italy and yourselves, I call upon you to quit in a war you cannot win. I warned you before that the United States is a mighty nation. They do not wish to destroy Italy, but you will make it possible unless you quit now for the honor of yourselves and Italy." The next day his neighbors and constituents read the same message in the *Baltimore News-Post*.[71]

While Big Tommy truly believed that America should use force when necessary, his daughter later supported the nuclear freeze and was even against a visit by a U.S. nuclear aircraft carrier to San Francisco Bay. Their differences really encapsulate the generational shift in the Democratic Party. Tommy personified the party of Harry Truman, one that was pro-defense and dropped the atomic bomb. Pelosi represents the party of Jimmy Carter.

Although Tommy may not have left his ethnic enclave, by the 1940s star politicians were coming to Little Italy. "He was good friends with Harry Truman," recalled Dominic "Fuzzy" Leonardi. "When Truman was running for president, Big Tommy went and picked him up and brought him to his house." He and the president drove to Little Italy in a 1936 Plymouth. Almost 60 years later there were still memories of Big Tommy as well as a few scenes reminiscent of what the neighborhood used to look like. In 2006, Leonardi and his friend Michael Trombetta, both eighty years old, would pass some time on most days sitting on a bench on Little Italy's High Street.

They both remembered other future presidents and vice presidents making the trip to the Baltimore neighborhood to see "Big Tommy." Among those who came to mind were Jimmy Carter, Ronald Reagan and, of course, native Spiro Agnew. "They all came down to see him," Trombetta said.[72]

Although Tommy was a master of white, ethnic neighborhood politics, the emerging black population was a huge test for him. According to author Michael Olesker, "D'Alesandro was an untutored man pushed and pulled by the same emotional tides as his constituents. He was dealing with a city council comprised of various white ethnics. Here, he was comfortable." But the blacks were growing in number, and they were becoming agitated. Big Tommy was in a bind: he could no longer ignore them, but he also had to appease those he owed his power to.[73]

By the 1936 presidential election, the black community and the working-class ethnic voters had shifted toward supporting the New Deal candidates. Roosevelt captured a decisive victory in Baltimore that year with a huge turnout, and his margin of victory there was greater than in other key northern industrial cities, such as Philadelphia, Pittsburgh and Chicago. The most significant factor in FDR's Baltimore win, though, was the fact that he made some inroads with the black vote in city wards that were solidly Republican, and he even prevailed in one ward.[74] And while the white working classes and blacks had become unified in their support of President Roosevelt, Baltimore as a city was still divided politically by race. It was a Republican mayor in 1943, Theodore McKeldin, who united these two voting groups. But D'Alesandro was not able to hold the coalition together. In 1947, Tommy received 68 percent of the white working-class ward vote, while the black wards cast only 44 percent of their votes for him. The rest of the black vote remained in the Republican camp. "East Baltimore had a mayor—but East Baltimore was white," wrote Kenneth Durr.[75]

During Tommy's mayoral reign in the 1950s, Baltimore's population swelled to almost one million people. However, by the end of the century it had declined by a third from that high point. Throughout that same period there was an even more dramatic racial shift in the city's population. Around 1950, Baltimore's population was 75 percent white; only 50 years later it was nearly two thirds black.[76] Whites left the security of their ethnic neighborhoods for new outlying communities. At the same time, the black population began to soar. There was one thing the bosses could not control: who moved out and who stayed.[77] And in the numbers there was new muscle. The old way of doing business would no longer work as well.

Numerous accounts reveal the black community's perceived lack of support from Mayor D'Alesandro. And a personal anecdote published in the October 13, 1951, edition of the *Afro-American* relates feelings of blacks toward their mayor. Baltimore residents Mrs. Juanita Jackson Mitchell, an attorney, and her mother, Mrs. Lillie Jackson, the city's NAACP president, had toured Europe earlier that year. Mrs. Mitchell shared a journal entry that she had penned while in Sardoni Riviera, Italy: "Please let us Baltimore colored citizens give Mayor D'Alesandro, who is reluctant to face squarely questions of racial discrimination, and State's Attorney Anselm J. Sodaro (who still hasn't appointed that qualified colored assistant to his large staff in spite of the number of vacancies he has had) a free trip back to Italy to see how their ancestral brothers treat colored people, so that they may come back to Baltimore and act like sons of God should have the courage to act on racial matters."[78] Clearly, they did not regard Big Tommy as their champion.

In 1958, Baltimore hometown boy and future Supreme Court justice Thurgood Marshall also had some words for Senate candidate and current mayor Tommy D'Alesandro, at the 95th Emancipation Proclamation celebration at a Bethel AME church in the city. At the time, Marshall was the chief NAACP legal counsel of New York, and his speech that evening included advice on racial tensions mounting over a bill introduced by Councilman Walter Dixon that would end segregation in public places. Marshall said, "I think you should write Mayor D'Alesandro and tell him that if he has ambitions to go further, that whether or not he gets your vote will depend, not upon what he promises to do when he's running for the U.S. Senate, but what he did when he had the opportunity to do [it] on this bill now." The mayor did not make the event and was represented by Colonel Richard C. O'Connell.[79]

On another occasion, Big Tommy took the opportunity to dedicate a new statue in Baltimore honoring Confederate war heroes Robert E. Lee and Stonewall Jackson. D'Alesandro, who had no Southern roots, nevertheless declared at the ceremony, "We can look for inspiration to the lives of Lee and Jackson to remind us to be resolute and determined in preserving our sacred institutions."[80]

Fingers pointed at Mayor D'Alesandro when a resolution to include blacks as delegates was ignored at the state Democratic convention. Black leaders charged that D'Alesandro's forces were in charge, and the final outcome was obvious: the delegation was all white. The Democratic black leaders believed that "if the Mayor had displayed any support at all of the resolution, the naming of a colored delegate would have been a simple matter." This time the leaders did not take the rejection lightly. It was time to defy the party bosses and strike out on their own. In contrast, the Republicans elected five black delegates, which included a delegate at large and two alternates, to their national convention.[81]

By 1959 nothing had changed with Big Tommy. The *Afro-American* reported in its February 28 edition that former governor Theodore McKeldin and state's attorney J. Harold Grady, two of the leading mayoral candidates, were in favor of legislation that would end public segregation, while the incumbent, Mayor Thomas D'Alesandro, had up to that point not supported such a measure.[82] What did change that year was who would be sitting in City Hall. D'Alesandro lost to Grady in the primary.

As journalist Mark Bowden put it: "The history of black political gains in Baltimore had been one of outrageous compromises with whites until the late 1950s, when Carl Murphy, publisher of the *Afro-American* newspaper, helped push several more independent black leaders into challenging the white machines." Finally, in 1958, Mrs. Verda Welcome, who came from a well-known black family in Baltimore, put together her own ticket and fought big-time boss and D'Alesandro ally Jack Pollack on his territory. Pollack lost that one. But always willing to do whatever he needed to win, he began forming his own integrated tickets.[83]

Years later, Little Tommy claimed that his father was an advocate of the black community. "He would see to it that blacks got city jobs, the fire department, that kind of thing. He thought housing projects were a good thing because they got blacks out of the slums. On integration, the school board people get credit for keeping things calm, but my father was fine. When the word came, he said 'Let's go.' Even though a lot of people were trying to tell him he shouldn't."[84] But his recollections are radically different from the actual experience of Baltimore's black community.

In part because of the times, young Tommy's history with his city's blacks was much more positive. Initially, he wanted to win and follow his father's course. So in 1963 he offered himself as a candidate for city council president, joining Republican mayoral candidate Theodore McKeldin on his ticket. Siding with the Republicans worked for Little Tommy. He won the election.[85] And in late 1963, he introduced Mayor McKeldin's Omnibus Civil Rights Bill, which was described in the *Afro-American* as the " 'boldest and most far reaching' civil rights legislation ever introduced in a major metropolitan city anywhere in the country." Little Tommy was confident that eight members of the council would vote for the measure and seven against. That left six members who he believed would be "persuaded to vote in favor of the ordinance." Councilmen from two districts, the First and Sixth, had traditionally opposed the civil rights laws.[86] Interestingly, "bosses" George Hofferbert and Big Tommy D'Alesandro, Jr., ran the organization that controlled the First District council seat until 1971.[87]

Little Tommy had returned home to his Democratic Party when he took over City Hall in 1967. His victory was resounding. He won all of the city's 555 polling places. But only four months into his first term as mayor, chaos overtook his city. It was April 1968, and Martin Luther King, Jr., had just been assassinated. Baltimore was one of the cities engulfed by rioting and burning, and for days it was on edge. Tommy really thought there was a trust between him and the black community. While on the city council, he had been a champion of civil rights legislation, even to the disdain of some whites. He had definitely made inroads. In sharp contrast to his father, he captured 93 percent of the black vote when he ran for mayor.[88] Little Tommy, however, never really got over the turmoil following King's assassination, and after one term he left politics behind. In many ways he was naive politically and had a "softer" side as a politician. When author Michael Olesker wanted to know if his father was "stunned" by his decision, Tommy replied, "He couldn't believe it. He thought I was crazy."[89] What Tommy observed as a child and young man were no longer the political realities. "One day I just woke up and decided I would rather not put up with the hassles of being mayor anymore," D'Alesandro recalled. "When I was in office it was like war, nothing like the days when my father was mayor or in the decades before that."[90] Besides, deal making got rougher for the bosses as they saw some of their power and patronage vanish amid the rebellious culture of the 1960s.

But there was another D'Alesandro who had the guts and fortitude to run and operate a machine. She would not only put up with the hassles of politics, but would see each obstacle as an opening for amassing power and furthering an agenda designed to change the country. She, however, had moved to California and was busy ensconcing herself in San Francisco society, paving her way into the heart of that city's political machine. Soon San Francisco would witness the rise of a new boss.

3

ON THE MOVE

Anybody who's ever dealt with me knows not to mess with me.[1]

Nancy Pelosi

During her 1987 congressional campaign, Nancy Pelosi described herself as a "rabid, foaming-at-the-mouth person in the Democratic Party," and she claimed, "I'm a hardened Democrat and have never voted for a Republican in my life."[2] It would be hard to offer a better self-assessment than this.

Two months later, Pelosi was sworn in as a member of the 100th U.S. Congress. It was a circuitous path she had taken from the rough, smashmouth political environment of Baltimore to the diverse and mean streets of San Francisco. And now she had reached the equally tough, partisan environs of Washington politics. It was June 1987, and Iran-Contra was at the epicenter of the storm brewing on Capitol Hill. But for Nancy D'Alesandro Pelosi, the U.S. Congress was just another sphere in which to "operate." To fully understand how she operates today as Speaker of the House, it is crucial to understand her rise to power and how she got to where she is. It is a story, in large part, about how fund-raising and money drive politics and can lead to the election of individuals with zero policy experience. Pelosi treats politics largely as the ability to raise money and gain access to resources. She is a machine politician in the truest sense, helping her allies and punishing her enemies.

But it is also a story about how much power money can bring. As a girl, Nancy saw patronage operating on a local level. And for Big Tommy it was more about the graft and less about an agenda. Once in San Francisco, however, her husband's associates catapulted her into a realm of money that would give her the power to make her a controlling force to be reckoned with. So she seized an agenda that would keep the money coming and would therefore grow her power. The more people who live under her agenda, the more money she receives and the more power she has.

Finally, this story reveals how Pelosi is, above all else, a highly energetic "operational" woman who is unabashedly hypocritical in trying to foist her intrusive liberal agenda onto the country. In a 2005 commencement address at Goucher College in Baltimore, Pelosi said, concerning her family, "Back in the day, they would have said that politics was in our blood; today they would say it's in our DNA." Blood or DNA, politics in the wrong person can be dangerous.

Several D'Alesandros were in the galleries of the U.S. Capitol for her swearing in, including her mother and Big Tommy, who was moved to tears.[3] And surely it was a moment of immense pride rooted in a father's love for his daughter. More than 30 years earlier, in 1956, Big Tommy had had the honor of introducing Speaker Sam Rayburn at the Emerson Hotel in Baltimore. He described Rayburn as a man "among American mortals." It is quite unlikely Tommy could ever have anticipated that his daughter's path would one day take her all the way to the seat once occupied by Rayburn.[4]

For Big Nancy, her daughter's swearing in was a moment in which her plans for her daughter had come to fruition beyond what she could have hoped for. She had been held back by traditions and responsibilities, but her daughter had transcended them. And Big Nancy had played a central role in that. Tommy III understood what it meant to his mother and told *The Baltimore Sun*, "The day Nancy was sworn in was one of the happiest days of my mother's life. She was the reincarnation of my mother's ambition."[5]

But Nancy had her own ambitions, too. And unlike her mother, she was able to get what she wanted. Not only did she go beyond the boundaries of her mother's generation, but she landed in a male-dominated sphere.

Pelosi writes in her book *Know Your Power*, "I was the first daughter in history to follow her father into Congress. Several times, Daddy expressed astonishment and pride that I had won in a district that was three thousand miles from Baltimore, without using the D'Alesandro name, and nearly forty years after he had served in the House."[6] She may not have used the D'Alesandro name, but the operational skills she learned from Big Tommy and Big Nancy proved to be, in comparison, invaluable.

Pelosi's historic ascension to the Speaker's chair has repeatedly been described as a "meteoric rise." And though she moved up through the ranks of a predominantly old boys' network quickly, the rise wasn't as surprising as that. Nothing in Pelosi's political life has been left to chance. It is a dangerous game to judge the driving force in someone's life, but her track record makes her motives unmistakable. Nancy is often quoted saying that she never intended to run for political office, but the party provided her with immense power. It was the deathbed wish of Congresswoman Sala Burton, widow of the imposing former U.S. representative Phillip Burton, that put questions about the veracity of that claim to rest. The dying Burton requested that Pelosi consider running for her U.S. House seat. Nancy claimed that her decision to campaign for the open seat was solely to honor Sala's request. But was it that simple? Was it left to fate? She is always laying the groundwork for what she has decided will be her next conquest.

As Nancy rocketed to stardom, the money she pocketed became much greater than anything she had seen in Little Italy. It is true that her parents were never wealthy. "She wasn't born with a silver spoon, growing up around here," said Marion "Mugs" Mugavero, who owned a confectionery in Pelosi's neighborhood for 59 years. "She grew up like the rest of us."[7] But her childhood certainly wasn't like those of the other children in working-class Little Italy. And while she may not have inherited wealth, she acquired the instincts and drive to grab influence and use it for personal gain. Early on, she experienced the perks of political power. One of the bonuses for Mayor D'Alesandro was a big black limo and a driver. Since Big Tommy's office at City Hall was about a mile away from Nancy's school, the chauffeur would drop her off at the Institute of Notre Dame in the morning as he drove Tommy to work. To avoid embarrassment, she would insist on walking the final block.[8] Her father had that car throughout his service as mayor, which spanned the entirety of her Baltimore school days, from first grade until her first year in college.

Besides getting rides in her father's chauffeured limo, there were other benefits that came with being the daughter of the mayor. One evening she found herself seated next to a dashing senator by the name of John F. Kennedy. She took the first lady of Baltimore's place at the head table at a dinner hosted by the United Nations Association of Maryland. Big Nancy had feigned illness, knowing it would be a great opportunity for her daughter.[9] That was a mayoral perk Little Nancy was completely thrilled with.

In 1960, she had another occasion to see the emerging Democrat star up close. This time it was in Los Angeles at the Democratic National Convention. An early supporter of JFK, Big Tommy was the Maryland Democratic national committeeman. Pelosi said that their family made the cross-country trip by train (Big Tommy was afraid of flying) to the convention, where they listened to Kennedy's acceptance speech outdoors at the L.A. Coliseum. The D'Alesandros were treated well, with, according to Little Nancy, "front-row seats and special access to the Kennedy events."[10] And even though Tommy no longer held an elected position of power, he was, no doubt, hoping the young president would reward him. But none of his rewards would ever compare with the resources his daughter would one day direct, manipulate and control.

The first place Nancy moved to from Little Italy was Washington, D.C. In the fall of 1958, her brother Nicky, his friend Peter Angelos, and Big Nancy moved her out of Little Italy—at least for the time—to Trinity College, an all-women's Catholic school approximately 40 miles from Baltimore and three miles from her future office. (It is now called Trinity Washington University.) It was pretty common for someone who left the neighborhood to eventually return. But both mother and daughter had bigger plans than Little Italy. Even early on, Pelosi's life would intersect with people who would one day be useful. Angelos was at the time a University of Baltimore law student who would go on to represent labor unions and become fabulously wealthy. He is the majority owner of the Baltimore Orioles and has contributed to several Democratic candidates,[11] including Harry Reid.

Once at Trinity, Nancy gravitated to politics. She signed up as a political science major and joined the Young Democrats. In 1960, she dove into JFK's presidential campaign, working as a volunteer.

The year 1961 would prove to be significant in Pelosi's life. On a frigid day in January, she witnessed President Kennedy take the oath of office outside on the East Portico of the U.S. capitol, the site of her future office. In contrast to the tough politicos of Baltimore's districts, the new, charismatic president inspired her. According to Pelosi, his words moved her generation to action. Her impact on making a difference could be grander than parochial politics. Pelosi said that Kennedy "made my generation believe that anything was possible."[12] Local boundaries like those marking Little Italy would never contain her ability to wield power and patronage.

A few months later, she met the man whose address and financial status would one day propel her into action for her venerated Democratic Party. Nancy got to know Georgetown student Paul Pelosi while taking a summer course titled "The History of Africa, South of the Sahara" at Georgetown's School of Foreign Service. She said, "I was from Baltimore, Paul was from San Francisco, and I like to say we met in Africa, south of the Sahara." But Nancy made herself clear right away. When she mentioned she was going to the dry cleaners to pick up her clothes, Paul naturally asked if she could collect his shirts as well. Not only did she forget about his shirts, but she said, "How could he *ever* have thought I would pick them up?" She went on, "After we were married, he once asked me to iron a shirt. That didn't happen either."[13]

Still, Pelosi proved a great partner for Nancy in her endeavors. He came from a connected San Francisco family, and is Italian, Catholic and, fortunately, a Democrat. His father, John Pelosi, was a member of the San Francisco establishment, and his money came from, among other businesses, a pharmacy and a long-term lease to operate concessions at Lake Tahoe's Squaw Valley ski resort.[14]

Before they wed, however, Nancy had her first brief career on Capitol Hill, working in Maryland senator Daniel Brewster's office as a receptionist. Strangely enough, one of her colleagues in Brewster's office was another young, determined aide by the name of Steny Hoyer.

The senator prized Nancy's family name. He had NANCY D'ALESANDRO etched on her nameplate and strategically placed her at the front desk. "Having the D'Alesandro family supporting me was very helpful," Brewster said.[15] Hoyer said that the other young members of Brewster's staff knew that she was a "big wheel because of her family."[16]

The New York Times announced Nancy's engagement to Pelosi, and following their 1963 wedding, Nancy made her next move. This time it was to New York City, where Paul had a position with the First National City Bank of New York.[17] Nancy gave birth to five children within a span of six years. Four were born while they were in New York. Like her mother, she had considered law school. But for now that would not be a possibility. Pelosi was a stay-at-home mom whose days were filled with feedings, diaper changes, and trips to the park. When she could eke out some free time, two things she enjoyed as part of her parenting "survival strategy" were *New York Times* crossword puzzles and chocolate ice cream. And that still holds true today. Somehow she did manage to find time to fit in a little volunteering during the 1966 midterm elections.[18]

For the young mother, politics had an undeniable draw. In fact, you could even say it was an obsession.[19] Like her father, Nancy liked being where the action was. In 1968, she attended the Democratic National Convention in Chicago with her father and brother Tommy. It was there that she witnessed Chicago mayor Richard Daley's rage when Connecticut senator Abraham Ribicoff accused the Chicago police of using "Gestapo tactics."[20] That event more than likely left an impression on her. Name-calling has become her signature. And one can only wonder if Ribicoff would have made the same accusation of the mayor of Baltimore, Nancy's brother Little Tommy, who just a few months earlier had sent the police in to aggressively put down riots in Baltimore. Furthermore, it is hard to imagine that Big Tommy, with his blue-collar and working-man sensibilities, would have handled the student rioters any differently.

Pelosi's second-eldest child, daughter Christine, claims that one of her first memories is of campaigning for Democratic presidential nominee Hubert Humphrey in 1968. She was two years old when she and her mother knocked on doors for their candidate.[21] It must have rubbed off on her, since today she is also immersed in politics. She is the author of *Campaign Boot Camp: Basic Training for Future Leaders* and heads up a PAC that trains both candidates and activists. Some of those candidates have won seats in the House. According to Christine, "My mom says that my political activism began in the stroller."[22] Pelosi was quoted as saying during her own first campaign, in 1987, "I have never not participated in a campaign no matter how little my babies were, if I was wheeling them in a carriage or carrying them in my stomach."[23]

Like Big Tommy, his daughter was imaginative and cunning, leaving absolutely nothing to chance. She started with small strategies while living in New York. Christine said, "Every year, right before Halloween, we went door-to-door through our apartment building with election leaflets. Then a few days later we returned for trick-or-treating." Her mom still isn't certain if there was a link between the treats and the leaflets.[24]

It was 1969 when the family made their big move to California, the place where Nancy's political fortunes would soar. For husband Paul, there were much greater opportunities close to home to amass his fortune. According to Pelosi, "Paul was offered an exciting job with a new publicly held financial services company located in San Francisco. It was a ground-floor opportunity in a brand-new market, at the dawn of the Silicon Valley tech boom."[25] But his real wealth would come from real estate investments. And Paul's hometown was good to him. According to the Center for Responsive Politics, a 2007 net asset value estimate put the Pelosis' holdings at between $35 million and $156 million, including real estate and bank account assets.[26]

The year the Pelosis arrived in San Francisco, the city was in the throes of a social upheaval. The city had always been known for the interesting characters it attracted, so it was only natural that it would be the site of a revolution. Only a few years earlier, 100,000 hippies had invaded the city's Haight-Ashbury neighborhood. (Pelosi would represent Haight-Ashbury years later.) The city's cultural transformation was unstoppable, and this turmoil gave rise to new political forces. In 1964, fiery Phillip Burton was elected to the U.S. Congress, and along with his brother, John, also immersed in California politics, his wife, Sala, and future mayor Willie Brown, he created the ruthless Burton machine—a political force that revolutionized the Bay Area.

Even though San Francisco was Democratic, Republicans had not yet been completely marginalized. In fact, during the years prior to the sixties, Republicans had City Hall for 52 years, and Eisenhower had been the city's choice in both his elections. Surprisingly, in 1972 Nixon captured 42 percent of the vote, and in 1980 Reagan made some inroads with 38 percent of the electorate. But that would be the Republicans' last stand. By 2000, George W. Bush drew only 15.5 percent of the votes in the city.[27]

And while there weren't infamous machines in San Francisco like those in Baltimore, there were influential people who could make you or shut you out. Political observer and University of San Francisco professor Corey Cook says the city's politics is not really a "get-out-the-vote-and-bust-some-kneecaps" machine like Daley's in Chicago. Instead, he says the key in San Francisco is connections that have endured for years "in a small politically engaged town with high political stakes."[28] As in Baltimore and Chicago, though, the outcome is tough, hardball leaders. Pelosi would utilize her lessons in patronage and coalition building to become a winner in the city's brutal political game.

Biographer Vincent Bzdek describes it well: "She learned the territory in those years, learned where the levers and valves of a complex political town were. She found that pretty, pastel San Francisco, so different in style and reputation from her down-and-dirty hometown of Baltimore, wasn't that different politically. Both cities are Democratic port towns with strong unions running the shipping industry and therefore deeply involved in each city's political life. Both cities are a gumbo of nationalities and political leanings. In 1940s Baltimore, when she was growing up, it was Italians, Poles, Jews, African Americans, and Irish all trying to mix together as the city slowly desegregated. In San Francisco in the 1970s, it was Asian Americans, gays, hippies, whites, blacks, and the suits of one of the West Coast's most important financial districts all maneuvering for power."[29]

Pelosi, however, wasn't caught up in the social chaos. She was too busy raising her children and money from among the city's elites, whose donations would support the candidates who were serving as the agents of all the upheaval. According to biographer Marc Sandalow, 25 years later Pelosi would describe her beloved city as the "capital of the progressive movement in this country."[30] She fit right in with the Bay City's Democrats. "I immediately felt at home," Pelosi said. "I was happy. I was surrounded by Democrats."[31]

But there was a war going on between two factions within the party. There was the Leo McCarthy wing and there was the Burton machine. Supposedly Pelosi met them both—McCarthy and Burton—at Democratic fund-raisers. McCarthy had held elected office in the city's apparatus since 1963, and at the time she met him he was a member of the California Assembly. He later went on to become assembly speaker, as well as lieutenant governor, and Pelosi, using her social connections, was an engine behind fund-raising efforts for his campaigns.

Paul Pelosi's brother, Ron, who was aligned with the McCarthy wing of the party, was an established player in the city's affairs in the 1960s and 1970s, even though he was by some standards considered a little more conservative than the politicos who would eventually aid his sister-in-law in her California political ascent. He served as president of the San Francisco Planning Commission and was elected to the city's Board of Supervisors in 1967, eventually becoming its president. John Burton claims that it was Ron and McCarthy who got Nancy linked to the political network that she would one day own.[32]

McCarthy became a treasured political mentor to Pelosi and backed her fund-raising machine. He once said of his friend, "I think she has now, through battle, really honed her own talents so they're much larger than they used to be. It's useful to call people to gain perspective, but she has become more self-reliant and she needs to become more self-reliant."[33] Sandalow described McCarthy as "a soft-spoken man with a priestly presence that masked his big political ambition."[34]

And then there was the all-powerful Burton wing. Phil Burton not only represented the city in the U.S. Congress, but he was a force to be reckoned with locally. He led the civil rights movement, the antiwar movement, the early environmental movement and the movement to forge all diverse San Francisco communities into one potent, liberal party. A testament to Pelosi's brilliant tactical skills, she learned how to navigate both wings without alienating either one of the party factions. She had kept her eye on Big Tommy as he mastered coalition building while he also appeased competing machines.

Even finding a house would be political for Pelosi. After living with Paul's mother for months with four young children, it was time to find a home of their own. The plan was first to rent, but there were problems with that. It was tough to find a suitable rental with all those children. Pelosi said that during their house hunt, some owners had told them "that they'd rather rent to people with four dogs than four young children." Finally, the ideal home became available, swing set and all. Nancy said she "was thrilled. Ecstatic." But an obstacle too big to overcome would be in the way. Just before the transaction was finalized, Pelosi asked the owner why their wonderful home was on the rental market. "Oh," the owner said. "My husband has been appointed deputy secretary of the Department of Health, Education, and Welfare, so we'll be going back east to join the Nixon administration."

Clearly that didn't sit well with Nancy, and she informed the real estate agent that she could not live in a house once occupied by Republicans. She explained to the agent, who seemed dumbfounded by the decision, "I could never live anyplace that was made available because of the election of Richard Nixon." According to Pelosi, her youngest daughter, Alexandra, who was not even alive at the time, says that story explains her mother well.[35] For Pelosi, the political can be deeply personal.

Soon, however, the Pelosis would find their perfect home on Presidio Terrace, next to the military base. The large, stylish home would be the ideal base for her operations. It was on a cul-de-sac that featured Tudor Revival, Beaux Arts and Mission Revival architectural styles. And the location couldn't have been more strategically savvy. As biographer Marc Sandalow put it, "It was not only the home of great wealth, it was also the home of great power." The neighborhood included the home of Joseph Alioto, the city's mayor, who lived just a few doors away from the Pelosis. It also was the site of Senator Dianne Feinstein's childhood home.[36] Feinstein must have loved it, because she eventually moved back, until 2006 when she traded her Presidio Terrace home in for a $16.5 million mansion in Pacific Heights and became a neighbor of the Pelosis.[37]

As a mother of five children, Nancy, as her mother had done, would become a master at multitasking. To her credit, she took her responsibilities as a mother seriously. But it wasn't long after her move to San Francisco that she started the juggling act—"mom and rabid Democrat."[38] But there was one huge difference between her and her mother: Little Nancy had financial means. While her husband, Paul, may not have shared her "passion" for politics, he did share his high-flying contacts and wealth. Paul brought a great deal to the marriage that allowed Nancy to polish her political skills and ultimately shine as a politician. His connections, in both the elite business community and influential social circles, and his money provided his wife with great freedom. During the 1970s and 1980s, she was able to "sacrifice" for the party, putting in untold hours volunteering for candidates and raising money for the party and its candidates.[39] But in less than 20 years, the sacrifice paid off big-time.

Pelosi worked doggedly to build her own political machine, but her success was not without some vital advantages. According to Michael Crowley, Pelosi possesses "three great skills" that shot her to the summit of the political ranks: "manic energy," "dazzling charm" (which she inherited from Big Tommy), and, most important, the "ability to raise big money."[40] But there was one more advantage she was able to add to her potent cocktail: easy access to money—a political boss's dream. According to Agar Jaicks, a Pelosi adviser for more than 30 years and San Francisco party activist, "If you travel in upper socio-economic circles, it's always good to tap those people. She became very good at it, and the better she got the more in demand she was."[41] And tap she did.

The value of her husband's contacts cannot be overestimated. Indeed, they are still significant. Donations made by wealthy Northern Californians help fund candidates in races Pelosi targets around the country. Some of her early introductions included venture capitalist William Hambrecht, who founded two high-tech investment banks that proved to be quite lucrative and is a close family friend who has been "a major source of financial backing for Pelosi's career"; philanthropist and activist Roselyne "Cissie" Swig, who had relatives living in the posh Presidio neighborhood and is the widow of Richard Swig, who was the chairman of the Fairmont Hotel Management Company; and John Freidenrich, a venture capitalist who was at many of Pelosi's early fund-raisers. Hambrecht and Freidenrich continued to donate over the years to candidates of Nancy's choosing around the country. Freidenrich has been quoted as saying, "I just have complete faith in her in not only her own positions, but that she will back people with similar interests."[42]

And over the years, her well of rich donors has never run dry. Those in her potent mix include trial lawyers, labor unions, progressive corporate executives, Washington power players, families with "old money," San Francisco elites, and husband Paul's business connections. Wealthy Oakland-based attorney Steven Kazan, who specializes in asbestos litigation, waits to take his orders from Pelosi before he writes any checks to candidates and House incumbents.[43]

Not only did she have the connections, but late Democratic Party icon Phil Burton deemed her home on Presidio Terrace the ideal setting for fund-raising. In fact, the first words Pelosi recalls Burton ever saying to her were "We'll use this for fund-raisers."[44] And fund-raise she did. One of the keys to her juggling act was her superior organizational skills, which she is still known for. According to biographer Bzdek, "Pelosi organized her house like it was a precinct headquarters."[45]

The operation inside her house resembled how things got done on Albemarle Street, back in Little Italy. "She modeled our house in San Francisco after the house where she grew up in Baltimore" is how her daughter Alexandra described her childhood years. "Our house was like a VFW hall. She'd be working the issues from there, stuffing mailers, having parties."[46]

Daughter Christine told CBS's Lesley Stahl, in a *60 Minutes* profile just a few months before Pelosi was elected Speaker, that her mother was the "disciplinarian and drill sergeant," making a comparison to how she would run the House. Stahl told Pelosi, "When I asked your daughter Christine how you rule, she said you were motherly."

To that Pelosi replied, "I guess it depends on your definition of motherly. If motherly means—we'll have order in the house, yes."[47]

Nancy Pelosi has cultivated the tightly drawn image of her earlier years as the consummate "soccer mom" driving her red Jeep Wagoneer, baking cookies for school parties and going on class field trips. While she may have done those things, that picture is highly distorted. She wasn't typical, in that she had immediate entrée into the wealthiest, most influential circles, including billionaires and political power brokers, the day she arrived in her new hometown. Nancy's springboard to San Francisco politics was as a "high society lady,"[48] and just 12 years after she arrived in the city she landed the position of California state party chairwoman.

But like any political boss, she understood well that to gain power you start where you are and then look to expand your territory. So she first became active in her own wealthy, exclusive neighborhood as president of the Presidio Terrace Association. Pelosi claims that during those early years, her closest friends from the neighborhood were "strictly Democratic." She also served on the L.S.B. Leakey Foundation. Pelosi said she met the Leakeys through billionaire Gordon Getty (who contributes to Pelosi's machine) and his wife, Ann.[49] The foundation's mission "is to increase scientific knowledge, education, and public understanding of human origins, evolution, behavior and survival." Its endeavors include supporting "projects that can shed light on how the behavior of modern hunter-gatherers and our closest living relatives, the great apes, may be similar to the way our hominid ancestors lived."[50]

But Pelosi got her first real break into the vortex of the San Francisco apparatus from a political player who noticed her talent and, like the bosses who recognized her father's potential, saw her promise for the party. It was her nearby neighbor Mayor Alioto. Alioto was a big name in San Francisco. His extended Italian family had deep roots in the city; they were involved in the establishment of the fishing industry at the famed Fisherman's Wharf. A lawyer by training, he was rich and had a keen mind.[51] Alioto served as mayor during the rough-and-tumble years of the late sixties and early seventies and knew what it took to come out on top. So when a seat opened up on the Library Commission, he appointed Pelosi. He told her it was time for her to be recognized for all her efforts. The new city librarian had spent time at Harvard and was ruffling some board members' feathers with the changes he wanted to make. For Pelosi, it was easy to understand the real reason for her selection. "I recognized instantly that the Mayor wanted to appoint one more friendly vote," she said. Alioto, however, was also thinking ahead. He told her the appointment would be helpful if she ever decided to run for office.[52]

All along the way, Pelosi claimed running for office was never a part of her plan. Still, whatever endgame she had in mind, she was fueled by both her own far-reaching ambition and the great plans Big Nancy had held for her. For Pelosi, it was a practical ambition that began with small payoffs and then plotted its way to great power. Mary Hughes, who has served the speaker for years as a political consultant, said Pelosi "gathered people together, always on behalf of a cause or someone else. So when the time came that it was for her, here was an army of people who were prepared to help her."[53]

Although she had aligned herself with the legends of San Francisco politics, it didn't take long before her Baltimore connections and the favor file validated her as a "real" player. Pelosi hit pay dirt with one of her fund-raising events in early 1976. The speaker was Governor Jerry Brown, who was already a friend of the Pelosi family. He had attended St. Ignatius High School with Paul's older brother David. When Nancy heard him at the fund-raiser, Brown was still strategizing his battle against the leading candidate for president, Jimmy Carter, and was determined to make his stand in the California June primary.[54] Pelosi, however, didn't agree with Brown's strategy. Her political instincts told her there was an opportunity for a Brown victory (and also one for her) in an earlier primary in Maryland. So to start things moving, she sought out McCarthy, who was Brown's campaign chair. She said to Leo, "If Jerry Brown wants to run for President, we shouldn't wait for California. By then it's going to be too late—there will already be a nominee. . . . Let's go to Maryland. We can begin the fight there."[55]

Like her father, who had seized a photo op with FDR on Maryland's Eastern Shore years earlier, Pelosi wasn't going to miss this chance. Her battle plan for the Maryland primary was ready, and in a campaign memo she detailed her winning strategy for Brown. Little Tommy would get things rolling, along with Nancy's high school prom date, Ted Venetoulis, Baltimore's county executive. At first they weren't convinced by the plan.[56] Fortunately, Maryland governor George Mandel owed Tommy a favor. D'Alesandro had helped Mandel secure the chairmanship of the Democratic caucus in the state legislature. Now Mandel would get the machine out to operate on Brown's behalf. It worked. Brown handed Carter his first primary defeat, winning 49 percent of the votes to Carter's 37 percent.[57]

It wasn't just the favor file that motivated Mandel. There was bad blood between Governors Mandel and Carter, because Carter hadn't supported Mandel's run as chair of the Democratic Governors Conference. "It was the first and only time that the old guard and the new wing got together in a political campaign," recalled Frank DeFilippo, Mandel's chief of staff and press secretary. "Marvin got all the old-line political bosses together and elected officials in the Hilton in Baltimore and said he didn't have any 'walking around money [payoffs] for this one, but I'll take care of you next time.' And they delivered the state for Jerry Brown."[58] The Baltimore machine was still working and reaping benefits for Nancy almost 3,000 miles away in California.

Pelosi claims, "That's the episode that took me out of the kitchen and put me into official party responsibilities."[59] Bill Press, who was a member of Brown's staff and in 1993 was elected chair of the state party, credited Pelosi for the governor's success in Maryland. "The secret weapon was Nancy."[60] And the reward for Pelosi was a big one. In the fall of 1976, Brown selected her as his choice to run for chair of the California Democratic Party. Pelosi, however, knew it was not yet time to go after such a big reward. "Please find someone else," she said. McCarthy suggested she instead campaign for northern vice chair of the California Democratic Party. She did and won.[61]

In her new position, Pelosi had an even more advantageous base from which to expand her power. She focused on the key weapons: money and people of influence. It was during this time that she joined forces with what was becoming the "political dynasty of Phillip Burton."[62] Burton had become a powerhouse in Washington, pushing his leftist agenda. In 1976, he lost to Texas congressman Jim Wright by one vote in the contest for House majority leader. He hadn't counted his votes carefully enough. Nancy Pelosi would never have let that happen.

Pelosi's Presidio Terrace home became, in the words of journalist Mark Barabak, "a party salon," where celebrities of the party would show up. It was where volunteers were energized about issues like the environment, economic policy and social justice[63] and, of course, where lots of money was raised.

By 1981, Pelosi had enough patronage to win a two-year term as state party chair. Just three days before Ronald Reagan's first inauguration, she commenced her new role as party chair, and it didn't take her long before she went after her fellow Californian. She attacked the new president's cuts in social spending and played the card that the only people Republicans care about are the rich,[64] one of Big Tommy's favorite ploys. However, it was none other than the wealthy citizens of the Bay Area whose money gave Nancy the power she now lords over the Republicans. And when the Republicans protested a move by Phil Burton—he had redrawn the district boundaries following the 1980 census to keep his brother John's U.S. House seat secure—Pelosi "assumed the role of junkyard dog," growling at the Republicans and calling them "sore losers." The district as designed by Burton encompassed five counties and even included an area across the Bay. When questioned as to how that could be right, Burton shouted, "It is at *low* tide."[65]

The party chair's number one job is to win elections. And Pelosi knew exactly how to do this: raise more money, get more people registered to vote, manipulate the ballots to favor candidates (something Big Tommy once alleged he had been a victim of) and launch partisan diatribes. There was one gentleman who unfortunately had the misguided notion that the state chair position could possibly be his. Nancy's friend and political ally Agar Jaicks recalls when Tom Hsieh, another party official, visited Pelosi in her office to inform her that he was going to go for the opening. Jaicks' office was next to Pelosi's, and from the volume of the conversation it was obvious there had been a pointed exchange. Hsieh left the meeting understanding that Pelosi definitely would be in charge. Jaicks said, "That told me one thing: Don't mess with Nancy."[66]

Her next goal was to convince the national party that the 1984 national convention should be held in San Francisco. Pelosi could show her talents on the national stage. So she started raising money and strategizing. She rounded up more than 10,000 volunteers from the shindigs she had organized.[67]

She faced a daunting assignment, however: she explained that she had "to portray San Francisco as an all-American, family-oriented city." For Nancy Pelosi, San Francisco *is* an all-American city. So when Mark Powelson, a San Francisco magazine editor whom the host committee had hired to produce a guide to the Bay City's neighborhoods, included comments from black residents concerned about the gentrification of the city, he raised Pelosi's hackles. She would not stand for that and promptly put him in his place, axing his comments. Powelson later said, "She seemed genuinely upset that people said critical things. She seemed to have a fairly skewed view of real people's lives in San Francisco."[68]

To accomplish her seemingly unachievable task, she enlisted some of the city's biggest players—civic leader and billionaire Walter Shorenstein, state Assembly Speaker Willie Brown, Mayor Dianne Feinstein, and the host committee, which she chaired.[69] Not only did she convince the party that her adopted hometown was a model city, but she also raised a ton of cash by 1984 standards—$2.5 million in private donations—to finance the event.[70] Pelosi was in full form during the convention. In her book *Sneaking into the Flying Circus*, Pelosi's daughter Alexandra described one of her mother's creative tactics. She wrote: "The first thing she did when there was a glitch in the convention schedule was order more food and alcohol for the reporters. She said that as long as they are eating and drinking they won't be writing bad stories."[71]

Her success with the convention hurled her from the small sphere of state politics into the realm of the Democrats' national operation. Besides making Geraldine Ferraro a star, the convention also introduced New York governor Mario Cuomo to the country, when he delivered the keynote address. Pelosi said, "He was spectacular as he presented a vision of 'the shining city on the hill.'"[72] A majority of Americans, however, preferred President Reagan's vision of a shining city. And following his landslide victory over Walter Mondale in November 1984, the Democrats were looking for a new national party chair.

Pelosi was "one of seven candidates seeking the ultimate political insiders' job."[73] Cuomo credited some of his success to Pelosi, and now it was his turn to help her. So when she entered the race for the chairmanship of the Democratic National Committee (DNC), "it was with the blessing of party kingpins such as Mario Cuomo and Daniel Patrick Moynihan."[74] Cuomo told Pelosi biographer Elaine Povich, "Nancy Pelosi was helpful, without even knowing it. She was helpful to me from the beginning of my career in 1983." This would prove to be a tough fight even for Pelosi. To get her offense rolling, she invited 150 Washington political movers and shakers to a big bash on Capitol Hill and hosted a fund-raiser in San Francisco to garner around $100,000, which she could use to persuade members of the DNC to vote for her.[75] She set up her headquarters in Washington, D.C., and at one point in the campaign she claimed she had more committed votes than any other candidate.[76]

Her main challenger was Paul G. Kirk, the party's treasurer and a Ted Kennedy ally. Knowing he was a formidable foe, Pelosi, like bosses always do, went on the attack, calling Kirk "unqualified and too closely tied to Senator Edward M. Kennedy." Claiming she was the one with the "credentials" (which she did not precisely identify), she asked, "Is [the party] served well with a message of Kennedy association for 15 years and labor connections? I don't think that's looking to the future. I would tell that to Ted Kennedy right here and now." She also had some words for organized labor. For good measure, she accused the unions of "trying to defeat her with a heavy-handed, 'antiwoman' campaign."

But this time labor wouldn't be on her side, and the money she raised couldn't pull votes to her camp. She leveled more charges, claiming, according to *The Washington Post*, "that labor leaders have been muscling their representatives on the Democratic National Committee to support Kirk." The real problem was that she didn't have as much muscle as labor. And she became really upset when she received reports that a labor official had referred to her as an "airhead." Pelosi said, "I can take the knocks. But . . . they made me angry." Cuomo supported her all along the way and said the attacks on her because she was a woman were old-fashioned and Victorian. AFL-CIO spokesman Murray Seeger said about the person accused of the attack, "He has certainly not called her an airhead, a female airhead or a Baltimore airhead. We don't talk like that." But one of Cuomo's assistants for labor affairs confirmed there had been a conversation in which something like that had been said. There were those in the party who recognized Pelosi's tactics for what they were: sour grapes.[77]

That would be the only race Pelosi would lose. And in response, she just toughened her resolve to raise more money, pursue more votes and help women and liberals get elected. She was now working like the ultimate boss while defying the image of one. "In 1985," wrote Marc Sandalow, "it was apparent that the image of a political boss was a brow-beating, cigar-chomping bull—perhaps a Tommy D'Alesandro—and not, as Pelosi's own hometown paper described her, the 'beguiling and dynamic operative in a size 4.'"[78]

Even though she lost the race, in some ways she won. Journalist A. Mellinkoff said back in 1985, "Nobody in political circles takes Pelosi lightly more than once."[79]

Party heads now knew what she was capable of. Recognizing both her fund-raising and fighting talents, Senator George Mitchell of Maine selected her to serve as the Democratic Senatorial Campaign Committee (DSCC) finance chair for the party's next battle—the 1986 midterm elections. That year the DSCC set a fund-raising record. Under Pelosi's tutelage, the committee raised $13.4 million. It was a big victory for the Democrats both in money and outcome. Republicans usually dominated in fund-raising for Senate races. But with Pelosi's shrewd skills, the Democrats did more than just become real contenders: they recaptured the Senate. Mitchell said, "Recruiting Nancy was one of the best things I did as Chairman of the DSCC. She was terrific."[80] Now they could foil the rest of Reagan's agenda.

It was in 1986 that Baltimore native Barbara Mikulski and Nevada congressman Harry Reid won their Senate seats. And during most of her 1987 campaign, according to *San Francisco Chronicle* journalist Jerry Roberts, Pelosi was "bragging about how she almost single-handedly wrested control of the U.S. Senate away from the GOP."[81]

Members of the Senate gave Pelosi her due for their victories, saying that she was the "single most important individual responsible for winning the Senate in 1986."[82] She would someday call all those favors in.

Within just a few months, Pelosi's San Francisco connections and her operational volunteer work would pay off enormously. With Sala's impending death from cancer, it was imperative to identify someone to carry on the Burton legacy of hardball politics. Phil's brother John had served in the U.S. House, representing an adjoining district, until 1982, when his cocaine addiction forced him to resign. So all that was left of the Burtons were their protégés. John Burton was taken aback by his sister-in-law's choice and said, "They told me Sala wanted Nancy to run for her seat. I thought they meant Nancy Walker." Walker was at the time a member of the city's Board of Supervisors.[83] But it wasn't Walker. It was Nancy Pelosi.

Although Burton wasn't convinced at first by his sister-in-law's choice, he came around. "[Sala] laid out every attribute, except fate, that would lead Nancy to be Speaker," Burton said. "She's smart, she's tough, she's operational, and she's good on everything we care about. Operational means you know what it takes to run campaigns and win campaigns."[84]

Pelosi's attributes paralleled those of another political intimidator: Phil Burton. A few months before her ascension to the speakership, John, who has remained a close Pelosi adviser, acknowledged that Sala knew what she was doing. Pelosi wasn't just someone who raised money. "Here it is, and everything Sala said Nancy had she has in spades," Burton said.[85]

Just a few days before Sala died, John read a statement from her recommending Pelosi as her successor. San Francisco's most powerful political family had bestowed their blessing on her. The Burtons had owned the seat since 1964, and 14 candidates were ready to fight for the opening.

Pelosi entered the ring for the special election for the Democratic nominee on February 14. Election Day was set for April 7, so time was short. Standing by her side as she announced her intent to run were, among other city leaders, her new campaign chair, John Burton, former mayor Joseph Alioto (the man who'd spotted her potential 15 years earlier) and two trailblazers of the lesbian movement, Phyllis Lyon and Del Martin. She immediately claimed to be the "front runner," though the polls showed otherwise. And her stand on the issues was hard-left liberal: AIDS would be a "very top priority," offshore oil drilling must be "banned," and foreign military interventions needed to be stopped.[86]

First, however, she had to get her machine oiled and moving. "I only had seven weeks to campaign," Pelosi recalled. "We had 100 house parties, and we got 4,000 volunteers to go door to door to man phone banks. I raised $1 million in seven weeks."[87] Of that total she borrowed $250,000 from husband Paul, while much of the rest were contributions from the favor file. "She essentially buried her opponents in money."[88] *She spent more money than the rest of the candidates combined.*[89]

Her district included The Castro, Haight-Ashbury, Chinatown, Golden Gate Park and Fisherman's Wharf, and as her father had done in Baltimore, she went door-to-door to ask for votes. It was time for the favor file. All those people she had helped before were now called in to get her elected. But there was one order of business that had to be taken care of right away. Since their Presidio Terrace address was not in the congressional district she would be representing, they moved to a rented home in Pacific Heights.[90]

As the race shook down, it looked as if the candidate to beat was Harry Britt, a member of the Board of Supervisors. Mayor Dianne Feinstein had appointed him in January 1979, in the aftermath of the assassinations in City Hall in late 1978. Feinstein had replaced slain mayor George Moscone, and Britt had succeeded Harvey Milk on the board. A rotund, handsome, friendly guy, Britt was openly gay and had been recognized for his efforts on what was becoming known as the AIDS crisis. He had served as president of the San Francisco Gay Democratic Club, and for some leaders in the gay community, this was their chance to have an openly gay representative speaking out in Washington.[91]

Nancy's husband, Paul, may not have shared his wife's obsession with politics, but he was an essential player. During her first run for Congress, he was intimately involved. Clint Reilly, Pelosi's consultant for her 1987 campaign, said that Paul had joined John Burton and Leo McCarthy, who was lieutenant governor at the time, to form the potent "triumvirate" that helped her pull off her slim victory over Britt.[92]

Early on, Reilly had sized up Pelosi's political realities. First, she would lose to the gay man for the nomination. Second, she couldn't win in the special election, since where she really needed to get the votes was from sections of the city that didn't vote for women. But Pelosi didn't buy it. "If your numbers are correct, I can definitely win," she told Reilly. "First of all, I will out-organize my opponents. Second, there's one thing you aren't recognizing about that part of town. They're Italian American. And they are going to vote for me."[93]

It was Reilly who thought up what was undoubtedly an appropriate slogan for the campaign: "A Voice That Will Be Heard." Twenty years later, he claimed that it was "prophetic."[94] With her money, she could even afford a commercial in the city's pricey television market. Handel's "Hallelujah" chorus rang out while images of children, a missile, the Golden Gate Bridge and the U.S. Capitol flashed across the screen. It ended with a deep voice reminding the voters of her theme: *"Nancy Pelosi: A voice that will be heard."*[95]

Two players who Reilly believed bolstered Pelosi's campaign were Fred Ross, Jr., and Marshall Ganz, considered at the time two of the country's premier political organizers. These two masterminds were "veterans of Cesar Chavez's Farm Labor Movement." Ross's father had mentored Chavez. As part of her bigger operation, they were instrumental. They collected a lot of votes by mail and rounded up enough volunteers to cover every precinct.[96] These two are still at work. Until recently, Ross was busy working for the Service Employees International Union (SEIU), and Ganz was a counselor in L.A.'s "Camp Obama" during the summer of 2007, "teaching key state organizers to share personal narratives and create compelling politics around human experience and emotion, rather than around issues."[97]

There were other reminders of Little Italy. Nancy's mother-in-law, Nana, and her friends, known as the Nana Brigade, gave her tips on how to snare the bingo players at the Catholic churches: keep it short, so they can get back to their game quickly. And before Pelosi left the church halls, she would "sweeten the pot." She said, "Sweetening the pot always got a big cheer."[98] That, of course, is how she gets other members of Congress to go along with her agenda when it in no way represents his or her constituency—"she just sweetens the pot" with more money. If that doesn't work, she's prepared to employ less benign methods. Besides giving advice on bingo games, the Brigade gathered around a table and went through the voter files identifying the Italian surnames from the neighborhood. They made sure those voters received handwritten postcards.[99]

During the campaign, there was a San Francisco–style live debate on KQED-TV, the city's public station, featuring the 14 assorted candidates. The Peace and Freedom Party candidate had to be "forcibly removed," and a female candidate who was a member of the Board of Supervisors challenged Pelosi. She brought up the fact that Nancy had money and couldn't understand most constituents' struggles. Pelosi got on the defensive about the cash and went on the attack. She tried to argue that her wealth was a good thing because it gave her greater "independence."[100] But, of course, why then did she keep a favor file like her father?

Even though she was a liberal, in this race she was actually considered the moderate. (Only in San Francisco!) But she personally went after Ronald Reagan to prove how liberal she actually was. One brochure identified her as "Ronald Reagan's No. 1 opponent." In another she took on the Reagan agenda. There was a letter that read, "Ronald Reagan has no compassion. Ronald Reagan has no vision. For the past two decades, I have battled Ronald Reagan whenever he has attempted to disenfranchise people, jeopardize our environment or risk our future. . . . Now as a candidate for Congress, I want to bring my longtime battle with Ronald Reagan to the floor of the House of Representatives."[101] Certainly many Americans would trade the Pelosi agenda for the Reagan agenda.

Yet her campaign also cleverly sought Republican voters. One of her mailings was a "Republican voter alert," with elephant logo and all. The mailer declared that Pelosi "will provide our city with the type of balanced representation that is long overdue."[102] What about Phil and Sala Burton? And compared with some of the other candidates, she probably did look pretty balanced. Pictures of her photogenic husband and children were also featured on her mailings.

Big Tommy telephoned his daughter daily. He was hoping she was using what he had taught her in Baltimore. Little Tommy finally flew out to see how things were going, or in journalist Mark Barabak's words, "to inspect the ground troops." He liked what he saw. He told Fred Ross, Jr., "This is how we did it in Baltimore."[103] When he returned home he told Big Tommy, "Dad, she's got a better organization than we ever had."[104]

There were other attacks flung at Pelosi during the campaign. One opponent hinted that she was an insubstantial candidate, saying she had been "crowned by the political power brokers."[105] The Britt campaign called her the "party girl"—of both the Democratic Party establishment and the rich and famous. Pelosi, however, was undaunted and said, "They warned us it would be brutal, that it would be a bloodbath and I'd be sorry I ever got in the race, but I wasn't frightened by any of that. My attitude is they'll take the low road, I'll take the high road, and I'll get to Congress before them."[106] Billboards and signs sprang up around the city with words like "dilettante" and "debutante." Dilettantes and debutantes are not good in street fights. Pelosi is. Unfortunately for her candidates, they didn't really know Nancy D'Alesandro. She was none of that. She was from Baltimore.

The race was close, but Pelosi won. She received 38,021 votes, or 36 percent, while Harry Britt received 34,031 votes, or 32.2 percent. A *Washington Post* story described her for what she does best: find money.

"Pelosi, a longtime Democratic fund-raiser who never before sought office, finished first in a 14-candidate race Tuesday for the seat of the late Representative Sala Burton."[107]

Like her father, Nancy knew how to snatch votes from several diverse groups. She got votes from minorities, women, gays, elderly Catholics and even Republicans. In fact, second to her money, the other major factor that got her into the House was the overwhelming support of Republicans in the district.[108]

On June 2, 1987, she easily won the special election. Her Republican challenger, Harriet Ross, received only 33 percent of the vote to Pelosi's 67 percent.[109]

Like Big Tommy, Nancy was off to Washington to represent a major city. And while the political environs of San Francisco and Baltimore were similar in the power of their muscle, the cultural issues Nancy came to support and embrace would have made Big Tommy cringe. He was a traditional Catholic with working-class sensibilities. In 1955, for example, he set off "a rebellion in the Baltimore art world," demanding that one of the paintings on exhibit as part of the "Life in Baltimore Show" be removed from the "city-supported" Peale Museum. The reason? The mayor saw the artist's painting of two nudes as "obscene" and "morally objectionable."[110] In contrast, daughter Nancy would go on to march in San Francisco's Pride Parade, held during the city's annual Lesbian Gay Bisexual Transgender Pride Celebration.[111] To survive and prosper in San Francisco politics in the 1980s, it was imperative to take a radical stand on the issues. When Pelosi ran in 1987, she said, "I'm running because I want to represent the progressive principles of this district. I'm not running because I don't have anything else to do."[112] But Pelosi's real agenda began to emerge: take her father's tactics, fuse them to the Bay Area's extremist agenda and ultimately reap great personal gain. How did she achieve this? Let me introduce you to the cast of radical characters who mentored and guided her.

4

LAUNCHING A HEAT-SEEKING LIBERAL MISSILE

In Baltimore, Nancy Pelosi had her father, "Big Tommy" D'Alesandro. In San Francisco she found Phil and John Burton. Besides her father's desk set, two of the many keepsakes that adorn her office are framed photos of him. One is from 1947, the day Big Tommy was sworn in as mayor of Baltimore. She is pictured standing by his side holding a Bible. The other is from 1987. This time the father is by his daughter's side as she takes the oath of office as a member of the U.S. House of Representatives.[1] Although she has kept a statue of Phil Burton in her office,[2] reminders of the late California congressman are not as conspicuous. But the messages he passed on to Pelosi are reverberating throughout the country to this day.

In some ways Burton, on his way to the top of San Francisco's political hill, worked like Pelosi's father as a ward heeler, although not in the true sense. He was a ruthless, pugnacious political boss in his own right in a state where political consultants invent celebrity politicians.[3] But nothing about Burton was manufactured. His operation wasn't a machine in the classic model. While Big Tommy worked on the patronage system, answering to the bosses, Burton answered to no one. He didn't give out jobs—except to Lim P. Lee, his key link to the Chinese community, and a few staff positions—or accept bribes.[4] His objectives were much grander than those of a typical East Coast boss, and the currency that mattered to him was power, not money.

But there was one huge difference between Big Tommy and Burton. Tommy was not ideological and, therefore, not nearly as dangerous. He cut deals in the back rooms of restaurants in Little Italy and in Baltimore hotels. His currency was parochial favors. Burton, however, was single-minded. He was driven by his beliefs and the power his agenda gave him. Biographer John Jacobs said, "Burton created and moved agendas that without him would not have existed."[5] For him, the whole world was his jurisdiction.[6] What did this all mean for Pelosi? Her own personal ambition infused with these models turned the daughter of a nonideological political machine into a heat-seeking liberal missile.

Soon after she arrived in San Francisco, Pelosi used her husband's influential network to claw her way into the city's hard-hitting political maze. And she was tough and smart enough to successfully work her way through all the inner machinations. Like Baltimore's, San Francisco's politics are rough-and-tumble, even cutthroat. The city's pastel, cultured image is a facade. Burton's brother John said, "If you can survive San Francisco politics, you can survive anything. It's like surviving g—d—Tammany Hall 50 years ago."[7]

Journalist Mark Barabak described the Bay City well: "San Francisco is a tough political town, far from the liberal monolith that outsiders perceive. It is home to a boisterous, personal and often brutal form of hand-to-hand politicking, which makes it unusual in California and may help explain why so many of the state's political leaders—from Hiram Johnson to Phillip Burton to Dianne Feinstein and Pelosi—have emerged from its roiling cauldron." Like the deceptive image of her beloved city, Pelosi's polished appearance belies who she really is: a cunning politician.[8]

Both cities have churned out potent political forces, yet they each have distinct underpinnings. According to journalist Rupert Cornwell, Pelosi "grew up not in the intense, idiosyncratic and tribal politics with which her adopted city [San Francisco] is identified, but amid the old-fashioned machine politics, of favours granted and favours called in, of the old East Coast cities." In her formative years, "Pelosi absorbed politics with her mother's milk, but on the other side of America."[9] What she did when she arrived in San Francisco was ingenious: Pelosi grafted the old-fashioned machine with the power of the intense, local politics and created an unbridled political engine.

Baltimore was a city founded on the necessary, while San Francisco was established on the unconventional. Not only did fortune hunters flock to the locale in search of gold, but it also became a haven for misfits and for those who possessed a potent stroke of individualism. The city was the ideal setting for a cultural rebellion and sexual insurrection. And the inspirational political chief of the uprising was Phillip Burton, a member of the United States Air Force, law school graduate and influential leader of the California Young Democrats. It's important to understand Phil Burton because he is the man who would, in the words of Pelosi biographer Marc Sandalow, "play a critical role in Pelosi's ascent."[10] It was Burton's example that Pelosi would follow. Her friends say, "Pelosi's ambition is to resurrect the House that Phil Burton built." Burton never became Speaker, but Nancy's triumph 30 years later was in some ways "sweet revenge" for his defeat by Jim Wright for majority leader. Not only is she a "Burtonista through and through," but her speakership is in many ways a memorial to Burton.[11]

Burton was a huge man both physically and temperamentally, and he liked to drink vast quantities of Stolichnaya on the rocks. As Jacobs describes him: "Burton was no ordinary adversary. He was a huge, burly man with unruly wisps of hair spiraling downward from his scalp. He had fierce brown eyes that always seemed poised to pop out of his head, a rasping voice he could magnify like a howitzer when necessary, the salty vocabulary of the San Francisco dockworkers he represented, and a presence that often left allies fearful and enemies totally terrorized."[12]

Like Big Tommy, Burton was a fan of FDR. In fact, Burton's fascination with politics had begun in 1936, when he heard Roosevelt on a campaign stump in Milwaukee. Another figure who impressed Burton was Dan Hoan, Milwaukee's socialist mayor. He served from 1916 until 1940, demonstrating to Burton how government leaders could hoard power for years by spending money on civic welfare programs.[13]

Phil Burton's views were completely outside of mainstream America. Yet he employed "terror, intimidation, the brute exercise of power, and total mastery of technical detail," all in the name of the poor, the unions, the environment and minorities, to increase his strength and upsurge his control. Jacobs said of Burton, "few politicians in American history who held his redistributive and ultraliberal views ever accumulated as much raw power as Phillip Burton in his prime."

Burton once told one of his protégés how to get what you want: "If you show them the depths of hell, everything else looks pretty good."[14] Even though his views were leftist, he amassed the power he needed to shove a lot of legislation through Washington. It was a lesson Pelosi learned well.

Often likened to Lyndon Johnson in his style, Burton would get right in his colleagues' faces and intimidate them. According to Larry Margolis, a top aide to Burton's California rival Jesse Unruh: "Saliva would pop out of his mouth while he told you what a prick you were and how he would get even."[15] While Pelosi, in her designer suits, may not be spitting saliva in someone's face, she often uses threats, intimidation, and strong-arm tactics, and she always gets even.

From the early years of his political career in California, Burton was known for, according to journalist Harold Meyerson, two qualities— "his political brilliance" and "his explosive temper." Meyerson said, "Nobody worked harder for liberal causes."[16]

When Burton was first elected to the California State Assembly, in 1956, it was with the help of George Hardy, who, for that time, had a pretty sophisticated communications network set up in his San Francisco basement at 240 Golden Gate Avenue—the "heart of the Burton Machine." Hardy was the head of his janitors' union, chartered by the Chicago "mob-run" Building Services Union.[17] This later became the Service Employees International Union (SEIU), which has been a staunch supporter of President Obama.

It was 1966 when all the parts of the Burton machine finally fell into place. Two of the other key components of the operation were Burton's brother John and friend Willie Brown, who were considered, at that time, important figures of the left in the Bay Area.[18]

From the 1960s until his death, in 1983, Phil Burton was the greatest political force from California. "Burton was a wild man, an unrestrained liberal who moved from grassroots campaigns to the California statehouse and finally to Congress," wrote Pelosi biographer Elaine Povich. And during those years he groomed those he identified as having some potential. One he "took under his wing" was none other than Nancy Pelosi.[19]

Burton liked what he saw in Pelosi. John Burton argues that his brother didn't really mentor Nancy, since she was already a pro, having grown up in Baltimore as Big Tommy's daughter. Pelosi agrees that the D'Alesandros got her ready for Burton. She said, "One of the reasons I got along with Phil is because I wasn't afraid of him. I knew a lot of people like him."[20] It didn't take long, however, for them to go head to head. Raising his voice, he tried to bully her. But Pelosi didn't back down. Burton admired her for that. "Burton grabbed her by the chin and shook it." Their friendship was sealed.[21]

Burton appreciated, according to journalist Harold Meyerson, Pelosi's "commitment to progressive values"—and knowing how to use the political system to see those values become laws for all to abide by. And Burton's list of values turned into laws is long and still alive today. He expanded government at every turn, creating a bill that established Supplemental Security Income (SSI) for the aged, blind and disabled; increasing the minimum wage; getting food stamps for strikers; and shutting down the House Un-American Activities Committee.[22]

Burton steered his machine through San Francisco's political landscape. His quest for power kept his political vision sharp. He was the first to see all the potential in the changing demographics. During World War II, thousands of blacks came for the jobs at Hunters Point shipyards, immigrants from Latin and Central America as well as Mexico settled in the Mission District, and Chinatown was burgeoning and in need of leadership. "Burton was the first politician with the imagination and intelligence to understand it, seize it and give it voice," wrote biographer Jacobs.[23]

Burton was "an architect of the city's powerful coalition of blacks, environmentalists, gays and working class voters."[24] He even brought the gay activists and police officers together near the end of his life.[25] Pelosi makes the most of this successful formula: build coalitions, even if you have to form them out of unlikely friends or enemies. Another Burton protégé, and today Pelosi's top lieutenant and key ally, is George Miller, California's congressman from the Seventh District. Miller knew both Burton and Pelosi, and he agrees that they had the same worldview and shared a common liberal agenda. He said, "There's a lot of Phil in her in terms of shared principles of government. Why people come to public service. Why people should be in elective office. What you're supposed to do if you get the privilege to have one of these seats in the Congress."[26]

In his pursuit of public service and power, Burton fashioned the congressional district seat that is now Pelosi's. As a member of the assembly, he got a place on the Elections and Reapportionment Committee following the 1960 census, and he exhaustively searched out how to design a district so it would best serve his ambitions. After the census, San Francisco was left with only four assembly districts. For Burton's plot to work, the Bay City needed to have five. So he manipulated the fifth assembly district into existence. He worked cunningly to produce that fifth seat: he would try to annex the fractions of entitlements from other cities. He said, "We have a lot of odds and ends. Santa Clara has three-tenths of a district [extra], 3.3." Obviously, he received opposition to that plan. His critics leveled charges that he was pumping up his city's census count by including all those on board ships in the harbor as well as prisoners at Alcatraz. Burton provided the staff of the committee with misleading information and proceeded to attempt to "draw one of the most left-wing congressional districts in the U.S. for himself by bunching the city's most liberal voters together . . . the new district would allow him to be as ultraliberal as he wanted to be." Since he knew his voters would be completely pleased with his legislative plans, he could zealously pursue his agenda in Washington instead of cultivating constituent loyalty at home.[27] Burton's crooked plot has given Pelosi the freedom to likewise work feverishly on her legislative agenda, undisturbed by the voice of moderation that holds most representatives in check. Since her first close election victory, in 1987, she has been reelected with an average of approximately 81 percent of the vote.[28]

Author David Frum claims that during the latter part of the seventies Phil Burton was the person who was really in charge of the House. Heavily backed by labor, Frum claims that it was Burton "who created the modern Congress." To appease Burton, in 1973, Congressman Wilbur Mills of Arkansas allowed a bill to go to the floor without the protection of the closed rule—the first time since the 1920s. As long as the closed rule was in effect, no amendments, except those from a committee, could be added to a bill from the House floor. Its removal, however, "triggered an explosion in the number of lobbyists employed in Washington." Frum writes: "If only [Burton] had not been so abrasive, difficult, tyrannical, ruthless—or possibly if that modern Congress were a more attractive and appealing thing—then perhaps the Capitol dome would have been named after him."[29]

Former San Francisco mayor Willie Brown has said of his friend, "Phil Burton was the most naturally gifted elected official or politician I have ever known or run across. All of his habits were tailor-made for politics. He had an appetite for detail beyond belief on every issue. He had an unlimited amount of energy. He had supreme confidence, and he was absolutely devoid of a need to be loved. I think Phil Burton believed that he could absolutely make a difference in any situation, and he usually did, and that drove him more than anything else."[30]

That description is in many aspects just as apt for Pelosi. When crafting legislation, she heeds *every* detail. During her health-care endeavor, Representative Debbie Wasserman Schultz (D-FL) said of Pelosi's abilities, "Very little that the speaker does is ad hoc. She is methodical, thorough, and detail-oriented. It was a masterful decision on her part for members to feel that they have an impact on the bill."[31]

And like Burton, she is not particularly concerned about her likability with the American people. *New York* magazine reporter Vanessa Grigoriadis writes that Pelosi likes to say, waving a hand, "I'll take the hit. I'll take the hit."[32] She is wildly unpopular around the country. But that doesn't bother her. "No, I don't care," she told Politico. "I certainly want to be trusted. I'm not particularly concerned if I'm liked." Unlike most leaders, she doesn't even commission her own national polls to see how she's doing. At election time, she's answerable to her leftist constituents in the Bay Area. She does have one burden with which Burton didn't have to contend: Pelosi must also keep her Democratic caucus troops in line. And while a number of members openly say they like and respect her, she is also feared.[33] Her voting record clearly is liberal, but she does have "a capacity for keeping all parts of her party happy," according to the *Almanac of American Politics*. No doubt part of the reason her troops follow her is for all the money she doles out.[34]

There are many parallels between Phil Burton's and Pelosi's operational styles. Early on, Burton knew his success would depend on who was beneath him. Like Pelosi on Presidio Terrace, he started working the territory he was in, orchestrating his way to power. He used the Young Democrats to train protégés, including his brother John, and then place them in key political positions. Another young activist was Henry Waxman, who would years later become a trusted colleague of Pelosi's and wage war with her on issues like AIDS, energy, and health-care reform. Burton believed that the Young Democrats was the place for dedicated liberals. In fact, its members viewed the People's Republic of China more favorably than the House Un-American Activities Committee.

Burton's drive for power was endless. First he had to conquer San Francisco, and he would not be satisfied until he was considered the city's "top elected official, the kingmaker who selected candidates for every office, no matter how seemingly inconsequential." During his ascent he came to understand the role money could play. Money was one area where he and Pelosi differed. He wasn't interested in accumulating it for himself. Nonetheless, he learned the importance of finding donors to underwrite candidates of his choosing. For his plans to succeed, he needed people in office who would vote for his far-left agenda.[35] This today is an indispensable tactic for the Speaker.

Interestingly, both Burton and Pelosi took advantage of Republican scandals, and funneled the money they raised from exploiting them to candidates they would in turn expect loyalty from once elected. Burton had had the foresight to seize and make the most of the Watergate scandal in 1974. He successfully persuaded the chairman of the Democratic Congressional Campaign Committee (DCCC), Wayne Hays (the Ohio congressman from the infamous Elizabeth Ray scandal), to allow him to determine which candidates should receive some of the campaign money in the 1974 midterm election.[36] His plan worked. When Burton ran for chair of the Democratic caucus, between 65 and 70 of the "Watergate Babies" cast their vote for him.[37] Pelosi did almost the exact same thing in 2006, exploiting the Republican scandals involving congressmen such as Mark Foley and Duke Cunningham as well as the fallout from lobbyist Jack Abramoff's conviction for conspiracy and fraud. She called it "the Republicans' 'culture of corruption, cronyism, and incompetence.'"[38] For candidates who were hoping to receive money for their campaigns, in return, Pelosi expected loyalty. She was elected Speaker in January 2007.

Pelosi flashes the cloak and dagger to get what she wants. Like Burton did, she uses issues that are tied not only to her ideology but also to her base of power to convince the national electorate that she is looking out for their interests in the name of justice. But justice for whom? In an interview for the November 1981 edition of *California* magazine, Burton said, "I like people whose balls roar when they see justice."

Pelosi claims that she and Burton had different means to achieving the same goals. She said, "My approach was quite different from Phil's. He would not be described as diplomatic or listening, or any of that. But we are both results-oriented." They both were passionate about their quest to right what liberals perceive as society's wrongs.[39]

Like Pelosi, Burton was set on climbing up the rungs of the House leadership. Usually secretive, he shared his ambition to one day be Speaker with a few friends. Once he had set that goal, he worked a little more stealthily on his legislation, and he chose his battles more carefully so as not to alienate too much potential support. He had achieved a great deal, but several of his colleagues still considered him "a wild man from the nation's kook capital."[40]

To move up, Burton would have to become a deal maker on some issues, an art Nancy had mastered after Big Tommy's example. So there were times he worked on legislation motivated above all for pure political gain. With his visions of leadership, Burton needed to find issues that would maneuver him into advantageous relationships with unlikely friends. Although he had zero coal miners in his district, he worked doggedly on their behalf to pass a bill to compensate miners with black lung disease. While he did it seemingly out of genuine conviction that the miners deserved it, in reality, he also wanted to make an impression on more than three dozen congressional "coal rats." Some of these coal rats were "very conservative southerners." One of these men was Congressman Hays, who called antiwar protesters "dirty hippies." The coal rats, however, might see Burton as a valuable ally if he could send them home with some money. "He would need these conservative colleagues for future deal making and his own leadership ambitions," wrote John Jacobs. Passage of the legislation would also strengthen his hand with another essential ally: leaders of powerful labor unions.[41]

Burton worked tirelessly. On his quest to pass the black lung bill, he would often ask those who were working with him on the legislation at 2 A.M.: "Do you know why we're going to win? Because we're going to outwork the bastards. They're in bed asleep. We're still working."[42] It looks like Pelosi is following in Burton's steps by using late-night and weekend votes to advance her radical agenda.

And Burton never cared about the price tag. Biographer Jacobs wrote, "In establishing the principle of a federal entitlement, he knew he could always manipulate the figures upward as he had with so many other programs." Burton is quoted telling a Democratic Study Group staffer assigned to his Welfare Task Force, concerning the Family Assistance Plan (FAP), "If we enact FAP, I'll bust the federal government within two years."[43] Those may also be Madam Speaker's thoughts on her health-care reform bill.

Shrewdness is another quality Burton and Pelosi share. Burton never allowed the spotlight to shine just on him when he worked on legislation. If his colleagues got their name on the bill and they were recognized publicly, they would be willing to appease him on what he felt were the "key points."[44] This is a tactic Pelosi cleverly employs as well. Whenever she holds a news conference, she directs her staff to round up as much media as possible. Once the cameras are turned on, she makes certain each colleague gets some good publicity, mentioning their names and how vital they have been in accomplishing the goal.[45] Of course, the end result is that the Speaker gets what she wants even if it is not what her colleagues had hoped for. She uses her coalitions to advance her key points.

John Burton has compared his late brother to Pelosi. He believes that no one has come close to being as "politically smart" as his brother was.[46] But he calls Pelosi the "nicer politician." John agrees, however, that they were alike in that they were both willing to make tough decisions, and at the same time some enemies, to get what they wanted.[47]

In his wife, Sala, Phil found the ideal match. Not only was she "as hardworking and as political an animal as her husband," according to biographer Jacobs, but she never tried to temper his fanatical drive.[48] She had ended up in San Francisco after her parents fled Poland in 1939, and in 1950 she met her husband at none other than a California Young Democrats convention.[49] Jacobs said of Sala, "She possessed a charm and gentle manner that Phillip utterly lacked. She cleaned up his messes, soothing and placating those he insulted or abused."[50]

Like Sala, Nancy can be charming. But the dying congresswoman saw something rare in Pelosi: she was from a similar political mold as her late husband. After Pelosi reached the Speaker's chair, Congressman Miller said, "Sala made a decision that changed the history of the House of Representatives and our country forever."[51]

Pelosi doesn't speak much about Phil Burton today. As bosses often do, they keep controversial figures at arm's length. She said, "[Burton] was quite a figure. He was a lion, really a lion." John Burton, however, claims that Nancy and Phil were tight.[52] She has also said that the Speaker she admires most is Tip O'Neill.[53] Yet Burton so offended Speaker O'Neill with his boorishness that O'Neill "could not stand to be in the same room with him."[54]

Pelosi avoids calling Burton her mentor, claiming she's forged her political path her own way. She said, "I certainly will be faithful to the ideal that Phillip and my parents believed in. But I have my own approach. I would hope that they would be proud of my success and what I know— that what I would do would be consistent with what he believed."

She continued: "But I am not—this is not about Phillip, and it's not about my father. It's about something that has happened in terms of how I have been shaped. I bring a woman to the table. I bring the changing nature of my district as part of it, the regional thinking that we have in California."[55] There is no question, however, that her relationship with the late Burton was one of mutual respect and understanding.

Since her election, in 1987, John Burton has been a key adviser in Pelosi's life. Those who know her well recognize Burton's influence. They say he "stands head and shoulders above the rest." He's not ready to admit to having that much sway, although they see each other when she's back in the Bay Area. Burton says, "Sometimes I'll have an idea—just an idea about something—so I might say, 'What do you think about this?' But trust me, she knows what the hell she's doing. It's in her blood."[56]

John Burton resurrected his career after retiring from the U.S. Congress in 1982 because of a major drug problem, including an addiction to cocaine. He was elected to the California State Assembly in 1988 and from 1998 to 2004 served as the president pro tempore of the state senate. Remarkably, Burton somehow managed to serve in the California legislature *while at the same time lobbying for clients in his private law practice.* The term "conflict of interests" apparently doesn't even exist in his vocabulary. As an elected state senator, Burton "maintained a lucrative lobbying law practice" housed in the Merchants Exchange Building in San Francisco. (Burton attempted to conceal the identity of his lobbying clients by working in partnership with another Bay Area megalobbyist.)[57]

Like his brother Phil, John is known for his temper, tirades and colorful language. An assemblywoman who has had her own battles with Burton said, "Politics is in his blood. It's not possible anymore in California for anyone else to have that muscle." He uses intimidation—grabbing other legislators in hallways and hanging up on people.[58]

After a huge victory as California's new state party chair in 2009, Burton said, "I am younger than Winston Churchill, the last time he was prime minister." He went on to hype all his experience in organizing the party he now leads.[59] Pelosi and her friend John Burton are still turning the machine's gears.

Phil Burton was always on the lookout for future political talent he could train and encourage. Besides Pelosi, another of his most successful protégés is Willie Brown.[60] Burton craftily restructured a district for Willie Brown. In 1962, Brown was defeated in his run for the California Assembly. But after Burton reworked things so the area would include more blacks, Willie seized it in 1964[61] and eventually became assembly speaker. The influence of Brown in San Francisco should not be underestimated. In fact, the machine was often referred to as the "Brown-Burton Machine." Willie was the one who authored and shepherded to passage the bill legalizing homosexuality in California in 1975, earning him the undying support of San Francisco's gay community. Another friend of Brown's in the seventies was Peoples Temple cult leader Jim Jones, an influential figure in the Bay City's political game. Brown said that he admired Jones and was quoted as saying in 1977, "In a tight race [for elected office in San Francisco] . . . forget it without Jones."[62]

Brown, like the rest of the machine, understood that money was the key to keeping their kind in office. During his time in the assembly, Brown himself estimates he raised almost $75 million to make certain both he and other Democrats were in office.[63] Throughout his mayorship, he was intensely loyal, showing patronage to his supporters. And the city payroll for "special assistants" increased hugely during his tenure. Brown's reason for the increase? Frederick Furth, Brown's lawyer, explained in a letter that the mayor needed to expand the payroll to "get important work done." He added that the past five years had been "remarkably productive." Even ex-girlfriends were receiving money from the taxpayers.[64] The colorful Willie Brown is still a player and is on the "list" of those who "whispers in [Pelosi's] ear."[65]

Leo McCarthy, another valuable mentor, left his own imprint on Pelosi. They were tight and stuck with each other. Until his death, he served as treasurer of her political action committee. Pelosi allowed McCarthy to really get to know her. And one thing was clear to Leo: she had an arsenal full of payback weapons. McCarthy once said, "When she meets someone who has done some conniving or tried to carve her up behind her back, she often will treat that person graciously, because she knows there are always an infinite number of ways you can retaliate."[66]

Over the past 40 years, Phil Burton and Nancy Pelosi, two San Francisco liberals, have transformed American politics and society. Burton "once bragged that he could round up 110 votes 'to have dog s—declared the national food.' "[67] Pelosi has many of Burton's talents but with a little more savoir faire. But it is ridiculous that these two staunch liberals, who represent a small sliver of the American electorate, have had such a dominating sway over the nation. Their vision is far removed from what the Founders believed. And Pelosi has surpassed Burton because she is tough like him, but can do it with a plastic smile. When Burton was elected Democratic caucus chair after the 1974 election, he achieved the number four position in the House leadership. During Burton's fight for caucus chair, *Wall Street Journal* reporter John Pierson explained what a Burton victory would mean: "It will be the first time . . . that a real liberal with a taste for power and ability to exercise it will have gained a position of leadership in the House."[68] It would be Pelosi, however, who would reach the top of that mountain.

5

FROM THE WHIP TO THE GAVEL

I pride myself in being called a liberal. . . . I don't consider
myself a moderate.[1]

—Nancy Pelosi, 1996

Seizing political power is seldom achieved through vacillation
or feebleness. Yet even by Washington standards, Nancy Pelosi's ascent
to the perch upon which her power rests has been marked by an unusual
ideological extremism, exacting ruthlessness, reprisals against former
friends and unprecedented money hustling. She deployed these political
tactics with methodical efficiency and unflinching resolve. And they
worked. From her 1987 entrance into the U.S. House of Representatives, to her plotting to land on influential committees, to her three-
year battle to seize the Democratic whip post, to her rise to Democratic
minority leader, to her promotion to America's first female speaker of the
House, Pelosi has displayed a shrewd self-discipline that has produced
a string of successes—for herself. The Boss's power base depends on
her unquestioning, unyielding commitment to the left's radical agenda.
Pelosi understood that winning the trust of House Democrats and the
financial backing of leftist donors would require that she toe the liberal
line consistently. And that's exactly what she did. In her first 20 years
in Congress, only once did Pelosi ruffle liberal feathers—when she supported the 1994 North American Free Trade Agreement.[2]

That Nancy Pelosi would one day become the mouthpiece and leader of radical leftist causes, however, should have been apparent from the start. When Pelosi first declared her candidacy for Congress, at the Jack Tar Hotel in Cathedral Hill, she had made a point to be flanked by John Burton, as well as by Del Martin and Phyllis Lyon, pioneers of the lesbian rights movement.[3] Given her district's sizable homosexual population, Pelosi's pandering to San Francisco's so-called LGBT (lesbian, gay, bisexual and transgender) voters might seem the work of a typical politician. But even by usual political standards, Pelosi's advocacy for special—not equal—rights for homosexuals has proven extreme. As the left-leaning *New Republic* magazine has conceded, Pelosi has fought "every conceivable battle for gay rights, even calling for legislation to mandate that the U.S. Olympic Committee allow gays to hold athletic competitions under the term 'Gay Olympics.'"[4] Pelosi's urgings fell on deaf ears. For a politician who prides herself in fostering "inclusiveness," such a separatist impulse could have pleased only the most extreme members of the lesbian, gay, bisexual, and transgender communities.

"The number one issue for my constituents when I first went to Congress in the late 1980s was AIDS," says Pelosi. "But I found out almost immediately that others didn't share my concern."[5]

Actually, the year after Pelosi became a member of Congress, President Ronald Reagan issued a directive to ensure equal rights for AIDS patients and banning discrimination. Furthermore, the Reagan administration had mailed out 107 million copies of a booklet called "Understanding AIDS," written by Surgeon General C. Everett Koop.[6]

Still, Pelosi's hyperbolic statement that some members of Congress lack compassion for individuals with HIV/AIDS was sparked by members' reticence to overfund research of a disease that, per capita, today receives exponentially more research dollars per death than diseases that kill hundreds of thousands more Americans annually. According to the FAIR Foundation's analysis of the 2011 National Institutes of Health (NIH) allocations, the NIH spends $2,429 per patient death attributable to cardiovascular disease, which claims 864,280 American lives annually. By comparison, for the 14,110 HIV/AIDS deaths each year, $225,656 taxpayer dollars are spent for every death, a feat of disproportionate spending achieved largely through the tireless work of

Nancy Pelosi and those beholden to the homosexual lobby's powerful array of special interest groups.[7]

Pelosi's demonization of her opponents' motives on matters involving AIDS remains a hallmark of what makes her a darling of the left. Tactically, Nancy Pelosi understood and heeded the lessons she had learned from Big Tommy; namely, that solidifying your base is the first step to seizing and expanding power. Her tactical decisions to consistently and aggressively advance her leftist agenda were part of a broader strategy designed to communicate her ideological commitment to liberal policies. After all, campaign donors and financial contributors like to know just what it is they're buying. An unreliable politician with a wishy-washy voting record is a hard sell. So Pelosi gave her donors precisely what they wanted: a reliable liberal who could be counted on to dig in her ideological heels and stand firmly and speak loudly on behalf of leftist causes.

Pelosi wasted no time. At her swearing in ceremony in the House, she was given the unusual opportunity to make extended remarks (congressional protocol dictates that most members simply say "Yes" to the oath of office and then remain silent) to mark the glorious occasion of her arrival in the Congress.

"Thank you, Mr. Speaker," she said. "I'm so honored to be here today with my family and with my father, Thomas D'Alesandro, a former member, and my constituents from the great city of San Francisco, which I'm proud to represent. In the course of my campaign, I promised that when I came to Congress, I would tell you that Sala sent me, and that I came to fight against AIDS."

According to Pelosi's dramatic recounting, as she uttered the words, some House members "looked stricken" and later pulled her aside to scold her. "Why on earth would you want the first thing anybody knows about you to be that your priority is to fight against AIDS?" In Pelosi's martyred retelling, she allegedly responded, "Well, that really is why I came here. It's one of my top priorities." In her breathless account, Pelosi adds: "It was just stunning to me that they would object to my mentioning one of the greatest health care crises in U.S. history. I thought, *Why would you say that to me? I just got sworn into Congress. And you're telling me that I shouldn't tell people I came here to fight against AIDS?*"[8]

In Pelosi's "they're evil, we're goodness and light" worldview, it would never occur to her that members might prefer to give initial priority to tackling and funding a problem like, say, cardiovascular diseases, which, according to the Centers for Disease Control, account for one out of every three deaths in America. No, clearly, allocating scarce resources to combat the nation's number one killer, instead of AIDS, which doesn't even rank in the top 15, must purely be a function of bigotry and prejudice.[9]

"Coming from San Francisco, I was appalled at how openly disrespectful some members of Congress were about people with HIV/AIDS, and even more disturbed that they would take their bigotry to the floor of the House," says Pelosi.[10]

Upon her arrival in Congress, Pelosi was eager to get placed on an AIDS health subcommittee, a coveted assignment. "I really didn't have much of a chance to be appointed. Fortunately, my colleague from California, Henry Waxman, who was the House's top crusader in the fight against AIDS, generously gave up one of his health assignments so I could serve."[11] It was a shrewd and classic example of her covering her demographic bases. During Pelosi's early campaign battles against an openly gay candidate like Harry Britt, for example, Pelosi's team had calculated that seizing political victory hinged on her winning at least 25 to 30 percent of the homosexual electorate in her district.[12] And although she defeated Britt narrowly, a visible placement on the AIDS health subcommittee would likely bolster her image back home with key gay and lesbian activist groups.

To further cement her image as a stalwart champion of LGBT causes, in her first week on the job, Pelosi broke new ground when she hired noted San Francisco AIDS expert Steve Morin to work in her Washington office, making him the first-ever congressional staffer hired to work primarily on AIDS-related legislative items. Soon, Pelosi began introducing a steady string of AIDS benefits legislation that would span the next 15 years of her career, including: the COBRA-Continuation Tax Disabilities Amendment of 1989, redefining Social Security requirements for disability payments to include individuals with AIDS-related complex,[13] opposing a constitutional ban on gay marriage, and supporting San Francisco mayor Gavin Newsom's decision to illegally license gay marriages. As a member of the banking committee, she also cowrote the Housing Opportunities for People with AIDS program to shuttle billions of dollars in housing subsidies to people with AIDS.[14]

Any Republican who questioned Pelosi's spending spree was met with scorn and mockery. When, for example, Republicans tried to thwart efforts to use taxpayer monies to foot the bill for distributing clean needles to drug users (presumably to reduce HIV transmissions from needle sharing among intravenous drug users), Pelosi shot back, "You'd think we're having a meeting of the flat earth society."[15] When Pelosi entered the Congress in 1987, the budget allocated $766 million for AIDS research and prevention. After almost 20 years of fierce and unflinching advocacy by Nancy Pelosi and others, "the federal government was spending more than $20 billion a year to battle the disease," according to Pelosi biographer Marc Sandalow.[16] Pelosi's early visibility on LGBT causes established her as someone whom activists could entrust with their message and their money. The national gay-and-lesbian magazine *The Advocate* hailed Nancy Pelosi as "one of the House's staunchest supporters of gay rights and a leader on HIV/AIDS issues since she arrived on Capitol Hill in 1987."[17] By firmly establishing her leftist bona fides right out of the gate, Pelosi quickly realized that funding her big-government designs would require jockeying for a seat on the powerful Appropriations Committee. Phil Burton had taught Pelosi that campaigning doesn't end on Election Day; rather, choice committee assignments come to those who engage in hard-fought politicking. According to *Washington Post* editor Vincent Bzdek, Pelosi's aides summed up Pelosi's how-to plan for her first mini-campaign for an assignment to the Appropriations Committee:

Step 1. Maintain constant contact. Send letters out to all the relevant members of the Appropriations Committee. Tell them you're running and why, and tell them you want their support.

Step 2. Solidify support. Ask to go before the next caucus meeting of the various caucuses that might help you plead your case, such as the California delegation, the women's caucus, the moderate "Blue Dog" Democrats, the Hispanic caucus, and so on, and talk to them personally, answer their questions. . . . Always know where you stand in terms of number of votes.

Step 3. Lobby members of the party's steering committee, because they are the ones who actually make the committee selections for the party. Get your delegation of supporters together and ask them to contact steering committee members. Try to figure out how each person can help you. It's complicated. And sometimes it takes a while, but "failure is not an option."[18]

Actually, for Pelosi, failure was an option. At least initially. Her first bid for Appropriations, in the early 1990s, failed. To hear Pelosi tell it, she was a victim of bias, and this time the prejudice was against Californians: "The people who were having their own campaigns (for the seat) were also saying, 'California has too much [representation],'" Pelosi complained. Indeed, California lawmakers who don't get their way have coined a phrase for this phenomenon. They call it the ABC syndrome— Anywhere, Anything, Anybody But California. And so, Representative Marcy Kaptur (D-OH) was installed on the powerful committee.[19]

However, when a new opening emerged, Pelosi had already built the strong network of contacts and favors laid out in her three-step plan to get what she wanted. With the personal help of Speaker Tip O'Neill, Pelosi accomplished an ambitious feat: she had won a prized seat on the powerful House Appropriations Committee after just three and a half years of being in Congress.

Big Tommy had himself been a member of the House Appropriations Committee.[20] Little Nancy had merely followed in her father's footsteps. Furthermore, she had learned the lesson of reciprocity her father had taught her with his favor file. You dole out money and favors to others, and soon they will feel indebted to repay your kindness and generosity by supporting you and your causes. And that is why Pelosi's early placement on the House Appropriations Committee was so important: it allowed her to do myriad fiscal favors for members seeking to bring home the pork to their districts. What's more, her Appropriations perch ensured that she would be able to bring her own bacon back to San Francisco, particularly as it related to funding causes likely to ingratiate her to segments of her LGBT constituency.

"It's important to my district and to the state of California," Pelosi said when she landed her seat on Appropriations. "From the standpoint of health, housing, transportation, it's important for us to be part of the decision-making. In times of tight fiscal policy, it's even more important to be at the table."[21]

Pelosi's self-important "seat at the table" allowed her to build strong bonds with Democratic powerhouses like Representatives John Murtha and David Obey, relationships that would later prove crucial in vaulting her into the leadership roles she craved.[22] It also produced controversial pork barrel projects designed to benefit her friends. As a monetary homage to one of her mentors, Lieutenant Governor Leo McCarthy, Pelosi saw to it that the San Francisco think tank he'd established, the Center for Public Service and the Common Good, at the University of San Francisco, received $1 million. As Pelosi biographer Elaine Povich put it, "Pelosi made no apologies for it. Her standard justification was that projects like the think tank are going to get federal money, anyway, and the money might as well go to her hometown."[23]

With her hand firmly planted in the Appropriations till to fund her visions of big-government grandeur, Pelosi also understood that grooming herself for ascension to still more serious leadership posts, such as on the Intelligence Committee, would mean boning up on her foreign policy credentials. Members of the Intelligence Committee hold a prized and powerful role. They know some of the nation's most sensitive and serious intelligence information. Membership on the committee is also a symbol of trust that adds heft to a member's leadership bio. So, in typical Pelosi fashion, upon entering the House, she began plotting to land herself a coveted appointment on a committee with serious foreign policy implications.

"You have two sides of a personality," said one senior Democratic staff member. "She has a very mechanistic, organizational way of looking at politics with an incredibly empathetic way of looking at policy. She is the most complete mix of political calculation and legislative strategist that I know exists in the Congress."[24]

Pelosi's calculations allowed her to plant her anchor on the House Intelligence Committee. Better still, with the power of incumbency on her side (her first nine reelection bids were won with a jaw-dropping average of 81.66 percent of the vote),[25] Pelosi would now have a high-visibility platform to amplify her district's pacifist, antiwar agenda. In

1990, during the first Gulf war, for example, following Iraq's invasion of Kuwait, Pelosi staunchly opposed military action and charged that President George H. W. Bush was "resorting to militarization in order to solve a conflict," using an "ill-conceived policy of violence," and was acting "illegally" in standing against Saddam Hussein's aggressions. During a January 1991 peace rally, Pelosi whipped the crowd into a frenzy when she turned President Bush's words on their head: "It is so important that you are here tonight to draw a line in the sand for George Bush." Even more incredibly, during a House floor speech, she explained that her opposition to protecting innocent Kuwaiti citizens from Saddam's brutality was also based on *environmental* factors. "The war cloud that would result from exploding oil fields and large-scale bombing of Kuwait, Iraq, Saudi Arabia, and other countries in the Middle East would doom the environment for many years to come," Pelosi thundered.[26] Strangely, when threats of rogue nations or terrorist organizations acquiring a radiological nuclear device are afoot, Pelosi and her environmental cronies seldom express urgency in thwarting the "global warming" and environmental fallout that would follow in the wake of a nuclear bomb detonating (not to speak of the hundreds of thousands of humans that would be destroyed as well).

Later, in 2002, Pelosi would leverage her ten years of experience on the House Intelligence Committee to help lead the Democrat opposition to President George W. Bush's decision to invade Iraq:

> It is from the perspective of 10 years on the Intelligence Committee that I rise in opposition to this resolution on national security grounds. The clear and present danger that our country faces is terrorism. I say flat out that unilateral use of force without first exhausting every diplomatic remedy and other remedies and making a case to the American people will be harmful to our war on terrorism. . . . If we go in, we can certainly show our power to Saddam Hussein. If we resolve this issue diplomatically, we can show our strength as a great country. Let us show our greatness. Vote no on this resolution.[27]

For her part, Pelosi persuaded 60 percent of House Democrats to stand against President Bush's decision to go to war, even as House

Democratic leader Dick Gephardt supported the measure. It was a pivotal stand for Pelosi, one that signaled to liberal House Democrats which side she stood on and how far she was willing to go in advancing her pacifist, anti-war agenda.

Indeed, one of the few areas in which Pelosi has ever shown much "spine" in terms of opposing aggressive regimes involves China. But her support always seems couched in the context of how it can benefit her electorally, not on more principled grounds of opposing Communism. Just as her father had ingratiated himself to the balkanized ethnic groups inside Baltimore, Nancy Pelosi has attempted to placate her Chinatown constituents by taking a hard line against the Communist dictates of the People's Liberation Army. Furthermore, she has been a supporter of human rights in Tibet. She applauded President George W. Bush's 2007 decision to present the Congressional Gold Medal to the Dalai Lama.[28] But even here, Pelosi couches her stance on issues in terms of remaining popular with her constituents, not on the broader grounds of opposing Communist tyranny. "Another issue important to my district is human rights, specifically what is happening in China. My district includes San Francisco's famous Chinatown, and many of my constituents were deeply concerned—as was I—when the Chinese government began to crack down on protesters who were demonstrating peacefully in Beijing and throughout China."[29]

In Pelosi's world, the political system is everything. It is the only thing. Every effort, every impulse, has a political calculation behind it, an angle to exploit for electoral advantage.

Bill Hambrecht, a San Francisco investment banker who specializes in Silicon Valley IPOs, is one of the top donors to Pelosi's campaign committee. As of 2006, Hambrecht had donated $38,000 to Pelosi and nearly $242,000 to Democratic causes. Before meeting Pelosi, Hambrecht says he sat on the political sidelines. "I had a political philosophy, but I was never involved in politics," said Hambrecht. But Pelosi's conviction that government could improve the world ignited something within him (and his wallet). "At the core of Nancy's being is a belief in the political system."[30] And it was this deep and abiding axial belief—that big government can solve and effectively control citizens' lives—that would spur her to aggressively pursue her leadership visions.

The storyline on Nancy Pelosi had long been that the San Francisco politician merely "fell into" politics following the untimely death of her friend Sala, and that she had never intended to climb into the leadership but rather wandered into opportunities as they came, first as Democratic whip, then Democratic minority leader, and ultimately Speaker of the House. The truth is much different. As the *Los Angeles Times* put it, "Her rise to a leadership role in Congress was more calculated, something she plotted and pursued for *years* [emphasis mine]."[31]

In early July 1999, Representative Loretta Sanchez (D-CA) hosted a small dinner gathering in Pelosi's honor at Barolo's restaurant on Capitol Hill. It was an informal gathering with a serious purpose. Those gathered had assembled to plot Nancy Pelosi's rise to the Democratic leadership. If, as Pelosi believed, Democrats could somehow win back the House in November 2000, Democratic minority leader Dick Gephardt would become Speaker of the House, Democratic whip David Bonior would rise to replace Gephardt as majority leader, and that, in turn, would leave a vacancy in the all-important spot of Democratic whip.

But there was an even more alluring possibility: if Gephardt ran for president of the United States (as many believed he would) and Bonior ran for governor of Michigan, whoever was elected whip would instantly become the new Speaker of the House.[32]

"The minute I decided to enter the race," said Pelosi, after defeating Hoyer for minority whip in 2001, "I decided to win. I wasn't going to ask people to support me and do a halfhearted race."[33]

Back in 1998, she had quietly tallied her likely level of support and found 80 votes. So following the dinner in 1999, Pelosi immediately went to work lining up her votes—she needed 108. Early indications led her to believe she was close. And that's when Pelosi, still well over a year away from the 2000 election, began kicking into overdrive. "Dinners, campaign appearances, letters to caucuses, team lunches, impromptu lobbying sessions in the hall" quickly ensued. Starting this early was unprecedented and irksome to many members, including Steny Hoyer and Representative John Lewis of Georgia, who was an "early casualty."[34] But Pelosi had her sights firmly set on her goal.

"In order to buck 200 years of history, if I have to start earlier than someone else, so be it," said Pelosi.[35]

Were Pelosi to become Democratic whip, she would be the highest-ranking woman in congressional history. She knew it wouldn't be easy. She needed a veteran insider as her field general, someone with heavy-weight credentials to manage her whip campaign. She turned to one of her closest allies and friends, Representative Jack Murtha. Murtha, who died in early 2010, is one of the most important figures in understanding Pelosi's climb. He served as her lead blocker, fiercest defender and closest adviser.

"If it hadn't been for Murtha," said one Pelosi backer, "Nancy wouldn't have a chance against the institution."[36] Catholic University politics professor Matthew Green agreed: "That alliance was absolutely essential because Murtha had a lot of connections, he was well respected among Democrats, was able to help her build relationships with members who might be suspicious otherwise. . . . I would suspect that Murtha saw in Pelosi the potential to become Speaker, saw that leadership potential in her, saw that she had the ability necessary to achieve power. I think to make that kind of decision to support a more junior member of the caucus over a long term means that you see something in that person and you want to take them under your wing and help them achieve their potential."[37]

As with Phil Burton, Murtha liked Pelosi's moxie. So he took her on. "She's talented. She's focused. She has an agenda to accomplish. She's got more energy than anyone I know," said Murtha.[38]

But the man standing in Pelosi's path was Representative Steny Hoyer of Maryland, as well as the so-called boys' club he and his seniority represented. Pelosi had originally backed Hoyer in 1991, the first time he had run for House whip, against David Bonior. But Pelosi and Hoyer's history went back further. In 1963, Hoyer and Pelosi had spent their younger years serving together in Maryland senator Daniel B. Brewster's office. That was where the seeds of rivalry were first sown. The reason may have been that Hoyer received a position working as an aide to Brewster, while Pelosi "was assigned secretarial work."

When asked if he and Pelosi were friends at the time, Hoyer replied that the term "friends" would make too much of their relationship. "We didn't run in the same crowd," said Hoyer. "Nancy came from an extraordinarily prominent family."[39]

Hoyer's political flame had been sparked when he was a sophomore at the University of Maryland, where John F. Kennedy showed up on campus in a Pontiac Bonneville convertible to campaign for president. The moment formed the man. Hoyer soon switched his major from public relations to political science, before going off to Georgetown Law. Then, in 1966, a 27-year-old Hoyer was elected to the Maryland State Senate from Prince George's County.[40]

Throughout his political career, Hoyer had established himself as a deal maker. As his chief of staff, Bill Cable, put it, "Mr. Hoyer's policy is that you've got to listen to all sides. Never close the door to anyone whether you agree with them or disagree with them." John Moag, who worked for Hoyer in the U.S. Congress and also when Hoyer served in the Maryland Senate, agrees: "He cares more about process than issues, per se. Good process ultimately produces good policy. This is a guy who's been compromising his whole life because he knows that's how it gets done."[41]

Hoyer had two factors working in his favor. First, he had seniority on his side. Second, he had strong ties to the Democratic establishment, most notably Minority Leader Dick Gephardt. But Hoyer's centrist sensibilities and pragmatic impulses were at odds with the more ideological factions of the Democratic Party. The pragmatist Hoyer versus the purist Pelosi. It was a fairly even match except for one key, distinguishing factor: money.

Pelosi deployed one of her most lethal tactical weapons against Hoyer: she buried him in a blizzard of dollar bills. Come Election Day 2000, Hoyer had raised and dispensed a remarkable $1.5 million to Democratic candidates. Impressive, to say the least. But Hoyer's efforts were nothing compared with Nancy Pelosi's West Coast money-raising machine. When the tallies had been counted, Pelosi had given a jaw-dropping $3.9 million to her Democratic counterparts to support their elections.[42]

As it turned out, all that money had been spent in vain; Republicans held the Congress, thus eliminating the possibility of a new Democratic whip. But the race resumed in May, when David Bonior announced he would be running for governor. Soon, the two rivals and their staffs were back at it—and at each other's throats. Voting for whip is done by secret ballot. That made vote counting a nerve-racking challenge. But Pelosi had learned how to count the votes by watching her father. She put 90 members on a public list to hold them accountable. She claimed to have a dozen more who'd asked to remain anonymous. Pelosi wanted certain victory, not speculation. That meant bringing out the knives. When Ellen Tauscher became the only California Democrat to publicly support Hoyer, she claimed that Pelosi began strong-arming her through intimidation tactics. Specifically, Tauscher alleged that Pelosi was trying to punish her by having her congressional district boundaries changed through a California redistricting plan.

"I frankly can't believe that [Pelosi] would risk the [House] majority to get a leadership post," said Tauscher, whom Pelosi had previously supported during Tauscher's successful reelection bid. Pelosi biographer Marc Sandalow wrote that when reporters asked Pelosi for comment on the redistricting matter, she snapped back, "It's not even worth my time to talk about."[43] And Pelosi's time was, indeed, worth something. She had tapped into her Silicon Valley and San Francisco money machines and raised a whopping $5 million for Democratic candidates this time around.

Pelosi's fund-raising dominance remains one of her most devastating tactical weapons. There are at least three reasons Nancy Pelosi is able to raise and disperse such massive sums of cash to Democratic candidates. First, because she comes from an affluent yet electorally "safe" district, Pelosi does not spend much money funding her own reelection campaigns and thus can give monies she would have spent on her campaign to candidates in more vulnerable districts. Even in the unlikely event that she ever finds herself in a tight race of her own, Nancy Pelosi is one of the richest members of the U.S. House of Representatives, with more than $25 million in assets, according to *Roll Call*. As the *San Francisco Chronicle* has reported, Paul Pelosi's investments include owning a portion of the Wine Country resort Auberge du Soleil, millions of dollars of stock in Microsoft Corp. and Disney Co., and owning a three-story commercial building in downtown San Francisco.[44]

Second, because of California's vast pockets of wealth, Nancy Pelosi is able to tap into the so-called California gold by excavating cash from California's richest citizens before exporting the gold across the country to candidates in tight races. Even prior to her career in Congress, she had been an active California fund-raiser and a state party chair.[45]

Third, Nancy Pelosi is unusually effective at money hustling because she understands—largely from the lessons learned in the rough-and-tumble Baltimore political world—that achieving one's own political ambitions is often a function of mastering jobs others find unappealing and even smarmy. As San Francisco political consultant Sam Lauter explained to the *San Francisco Chronicle*, "Pelosi's rise in the Democratic Party has been fueled by her willingness to take on the unpopular jobs necessary to build the party, whether it's licking envelopes or asking for money."[46] Other Democrats have lamented the swank parties she hosts and the lavish donor base she courts. "She's just a fund-raiser," one senior House Democratic aide complained. "A wealthy woman with a lot of wealthy friends."[47]

Still, even with Pelosi's money bullet train blazing along, tensions were growing in the whip race. Pelosi believed Hoyer's camp was leaking negative information about her to the press to undermine her chances of winning. Moreover, Pelosi had grown increasingly annoyed that the whip race had been framed as Hoyer the moderate against Pelosi the leftist. It was, of course, a reasonable way to frame things. But she felt such positioning detracted from her place in the spotlight. So she began lashing out at the press.

"Here I am on the brink of making history," Pelosi lectured. "Here I am on the brink of changing the way people think about these issues . . . and you are stuck on a record that has no real significance. You're talking new-old. You've got to reject that because that's holding you back. There's no real difference in our voting record. This is about how you do things. You're stuck in tired old assumptions of the past. You're being spun."[48]

It was the real Nancy shining through. As President Obama's chief of staff, Rahm Emanuel, puts it, "She has a mettle to her that is disguised by a wonderful smile." Another senior House aide adds, "Nancy Pelosi is a take-no-prisoners type of politician."[49]

As the date of the whip election—October 10, 2001—drew closer, the battle between Hoyer and Pelosi came to a temporary pause when terrorists turned airplanes into missiles on September 11. Like all Americans, Pelosi expressed grief and outrage at the atrocities Al Qaeda had committed against the United States. But just weeks after the attacks, Democrats were back to political business as usual, revving up for the whip vote.

"We've all put it on the back burner for the past three weeks," said Pelosi. "Fortunately for me, I had my votes lined up before. I can ignore the race for three weeks. I wish the election were right now. I'm in excellent shape."[50]

Prior to the vote, Hoyer and Pelosi engaged in some psychological gamesmanship. Each made statements that the other candidate's supporters had lied to them and that their count totals were wrong. Pelosi had seen her mentor Burton endure a painful one-vote loss to Jim Wright on a similar leadership vote. So she had been exacting in counting and recounting, confirming with members and reconfirming. Team Pelosi even issued 7:30 A.M. wake-up calls to the more than 100 members who had pledged their support.[51] Her meticulousness and arm-twisting paid off. True to form, Pelosi had counted her votes almost perfectly. On October 10, with a 118-to-95-vote majority, Nancy Pelosi became the highest ranking female congressional leader in U.S. history.

"My votes were so right on the money," bragged Pelosi.[52] "This is difficult turf to win on for anyone," Pelosi said. "But for a woman breaking ground here, it was a tough battle. We made history, now we need to make progress."[53]

Hoyer was all sour grapes. "If she hadn't been a woman or from California, I think we would have been okay. Gender and geography in this case were overwhelming. *C'est la guerre.*"[54]

Pelosi's meticulous planning, excruciating attention to detail and vote counting, and endless money geyser had been precisely the tactics necessary to break through the so-called marble ceiling, as she put it. Feminist groups were abuzz.

After years of plotting and strategizing, she was now poised to catapult herself to the two rungs that remained above her—Democratic leader and Speaker of the House. On the day of the vote, the late veteran legislator Representative Tom Lantos (D-CA) issued a prediction: "She's clearly on the way to becoming the first woman speaker in the United States."[55]

The comment wasn't just prescient; it also presaged a severe new code for enforcing obeisance to the dictates and demands of the Democratic leadership. As members soon learned, no one crosses Nancy Pelosi without paying a price. And nowhere was that more clear than in the way she treated veteran lawmaker Representative John D. Dingell (D-MI) in the wake of his decision to support Hoyer over her during the epic battle for Democratic whip. For Pelosi, Dingell represented a prime opportunity to send a message to all Democrats. She would not tolerate disloyalty of any kind, regardless of seniority. So, when Dingell, the longest-serving House member, found himself in the Michigan primary battle against Lynn Rivers, Pelosi dispatched a $10,000 check from her massive war chest to Rivers, not Dingell. It was an unprecedented move; members of the leadership seldom if ever oppose a sitting member of Congress in a primary. Pelosi's move was the shot heard round the Democratic world. It sent a loud and clear message: disloyalty and defection will come at a price—literally.

"Her biggest weakness," said one House leadership aide, "is she views the world in two camps: 'those who are for me and those who are against me.' She'll have to get over that if she's going to succeed."[56]

But she didn't get over it, and she *still* succeeded. In fact, one might argue that she succeeded precisely *because* she held grudges and never forgot past "betrayals." When asked about why she'd decided to shoot Dingell a heat-seeking money missile, Pelosi replied, "[Rivers] was for me. [Dingell] was not."[57]

Pelosi's role as Democratic whip would be short-lived, however. In the wake of the Democrats' 2002 congressional defeat, Minority Leader Dick Gephardt announced he would be stepping down to run for president. The instant Gephardt made his announcement, Pelosi picked up the phone and began a 36-hour blitzkrieg of phone calls. It was a sight Pelosi's children had seen many times before. "I remember her throughout my childhood with a telephone glued to her ear," remembers daughter Alexandra, the youngest of the Pelosis' five children. "In the name of the Democratic Party, she's been on the phone for 32 years."[58] Pelosi's speed in working the phones was not random. It was a trait she had learned from her mentor Phil Burton, whose phone banks stood ready for deployment at a second's notice. Like Burton, Pelosi had lined up her votes well in advance. Her opponents for Democratic minority leader were Representative Martin Frost (D-TX) and the young Representative Harold E. Ford, Jr. (D-TN). Neither stood a chance. Frost hit the airwaves and got in front of as many TV cameras as possible. As Pelosi remembered it, "Everyone said, 'How come you're not on TV?' I said, 'They're on TV, I'm on the telephone. That's where the votes are.'"[59]

Within 36 hours, Frost had pulled out and thrown his support to Pelosi. Ford, then 32 years old, stayed in. On November 14, 2002, House Democrats elected Nancy Pelosi as their minority leader. It was a landslide—177 votes to Ford's paltry 29. Her working of the phones, however, had been a mere formality. It was the flexing of Pelosi's money muscles that, once again, had won her the day. She had almost doubled her previous fund-raising record, raising between $7 million and $8 million, which she then divvied up among more than 100 Democratic candidates, not including the $722,000 she doled out to candidates from her leadership PAC and her personal campaign funds.[60]

"It took us three years to win the whip's race, and 36 hours to win [the minority leader race]," said one Pelosi aide.[61]

The speed and lethality of Pelosi's machine was growing. She had honed her skills to operate with blinding speed. She had enforced a code of reverential fear among allies and enemies. Retaliations against rivals and defectors were now administered unflinchingly, just as Burton had taught her to. Her tactical proficiency in mining and shuttling mountains of California gold to Democratic candidates around the country now impressed even her biggest critics. As she assumed the leader's role, the Boss was now primed and ready to kick her operation into maximum overdrive.

6

POUNDING THE GAVEL

If people are ripping your face off, you have to rip their face off.[1]

—Nancy Pelosi

No sooner had Nancy Pelosi won the race to become Democratic leader than she began a series of Mach-speed maneuvers to consolidate and expand her power. She knew the importance of committee assignments, and she treated cherished spots on select committees as the form of patronage she'd seen Big Tommy dole out back home in Baltimore. Loyalty was to be rewarded, disloyalty punished.

"When she fights, she wins . . . and those that stand in her way not only lose, but she never forgets," said Democratic strategist Mark Siegel. "Cross her once, she crosses you off the list."[2]

Being "crossed off her list" meant that important and influential committees were to be packed with her fiercest and most loyal friends. Members who had dared to buck her rise to power by backing Representative Steny Hoyer would receive lesser committee assignments. When the choicest spots opened up, Pelosi carefully installed older, docile Democratic members whose loyalty was assured and whose lack of ambition was self-evident.[3]

Pelosi's managerial style, both as minority leader and Speaker of the House, remains fixated on details. The details in which she is most interested involve eschewing bipartisanship, ensuring obeisance in voting, obfuscating her hypocritical stances in domestic and foreign affairs, keeping the money machine churning out boatloads of campaign cash, and rewarding loyalty.

Upon assuming her role as Democratic minority leader, Nancy Pelosi immediately began laying the groundwork for a new code of Democratic Party unity. In many ways, she applied to her new leadership position as Democratic leader the same party discipline tools she'd used as Democratic whip. One of Pelosi's long-standing allies, Palo Alto congresswoman Anna Eshoo, explains:

> She understands in a very sophisticated and profound way what unity is. It's not that it begins and ends with party discipline, to be loyal to a party, but that if you are not unified, the doors in front of you will be locked. You can't do anything unless you bring a unified position to whatever you are doing.[4]

Indeed, for all of Pelosi's talk about bipartisanship, those who know her best say that bipartisan efforts are anathema to her political makeup. Talk of bipartisanship is all a political head fake. For Pelosi, ramming legislation through the political pipeline suits her just fine. "Nancy really doesn't care about Republicans, because she doesn't believe the whole bi-partisan thing exists," said one of Pelosi's close associates. "Her attitude is, 'God bless their souls, but these people don't believe in global warming. They just don't agree with us.'"[5]

As Democratic minority leader, Pelosi's disinterest in reaching across the aisle allowed her to achieve a rare level of Democratic unity in the House. Under Pelosi, according to the *Congressional Quarterly's* 2005 study of the past 50 years of Democratic House voting trends, Democrats were more unified as a voting bloc than ever before, voting together an astonishing record 88 percent of the time.[6] For a liberal who espouses the importance of open-mindedness and of including a diverse chorus of opinions and perspectives, Pelosi seems curiously insistent on robotic groupthink. Indeed, to achieve her goal of climbing into the speakership, Pelosi knew she would need to present Democrats as a unified opposition against the policies and leadership of President George W. Bush. Doing so, Pelosi understood, would project an air of strength that would redound to her fundraising efforts.

Pelosi sees bipartisanship as the political equivalent of sleeping with the enemy, a sin wealthy leftist donors are unlikely to forgive.

According to *Time* columnist Perry Bacon, Jr.:

> To condition Democrats for this fall's [2006] midterm elections, she has employed tactics straight out of DeLay's playbook: insisting other House Democrats vote the party line on everything, avoiding compromise with Republicans at all cost and mandating that members spend much of their time raising money for colleagues in close races. And she has been effective. House Democrats have been more unified in their voting than at any other time in the past quarter-century.[7]

Even less useful than bipartisanship to Pelosi is perceived weakness. For Pelosi, public displays of weakness are the gravest sin. "I'm not big on showing weakness," says Pelosi. "It's not my thing."[8]

As *New York* magazine reporter Vanessa Grigoriadis noted, Pelosi cares little about her public opinion ratings, or how her fierceness may offend people, so long as she does not portray frailty. "To look weak in public, well, that's Pelosi's worst nightmare," writes Grigoriadis. "If need be, she's willing to be hated. Not caring makes Pelosi powerful. She'll listen to her poll numbers from her staff, but she doesn't really process them."[9]

Nowhere was this feature of Pelosi's leadership more evident than in her consistent and staunch opposition to President George W. Bush's prosecution of the war on terror, particularly as it related to the president's decision to invade Iraq.

"She really hates this president with a passion," said former Democratic congresswoman Pat Schroeder. "Everything he has stood for and he and [Vice President Dick] Cheney have done is the antithesis of what she believes in."[10]

Pelosi's antipathy toward President Bush's domestic agenda, coupled with her vehement opposition to the Iraq war, proved a lucrative fund-raising combination. Indeed, by the 2004 election, during her two years as Democratic minority leader, Pelosi had netted $30 million for Democratic candidates, trekked to more than 25 states and 115 cities, and participated in more than 130 fund-raisers.[11] Still, while Pelosi's and many Democrats' antiwar views may have resonated with leftist activists and donors, come Election Day, voters stood solidly beside President George W. Bush, reelecting him over John Kerry. It was a setback to Pelosi's designs on the speakership, but one that merely motivated her to recommit the next two years to building an even stronger organizational network to catapult her into the Speaker's office. Pelosi's two operational dictums—"organize, don't agonize" and "proper planning prevents poor performance"—became her rallying cry for a highly coordinated and meticulously executed two-year strategy to win back the Congress and seize her place as the nation's first female Speaker of the House.[12]

First, Pelosi homed in on developing a Democratic message she could market to voters. So she turned to the masters of messaging, top marketing executives in the high-tech industry. Pelosi wanted to learn how to sell Democratic candidates and policies like an iPod. According to Pelosi, the Silicon Valley marketing mavens first advised that she and the more than 250 Democrats in the House and Senate should boil down their ideas to a manageable handful of simple principles and priorities. The result, says Pelosi, was six key priorities that coalesced into something called the "Partnership for America's Future." Having dutifully completed the marketing homework, Pelosi and her gang unveiled their plan to the high-tech gurus.

"Your six ideas are very good," they told Pelosi, "but timing is everything. If you go forward with them now, President Bush can crush you right under his heel. He has the bully pulpit. He is the President of the United States, you're the minority. You have so little power. You can't compete unless you take him down a few pegs first. That's the way it's done in the private sector."[13]

Pelosi had her marching orders. She would engineer a smear campaign against the president that would trash his ratings, contrast Democratic positions with the president's, and then—and only then—roll out their "New Direction—Six for '06" campaign platform.

Pelosi's first target of attack came early in 2005, when President Bush announced that he supported efforts to allow taxpayers the option of investing a portion of their Social Security in nongovernmental vehicles to achieve greater financial gains. Pelosi and Senate minority leader Harry Reid pounced immediately. The goal was to whip up fear among seniors that the president was intent on "privatizing Social Security" and bankrupting seniors' life savings through risky private investments. It was a classic strategy of demonize-and-destroy. When some Democrats proposed offering a positive alternative to the president's proposal, the Boss immediately shot down the idea and enforced a code of "Just say no."

"Social Security is our plan," Pelosi and Reid told Democrats. "The only way we can beat President Bush is to focus on the shortcomings of *his* plan." Pelosi's strategy of demonize-and-destroy had begun to move the needle of public opinion in the Democrats' favor. Even so, Pelosi advised Harry Reid that a victory would be no cause for celebration; maximum pressure must be applied consistently and without ceasing. "If we win on this, we can't just take this issue off the table. We must create a two-pronged attack," Pelosi told Reid.[14]

Soon, Pelosi and Reid found a rhetorical framework in which to wrap their Republican attacks. They would lob the alliterative charge that Republicans had created a "culture of corruption, cronyism, and incompetence."

It was a phrase in search of an issue to exploit. Democrats didn't have to wait long. On August 29, 2005, Hurricane Katrina, the most expensive and third-most-intense storm ever to hit the U.S. mainland, ravaged the Gulf Coast. Pelosi now had her tragedy to exploit, one she could use as a wedge to take down the president, just as she and her high-tech marketing cronies had strategized. Shortly after the storm hit landfall, Republican and Democratic leaders met with the president at the White House. Immediately after the briefing, Pelosi darted toward the press.

"When I met the press outside the White House, all I said was, 'I suggested to the president that he fire Michael Brown.'" Bush had exacerbated matters when he defended "Brownie" and claimed the director was doing "a heck of a job." The day after the White House meeting, even as the disaster relief efforts were freshly under way, Pelosi launched her attack against the president. "This president is in denial. He is therefore dangerous."[15] Soon, with the help of liberal members of the media, as well as Hollywood leftists like rapper Kanye West, who, on

September 2, declared during a nationally televised Hurricane Katrina relief effort that "George Bush doesn't care about black people," Pelosi's plan to destroy the president's public standing was working brilliantly.

"The Democrats had successfully pulled back the curtain to reveal the Republicans' culture of corruption, cronyism, and incompetence, and the President's approval rating dropped to 38 percent," Pelosi boasted. "Soon came the time for differentiation. We spelled out how our proposals and legislation were different from theirs. We *defined* ourselves, which was part two of our strategy. Only as the midterm elections of 2006 approached did we announce our 'New Direction—Six for '06' platform:

- Real Security: at Home and Overseas
- Prosperity: Better American Jobs, and Better Pay
- Opportunity: College Access for All
- Energy Independence
- Affordable Health Care
- Honest Leadership and Open Government"[16]

It was a well-honed and tested message designed to pick up at least the 15 critical seats that would be needed for Democrats to take over the House. Almost as if on cue, in September 2006, just weeks out from the midterm elections, Democrats were handed an electoral gift when Representative Mark Foley (R-FL) became embroiled in a national scandal involving an underage House page. The ensuing scandal surrounding Foley's texting and targeting of underage male House pages for sex dealt a major electoral blow to the GOP that deflated Republican turnout and emboldened Democrats to try to win control of the House. In typical fashion, Nancy Pelosi wasted no time seizing on the scandal to inflict maximum political damage. In fact, she helped lead the ethics charge against Foley, saying that Republicans who had known of Foley's vile behavior had broken faith with voters.

Pelosi's strong stand against gay pedophilia stands in sharp contrast, however, to her 2001 decision to participate in the so-called Pride Parade, a parade that the *San Francisco Chronicle* dubbed "the granddaddy, grandma and grandtrannie [as in transvestite] of 'em all." That year's San Francisco Lesbian Gay Bisexual Transgender Pride Celebration grand marshal had been none other than the legendary homosexual activist Harry Hay, a leader with connections to the Communist Party in the 1930s who founded the Mattachine Society, an organization that the *Chronicle* dubbed "the first sustained homosexual rights organization in the United States."[17] Hay was celebrant 31 in the parade. Representative Nancy Pelosi was celebrant 34, a marching position that placed her but steps behind Hay. Oddly, however, Pelosi did not erupt in protest against Hay. This seems odd. After all, Harry Hay was a strong advocate of man/boy love. In fact, the North American Man/Boy Love Association (NAMBLA) was such a fan of Harry Hay's pro-pedophilia opinions that it made available a collection of his beliefs that there is great benefit in young boys having sex with older men.

"Because if the parents and friends of gays are truly friends of gays," Hay said during a 1983 New York University forum, "they would know from their gay kids that the relationship with an older man is precisely what thirteen-, fourteen-, and fifteen-year-old kids need more than anything else in the world."[18]

Just one year later, in 2002, Pelosi used the upcoming celebration as an occasion to honor the first openly gay police officer in San Francisco to lose his life while on duty, and to voice her support for the LGBT community. Pelosi said on the House floor, "This weekend marks the 32nd annual San Francisco Lesbian, Gay, Bisexual, Transgender Pride Celebration entitled, 'Be Yourself, Change the World!' This is our time to celebrate San Francisco's proud history of advocacy for equal rights for lesbian, gay, bisexual, and transgender persons and to recognize the important contributions the LGBT Community makes to our City and to our nation."[19]

When the Foley affair broke, Minority Leader Pelosi issued the following condemnation: "Republican leaders admitted to knowing about Mr. Foley's abhorrent behavior for six months to a year and failed to protect the children in their trust. Republican leaders must be investigated by the ethics committee and immediately questioned under oath."[20]

Yet when it came to San Francisco's celebrated homosexual champion and man/boy sex advocate Harry Hay's participation in the parade, and his marching just feet in front of Pelosi, the San Francisco congresswoman was strangely silent. No protests. No condemnations of Hay's involvement in or advocacy of similarly "abhorrent behavior" as that of Foley. No harsh alarms sounded to parents in the community. Silence.[21]

The Foley scandal fit perfectly into the corruption narrative Pelosi and Reid had anchored in the minds of the media and the electorate. With just weeks to go, Pelosi's attack strategy, hard work and meticulous planning all appeared to be culminating in a perfect electoral storm. "Many Democrats are getting super excited about [the prospect of] the first woman speaker," said Democratic Congressional Campaign Committee (DCCC) staffer Kori Bernards.[22] But Pelosi's enthusiasm to "crack the marble ceiling," as she would put it, did not shake her focus.

"She's as savvy as you can get," says Representative George Miller (D-CA). "She has a tremendous field of vision. She sees where players are; she sees where an issue is." Miller compares Pelosi's political acumen to the basketball prowess of Magic Johnson. "You know exactly who he's going to pass the ball to, except he doesn't pass it to that person. He flips it behind him, and that person takes and dunks it. He knows where the players are on the court, and she brings that kind of vision to politics."[23]

More to the point, Pelosi knows how to *fund* the players on the court. And, once again, Pelosi unleashed her go-to move: raising unprecedented sums of money. Part of Pelosi's fund-raising acumen involved leveraging her title as minority leader. "Since Nancy started signing our mail, we've had over a million dollars a month for over 10 months in a row now," said Bernards.[24]

Still, just as with her past fund-raising efforts on behalf of her bid to become Democratic whip, Pelosi possesses a seemingly preternatural ability to turn on the charm, leverage relationships and become a veritable ATM machine to dispense cash to Democratic candidates, thereby ingratiating herself to them and building up goodwill to be called in as favors at a later date.

"She is very good at the personal, retail level of this stuff," said Steven Kazan, an Oakland lawyer who specializes in asbestos lawsuits that have pumped $30,400 into the DCCC's coffers. "With the House of Representatives, I long ago decided that I could not figure out what races were important," said Kazan. "When someone calls [for a campaign donation], I tell them, 'Nancy Pelosi is my leader. If your name is on her list, I'll give you some money. If it's not, I'm real sorry, but take it up with Nancy.' "[25]

But beyond Pelosi's skill in building relationships with donors, the Boss seems to possess a stomach for fund-raising that others disdain. "Not everyone wants to do this," says a liaison to big donors in the area. "She makes you." Others agree. "When she helped you to get into office to vote one way and then you don't," says a friend, "well, that's what gets her."[26]

It's all part of the speaker's applied pressure techniques. Operating behind the scenes, Pelosi aligns important donors from key constituencies to lean on members to vote her way. A telling example of this occurred when freshman congressman Zack Space, a Greek American member from a vulnerable Ohio district, was waffling in his support for the global warming bill. As soon as the speaker learned about Space's indecision, she picked up the phone and began dialing powerful Greek American donors. She then asked the donors to contact Representative Space directly to weigh in with their support for the bill. The day following their calls, Space decided to support the legislation.[27]

However unseemly, Pelosi's tactics had a powerful net effect. With her future speakership on the line, Pelosi's 2006 dash for cash yielded record-shattering results. In 2006, Minority Leader Nancy Pelosi raked in a jaw-dropping $60 million for Democratic candidates. By comparison, former leader Dick Gephardt had raised a measly $2.5 million for candidates from 1990 to the 2000 election. All told, between 2000 and 2006, Nancy Pelosi had been responsible for amassing more than $140 million for Democratic candidates.[28]

It was an investment that paid historic dividends. Picking up 31 seats, Democrats easily cleared the 15-seat hurdle necessary to regain control of the House, thereby placing Nancy Pelosi two heartbeats away from the presidency.

On January 4, 2007, Nancy Pelosi, 66, took the oath of office and was sworn in as America's 60th Speaker of the House and the first female to occupy the office. Amid effusive pageantry and fawning media attention, Pelosi positioned herself as the standard-bearer of progress for all American women. "We made history and now we will make progress for the American people," she declared. The record-breaking fund-raiser then added, "We will not be dazzled by money and special interests."[29]

The historic nature of Pelosi's rise to power may have been unprecedented, but the tactics she has used to wield and expand her power as
Speaker of the House are not. In many ways, Pelosi's political tactics are
quite predictable and consistent across the trajectory of her career.

First, right from the start, Madam Speaker exhibited her trademark
ambitious, Mach-speed style to ram her agenda through the political
pipeline. In the fall of 2006, Pelosi promised to "drain the GOP swamp"
with an ambitious agenda if the Democrats won control of the House
and she got hold of the gavel. That agenda would include: instituting
rules that would sever ties between lobbyists and legislation, implement
all recommendations from the 9/11 Commission, raise the minimum
wage to $7.25 an hour, cut the interest rate on student loans in half, foster
direct negotiations between the government and pharmaceutical companies for Medicare drug prices and expand federal funding for additional
types of stem cell research.[30] And in January 2007 she followed through
on her promise. As each bill passed, Pelosi reportedly banged the gavel
so enthusiastically that it left a small dent in the lectern.[31]

Second, as she has done in the past, Pelosi began her tenure by
attempting to reward her loyalists and marginalizing her rivals. Even
before she assumed the speakership, Pelosi had suffered a political blow
when her decision to support her longtime ally and the manager of
her whip campaign, Representative John Murtha, for the number two
House leadership post over her archrival, Representative Steny Hoyer,
backfired. It was an important statement of loyalty on her part, a clear
sign that old alliances would remain in her new role as speaker. Nevertheless, wanting to project an image of unity, Speaker-elect Pelosi
sounded a conciliatory tone. "I look forward to working together with
[Hoyer] in a unified way," said Pelosi. "We've had our debates; we've
had our disagreements in that room. And now, that is over. As I said to
my colleagues, as we say in church, let there be peace on Earth and let
it begin with us. Let the healing begin."[32]

For public relations purposes, Speaker Pelosi may have buried the
hatchet with Majority Leader Hoyer, but she maintains a tenuous relationship with an array of other adversaries, each of whom she has tried to
steamroll. In contrast to her father's "favor file," reporter Glenn Thrush
says that Speaker Pelosi also maintains a "disfavor file in her head—a roster

of those whom she believes have screwed up, betrayed her, challenged her or merely annoyed her." Pelosi allies contend that the list is real.[33]

Chief among these individuals is Representative Jane Harman, the hawkish California Democrat whom Pelosi had tapped in 2003 to serve as the ranking Democrat on the House Intelligence Committee. Harman, a Harvard Law graduate, was in line for the chairmanship of the powerful committee until Pelosi pulled the plug on her onetime friend when Harman failed to protest the Bush administration's "alleged abuses of intelligence." Harman made the mistake of launching a boisterous and vocal bid for the chairmanship. The Boss dug in her heels and made an example of Harman, denying her the coveted chairmanship. Later, in 2009, it was revealed that Harman's phones had been wiretapped by the National Security Agency and that Speaker Pelosi had been notified that Harman's phones were bugged but was legally prevented from tipping off Harman. The reason for the phone tap remains unclear, but Politico reported that "nobody would be paying much attention to the old-news internecine battle [between Pelosi and Harman] had *CQ* and *The New York Times* not reported that a suspected Israeli agent was wiretapped several years ago allegedly offering a deal to Harman."[34] Harman vigorously denies the allegations.

Another person Speaker Pelosi has in her crosshairs is Representative Heath Shuler (D-NC). Shuler raised the Boss's ire when he voted against both bank bailouts and President Obama's stimulus package. Shuler's comment that "House leadership and Senate leadership have really failed" on the stimulus package didn't sit well with Pelosi.[35]

Representative Greg Meeks (D-NY) and Representative Edolphus Towns (D-NY) also joined Pelosi's hit parade when they supported the Central American Free Trade Agreement (CAFTA). Meeks doubly angered Madam Speaker when he had the audacity to vote for Republican bankruptcy and tort reforms. As Pelosi has said in another context, "Anybody who's ever dealt with me knows not to mess with me."[36] The Speaker put her muscle where her mouth was and threatened to strip Towns of his Energy and Commerce Committee seat. Towns's chief of staff, Karen Johnson, said, "[Pelosi] can't be any angrier at Mr. Towns than she was at Steny Hoyer. If the healing is to begin, it should begin with Mr. Meeks and Mr. Towns."[37]

Yet for all her vindictiveness and insistence on Democratic voting discipline, perhaps the Speaker's most dangerous tactic is her erratic way of lashing out and issuing serious charges and attacks against others when clearly she has been exposed engaging in political hypocrisy and scandal of her own creation.

To date, Nancy Pelosi's greatest and gravest hypocrisy has come on the issue of whether or not she knew that the CIA was engaged in so-called enhanced interrogation techniques (EITs), most notably waterboarding. Given Pelosi's strong support among the blame-America-first crowd and her San Francisco antimilitary, anti-war constituency, one would imagine that as ranking member of the House Intelligence Committee, Nancy Pelosi would have shouted down the CIA's use of such ghastly torture techniques as dribbling water down a terrorist's nose to get him to speak. But that's not what happened. Not at all. To hear Pelosi tell the story, she and her fellow committee members were bamboozled by the CIA.

"The CIA briefed me only once on some enhanced interrogation techniques, in September 2002, in my capacity as Ranking Member of the House Intelligence Committee. I was informed then that Department of Justice opinions had concluded that the use of enhanced interrogation techniques was legal. The only mention of waterboarding at that briefing was that it was not being employed."[38]

In fact, according to the CIA chronology of events, Pelosi received a September 4, 2002, waterboarding briefing on Abu Zubaydah.[39] One of the other members of Congress present was the chairman of the House Intelligence Committee, Porter Goss, who would later serve as CIA director from September 2004 to May 2006. Goss strongly disagrees with Pelosi's convenient retelling of events and remembers the CIA briefing quite differently. In a 2009 *Washington Post* article, Goss wrote that he was "slack-jawed to read that members claim to have not understood that the techniques on which they were briefed were to actually be employed; or that specific techniques such as 'waterboarding' were never mentioned." Goss went on to write that members "understood what the CIA was doing," "gave the CIA our bipartisan support," "gave the CIA funding to carry out its activities" and even "asked if the CIA needed more support from Congress to carry out its mission against al-Qaeda." Goss recalls that not a single objection was made.[40]

Pelosi's decision to play politics with national security was bad enough. But it was her decision during a rambling and embarrassingly bumbling May 14, 2009, press conference to turn her rhetorical guns on the CIA that sparked a firestorm. In typical Pelosi fashion, when finding her back against the wall, the Boss lashed out, blasting away at anyone and anything if she considered it politically advantageous to do so. First, she slammed the CIA. "They misled us all the time," Pelosi charged. Then it was all the Bush administration's fault. "They misrepresented every step of the way, and they don't want that focus on them, so they try to turn the attention on us."

Pelosi's press conference performance was a disaster. Reporters pounced on her sputtering, bumbling, evasive answers. With each follow-up question, her answers grew more opaque and bizarre. Bafflingly, Pelosi actually confessed that, as early as 2003, she had, in fact, known that waterboarding had been used. "I wasn't briefed," Pelosi said. "I was informed that someone else had been briefed about it."[41]

The next day, former Clinton White House chief of staff turned CIA director Leon Panetta issued a statement rebutting Pelosi's allegations that the CIA had misled the Congress. "Let me be clear: It is not our policy or practice to mislead Congress," said Panetta. "That is against our laws and our values. As the Agency indicated previously in response to Congressional inquiries, our contemporaneous records from September 2002 indicate that CIA officers briefed truthfully on the interrogation of Abu Zubaydah, describing 'the enhanced techniques that had been employed.'"[42] As Jed Babbin, former deputy undersecretary of defense for President George H. W. Bush, pointed out, Panetta's use of the past tense—"that *had been* employed"—makes it clear that Pelosi was fully aware that waterboarding had been used but did nothing in response, a clear contradiction to her breathless protestations about Republicans' love affair with "torture." "She is caught between the facts and her own radicalism in condemning the CIA," wrote Babbin.[43]

Former Speaker of the House Newt Gingrich condemned Pelosi's statements against the CIA and called for her to step down as Speaker. "The case against Nancy Pelosi remaining Speaker of the House is as simple as it is devastating: The person who is No. 2 in line to be commander in chief can't have contempt for the men and women who protect our nation," wrote the former Speaker. "America can't afford it."[44]

Representative Peter King (R-NY), the ranking member of the House Homeland Security Committee, joined Gingrich in his outrage against the Speaker's actions and called for Pelosi to temporarily step down until her allegations were investigated. "She's made some serious charges and should step aside until she proves them."[45]

Even Democratic stalwart and Clinton strategist James Carville conceded that Pelosi's performance had been an embarrassment. "I'm sure if she could have it back, she would have done the whole thing over."[46]

As Democratic minority leader and now as Speaker of the House, Nancy Pelosi has proved herself to be a fierce and resilient political animal. There is nothing new about politicians aggressively pursuing their goals or fighting hard to rise up the leadership food chain. However, Pelosi has employed a severe brand of enforcement from her Democratic caucus, meting out unbending punishments for defectors and rewards for those who fall in line.

"If you take the knife off the table, it's not very frightening anymore," said Pelosi.[47]

When the Boss deploys her arsenal of tactical weapons, sometimes, from the outside looking in, Pelosi's managerial style can appear haphazard and ineffective. Nowhere was this clearer than during the yearlong war over enactment of President Obama's health-care boondoggle. For a while, it appeared that Pelosi had begun to lose her grip on the gavel, that years of recriminations and political kneecapping had finally taken their toll on the Speaker's ability to ram through and enact her far-left radical agenda. But like the political bosses of old, she, too, had a few aces up her Armani sleeves. "The Speaker always carries a number of votes in her pocket," said the critically important Representative Bart Stupak (D-MI), one of the Democratic holdouts who eventually caved to the Speaker's demands. Stupak said that the Speaker had already brokered enough backroom deals and applied enough party pressure to give herself a vote cushion if she needed it.[48] Indeed, what for a time looked as though it might spell the Boss's undoing, the health-care bill further confirmed that if anyone wants to pry the Speaker's gavel from Nancy Pelosi's hands, he or she had better be prepared and come armed to the hilt.

7

THE BIG POWER GRAB: HEALTH CARE

We don't have to start with a sledgehammer to convince
people of our point of view, but we have to be fully prepared
to go to that place. I always say start with a feather and then
you can end up with a steamroller.[1]

—Nancy Pelosi

President Obama may have been the one who glided his 20
signing pens across the surface of the historic health-care reform bill on
March 23, 2010, but the not-so-secret weapon who had maneuvered in
the depths of the plan was Nancy Pelosi. Indeed, "Fired up, ready to go"
and "Nancy, Nancy" were the cheers heard in the East Room.[2]

Since becoming Speaker, Pelosi has set her sights on two massive legislative targets: health care and energy. The former is literally a matter
of life and death. Moreover, meddling with health care—unlike, say, the
tax code or even the environment—presents immediate and life-altering
medical choices that can have dire consequences. Despite the moral heft
of such an issue, unforgivably, Pelosi found a way to drown health-care
"reform" in a sea of government exploitation and incompetence.

For leftists like Pelosi and Obama, health care represents the Holy
Grail, a massive slice of the federal fiscal pie, totaling one sixth of the
U.S. economy. Better still, as the Boss and Obama fully understand,
once health-care authority has been centralized and the left's utopian
vision of "redistributive justice" has been realized, citizens are unlikely
to unwind such massive entitlements.

Just before passage of the "historic" health-care measure, the Speaker claimed, "Our economy needs something new, a jolt. And I believe that this legislation will unleash tremendous entrepreneurial power into our economy." She said, "The best action we can do to create jobs and strengthen our economic security is pass health care reform."[3]

But government intrusion has never unleashed anything but more taxes and more control. If you can command vital areas of people's lives, you can control people. The Speaker's agenda is simple: seize power. After all, power equals control. And that's what the left is all about: "spreading the wealth around" to maintain control over human actions and outcomes.

At first glance, it appears that the Speaker is just trying to impose more colossal government solutions. But a closer look at these two issues reveals something even more sinister. Just as Big Tommy opened the government coffers for his friends in Baltimore, a centralized, far-reaching government response to health care and the environment would allow Pelosi and her allies to distribute patronage on a grand level. Friends will be rewarded and enemies punished, especially her loathed adversaries, like the insurance industry and oil companies. And political opponents will be shoved to the sidelines, denied any of the government largesse. The more centralized the control, Pelosi understands, the greater the influence of the power broker. According to journalist Richard E. Cohen, during the health-care debate, Pelosi "centralized perhaps unprecedented control in the speaker's office." The bill was so tied to her that Minority Leader John Boehner (R-OH) called the legislation "Pelosi's bill."[4]

On March 21, 2010, Nancy Pelosi's House passed a sweeping $938 billion health-care bill. The last one to speak before the vote was the Boss, cementing her place in history. "We will be joining those who established Social Security, Medicare and now, tonight, health care for all Americans," she said. "It is with great pride and great humility that we undertook this great act of patriotism that occurred on the floor of the House," said Pelosi.[5] Her great act of "patriotism" was, in fact, a grand heist of taxpayers' money and an unalterable assault on the world's most expert health-care system. As usual, Pelosi's deployment of hard-ball tactics and jaw-dropping power plays would reshape the legislative landscape and pave the way to passage.

Some of the early provisions of the Patient Protection and Afford-able Care Act, along with the Health Care and Education Reconcili-ation Act of 2010, include, among others, an insurance mandate, health care exchanges, insurance rules, federal subsidies and an expansion of Medicaid.[6] Of course, this is only the beginning of the power grab.

The Wall Street Journal wrote in November 2009, "Democrats have dumped any pretense of genuine bipartisan 'reform' and moved into the realm of pure power politics as they race against the unpopular-ity of their own agenda. The goal is to ram through whatever income-redistribution scheme they can claim to be 'universal coverage.' The result will be destructive on every level—for the health-care system, for the country's fiscal condition, and ultimately for American freedom and prosperity."[7]

Hardly utopia.

Like an experienced boss, Pelosi framed health care as an ethical issue. Delay, she claimed, would be immoral. "In the Book of Hebrews it is written: 'Make level paths for your feet, so that the lame may not be disabled, but rather healed,'" Pelosi said at a Hispanic prayer breakfast. "Today, creating those 'level paths' means providing health care access for all."[8]

Pelosi and her leftist allies have long fantasized about taking over heath care. In fact, her mentor Phil Burton said in 1964 that anyone needing free health care should have it, even though he admitted that his father, who was a doctor, didn't agree.[9] Pelosi has tried to convince the public that her power grab is altruistic. She said, "Nothing is easy. It's challenging to get the job done and live up to the expectations and the hopes of the American people, as the president has taken them all to a new height. . . . This is what I've hoped, prayed, dreamed and worked for. And it absolutely goes beyond my expectations of what it could be."[10]

In March 2010, a few weeks before the "historic" event, Pelosi yet again hailed the wonders of her health-care bill in a speech at the Leg-islative Conference for the National Association of Counties. "I don't know if you have heard that it is legislation for the future, not just about health care for America, but about a healthier America. . . . Prevention, prevention, prevention—it's about diet, not diabetes. It's going to be very, very exiting."[11]

But David Gratzer, a physician and senior fellow at the Manhattan Institute, who grew up in Canada and is intimately familiar with that country's government-run system, more accurately stated the reality of the cost of the contentious health-care debate. He wrote, "The year 2009 has been about passing 1,100-page bills [which eventually mounted to a 1,990-page House bill] without reading them because of the urgency; dumbing down health policy to cartoonish simplifications with miracle cures (prevention), easy choices (a blue pill and a red pill), and villains (insurance companies and doctors); and reworking one-sixth of the nation's economy with practically no discussion."[12]

So voluminous was the first bill that many of the 256 Democratic caucus members had trouble understanding the legislation, even when it was in its early, 1,000-page stage. To aid them, their House leaders organized a five-hour seminar. Ways and Means Chairman Charles Rangel (D-NY), one of the bill's coauthors, admitted that all the reams of paper were difficult to understand. He said, "The bill is so complex." The response to the seminar was, according to Rangel, "overwhelming."[13] But for Pelosi and her allies, complex and arcane "solutions" work best, since they rely on insiders to interpret them and guide people through them.

Both her colleagues and outsiders recognized Nancy Pelosi's talents during her push in 2009. "Think of how many speakers in the past have tried to get to this point," Rules Committee Chairwoman Representative Louise Slaughter (D-NY) said. "She got here."[14] But to get to where she did required strong-arm tactics and deal making beyond what the usual Washington game requires. According to author and social critic Camille Paglia, "In shoving her controversy-plagued health care reform bill to victory [in the House] by a paper-thin margin, she conclusively demonstrated that a woman can be just as gritty, ruthless and arm-twisting in pursuing her agenda as anyone in the long line of fabled male speakers before her. Even a basic feminist shibboleth like abortion rights became just another card for Pelosi to deal and swap."[15]

All her lessons in deal making go back to the backroom politics Big Tommy engaged in. Weeks before the November 2009 vote, "Pelosi ruled her ideologically divided caucus not as a San Francisco liberal but as the daughter of Thomas D'Alesandro, Jr.," according to Los Angeles Times journalists Faye Fiore and Richard Simon.[16] She knew what counted most: the votes. "When I take this bill to the floor, it will win," Pelosi declared in July that year on CNN's *State of the Union*.[17] And when House GOP leader John Boehner hinted that she didn't have the votes in March 2010, Pelosi was quick to respond. "I'm never dependent on Congressman Boehner's count. I never have."[18]

Representative Slaughter said, "She counts from the bottom, then she counts from the top. She could lay out any bill like a deck of cards." And she knows what she needs to do to get things done. Another House member called her leadership style "kid gloves and a hidden stiletto." Throughout the long debate, she cajoled and made compromises to amass the votes she needed. She even persuaded departing congressman Robert Wexler of Florida to not leave for his new job until the deal was sealed in the first House vote.[19]

Representative Gerry Connolly (D-VA) praised Pelosi's talents. "She is a very skilled inside player. She possesses the entire panoply of insider skills. She knows when to cajole, exhort, step back, when to make an implied threat, and when to listen." And ally representative Anna Eshoo of California said of her friend, "She is the best vote-getter that I have ever met. She is like a nuclear submarine."[20]

When compromise or bullying didn't work, bribes were offered. To secure Representative Dennis Cardoza's vote in November 2009, House leaders and the White House coughed up an additional $500 million for medical schools in rural areas. Cardoza is a California Democrat from a low-income district in the Central Valley that's been hit especially hard by home foreclosures. Just three days before the vote, Cardoza said, "The unwillingness to focus on what is important in a member's district with serious crises affects our malleability." After receiving his generous payoff, he complied with the Speaker's wishes.[21] While Cardoza's concerns for his district were no doubt genuine, what was more pressing and real to the Speaker was whether or not she could count on his vote and how much it would cost.

Still, Pelosi couldn't keep the biggest bribe from the public's view. When tensions between President Obama, Big Labor and Speaker Pelosi became public, the Democratic leadership tried to hoodwink voters into believing that the health-care plan's massive price tag would be paid for by socking it to the "rich" with more taxes. Obama was in favor of the "Cadillac tax," a name, according to *National Review* editor Rich Lowry, "redolent of corporate executives cackling in their Escalades over their cushy benefits." The 40 percent excise tax, which was in the first Senate bill, would strike high-end employer-provided insurance plans. However, it didn't take long for labor unions to realize that *they* were the rich—not the fabled fat cats smoking cigars—since labor leaders are notorious for securing cushy insurance plans with their employers. Soon a coalition of public-employee unions shot a letter off to congressional leaders. "While the excise tax is slated to be imposed on the insurers on so-called high cost plans, the tax will be passed on to enrollees in the form of higher premiums, co-pays or reduced benefits. Characterizing this tax proposal as a 'Cadillac tax' is a misnomer. It hits the average blue collar and white collar employee."[22]

Pelosi knew she had to protect one of her biggest allies—organized labor. Early on, before either chamber voted on health care, the Boss stood up for the labor unions, trying to ease their concerns that their insurance plans might be slapped with a tax. In mid-October 2009, the Speaker said, "I want to send our company to the table with the most muscle for America's middle class."[23] She said the Cadillac tax was a hit on the middle class. Taxes for her plan were supposed to hit just the "rich." Finally, in early January 2010, during the flap over the president's disingenuous pledge to air health-care negotiations on C-SPAN, she was ready to strike. Pelosi told a reporter smugly, "There are a number of things [the president] was for on the campaign trail." She, of course, was referring to his Cadillac tax. An aide defended her, saying it wasn't a stab at the president. But a leadership staffer recognized what she was up to. "It's strategic. She's staking out her territory."[24]

Labor was clear: either give us what we want or we will not show up for the November midterm elections. To appease them, President Obama met with a dozen leaders in January, including James P. Hoffa of the Teamsters and Richard Trumka of the AFL-CIO, to privately work out a bargain. A labor-leader spokesman said the White House had requested that the unions not talk to the news media about the meeting.[25]

While the president was busy at the White House bickering with union leaders, Madam Speaker was in Detroit, at the North American

International Auto Show, congratulating Big Labor on their achievements using the more than $100 billion bailout from taxpayers. The Boss liked what she saw. And she outshined the industry's new models. She had given them cover, and they, in turn, treated her like industry royalty. Pelosi declared, "We came to listen, to learn, to observe, to measure, to judge what has happened to the investments that were made. . . . We've been impressed. We have confidence in what has been accomplished, and we'll be back next year again." She was "like a conquistadora presiding over the conquered."[26]

But while the "conquistadora" was cozying up to her friends in Detroit, Obama was "wrangling behind closed White House doors under the demanding gaze of big-labor bosses." After two days, a deal was struck. Labor unions wouldn't have to worry about the 40 percent tax on their first-rate, loaded insurance plans until at least 2018. The rest of America's laborers with such plans would have to start paying at once.[27] The cost of the deal: government employees covered under collective-bargaining contracts as well as other union members would save at least $60 billion over the years they were exempted, while other hardworking, tax-paying Americans would have to pay around $90 billion. The leaders were ecstatic. George Boncoraglio, regional president of the New York State Civil Service Employees Association, boasted, "We can live with it. We have an agreement that nothing will be taxed until 2018." Besides Hoffa and Trumka, another heavyweight at the table in the White House was Andy Stern, head of Service Employees International Union (SEIU). Stern has gotten to know the layout of the White House well. Visitor logs reveal that he was a guest more than 20 times during the first year of the Obama administration.[28]

Rich Lowry summed up the outcome of Pelosi's and her Democratic minions' strong-arm deals: "This Labor Loophole stands in the finest tradition of the Louisiana Purchase and the Cornhusker Kickback. With no possible public-policy justification, it puts the awesome power to tax and spend at the service of nakedly political ends."[29] While these aptly named deals didn't come to complete fruition (the Louisiana Purchase survived), they represent a glaring and disturbing truth: no price was too high to gain control of the nation's health-care system.

The final reconciliation bill delayed a tax on all Cadillac health-care plans until 2018, even though there was an attempt to permanently exempt union members.[30] Still, labor has no need to lose any sleep as long as Pelosi and her allies are in control. They will make certain that the unions are out of the tax collector's way.

A boss encourages people to look to them for protection by invoking fear and making use of scare tactics, the very tactics Pelosi accused President George W. Bush of using to justify the Iraq war. But while the Iraq war is debatable, there were real enemies and real threats. Bosses *create* threats. Just as the inner-city bosses instilled a fear of blacks to consolidate their power, liberals manufacture panic to secure their power. To accomplish this, Pelosi set up her game similar to the way Big Tommy did in Little Italy. It was the game of us-versus-them. Leftists like Nancy Pelosi want voters to think they are on the side of the average American while conservatives are on the side of the rich, out to steal the dream from everyone else. The truth is: her "us" means her liberal colleagues, wealthy friends and any helpless person she can entangle in her web through her claims that health care is in a state of crisis ready to implode at any minute. "Them" includes the insurance companies, the drug companies, the Republicans, town hall protesters and anyone else who disagrees with the Democratic leadership that has politicized the issue for their advantage. As Pelosi breathlessly asserted: "This is the fight of our lives for the people that we represent, for their health."[31]

Nancy Pelosi wants us to believe not only that the country's health care was sliding to the brink, but that the system had failed and was ill suited to take good care of people. In 2008, Pelosi wrote in her book *Know Your Power* that a leading scientist, whom she leaves unnamed, told her that the present model for health care is obsolete.[32] And during her House floor speech just before the March 2010 vote, she said, "This legislation will lead to healthier lives, more liberty to pursue hopes and dreams and happiness for the American people." She went on, "We all know that the present health care system and insurance system, health insurance system in our country is unsustainable. . . . It simply does not work for enough people in terms of delivery of service and it is bankrupting the country with the upward spiral of increasing medical costs."[33]

However, a worldwide population-based study, published in August 2008 by the highly regarded British medical journal *Lancet Oncology*,

concluded otherwise. The findings: America treats cancer more successfully than Europe or Canada, with a better survival rate for 13 of the 16
most common cancers. When compared with his European counterpart,
an American man has a nearly 20 percent better chance of surviving for
five years after a cancer diagnosis. American women benefit from their
country's health care as well. They have a 7.2 percent better chance of
living for five years following a diagnosis than women do in Europe.
Sally C. Pipes, author of *The Top Ten Myths of American Health Care*,
wrote: "Perhaps that's one reason why tens of thousands of foreigners
come to the United States every year for medical treatment. They're
usually seeking advanced and sophisticated procedures that are simply
unavailable—or rationed—in their home countries."[34] But these facts
and statements mean nothing to Pelosi; they don't advance her agenda.

The health-care problem becomes worse when the numbers of
uninsured Americans are exaggerated. Google the phrase "46 million
uninsured" and around 25,000 hits will pop up. But, according to Pipes,
"While it's not technically wrong to say that there are roughly 45.7
million uninsured, it's grossly misleading to use this number as an
indication of a crisis."

This number comes from the U.S. Census Bureau's *Current Population Survey* (CPS). But the Census Bureau itself says, "health insurance
coverage is likely to be underreported on the CPS." And consider the
following about those who are part of the uninsured. Of that mythical quoted number of close to 46 million "Americans," more than ten
million are not U.S. citizens. Then there are those who are voluntarily
uninsured. Nearly eighteen million of the uninsured live in homes that
have yearly incomes exceeding $50,000, and almost ten million of
them have yearly incomes over $75,000. Moreover, some of those are
Americans between the ages of nineteen and twenty-nine, who make up
not only one of the largest but also one of the fastest-growing sectors of
the uninsured population. They are young and generally healthy and, if
not covered by their employers, are just choosing not to have coverage,
pocketing the cost of a monthly insurance premium. In short, to speak
of 46 million uninsured is highly inaccurate.[35]

One of the biggest obstacles on her quest to take over the health-
care industry was the insurance companies. Nancy Pelosi's repeated

name-calling made it unmistakable who she believed was enemy number one. Pelosi has branded them "immoral" and the "villains," and, according to her plotline, they are contributing to the demise of the country's health. Not that this should get in the way of taking their money, mind you. In the '08 election cycle, Pelosi's PAC and personal campaign account collected $177,000 from these immoral villains.[36] In response to their resistance to her House-backed public option, Pelosi said, "I think it is pretty clear that we want a strong public option in the legislation. Insurance companies [are out there in] full force carpet-bombing and shock and awe against the public option—so much so that the American people doubt the plan or are uncertain about it, until you tell them what is in it."[37] The reality is, the major strike the insurance companies released in the information war was an irritant to the Speaker. And the fact is, the more citizens learned about the public option, the more concerned they became that it would reduce competition, lead to a decline in the quality of care and result in rationing. Even liberal journalist Camille Paglia conceded that neither the insurance companies nor the drug companies are solely to blame for the spiraling costs of health care. To continually demonize the pharmaceutical industry and insurance companies "is a demagogic evasion."[38] But that is exactly what Pelosi continues to do in her crusade to legislate in a manner that grows the government's power.

She even got personal with the insurance companies. Colleagues and friends concede that one of the reasons Pelosi targeted health care was because she is a woman and a mother. Moments before the final vote, the Speaker said, "After we pass this bill, being a woman will no longer be a preexisting medical condition." The next day she said in an interview, "My sisters here in the Congress, this was a big issue for us."[39]

It only took the Boss hours after the president signed his name to the bill to deliver words of warning to these villainous companies. They had better not assume that they are "automatically included" in the new health exchanges that begin in 2014. Pelosi added, "Unless they do the right thing, they're not going in. They will be relinquishing the possibility of having taxpayer-subsidized consumers in the exchange."[40] The enemies had been put on notice.

Yet it was these very companies that were going to be expected to contribute generously to the government's plan. In July 2009, Pelosi told Politico that "she will push to 'drain' more savings from the medical industry—hospitals, pharmaceuticals companies and health insurers—than they have given up under current health-reform agreements with the Senate and White House." When asked if these segments could do more, Pelosi said, "Frankly, I think all the money [to pay for health reform] could be drained from the system, if they were willing to do that."[41]

Most alarmingly, however, is what the Boss had in store for the drug and medical-device companies. Pharmaceutical research and development is the lifeblood of new cures and lifesaving discoveries. In fact, the newer, more effective drugs significantly reduce medical costs. For example, from 1980 to 2000, for every 100 patients, the number of days spent in a hospital plummeted from 129.7 to 56.6, a drop of 56 percent. In 2000, Americans spent 206 million fewer days in hospitals, according to Medtap International, which provides health economics and outcomes-research services. These statistics are the result of new drugs created by pharmaceutical research and development. The newer drugs even lowered mortality rates. One study found that for patients who took medications during the first six months of 2000, the ones who took newer drugs were less likely to die by the end of 2002.[42] So does Nancy Pelosi understand that money spent on cutting-edge research for new wonder drugs and treatments will now, instead, be used to subsidize treating the runny noses of children whose mothers take them to the doctor for taxpayer-funded services?

Initially, the pharmaceutical industry agreed to bring $80 billion to the negotiating table to help supplement the massive overhaul. The reason: it was ordered to play the game by returning some of its profits or it wouldn't be allowed to pull up a chair at the table. But that wasn't enough for Pelosi. According to Henry Miller, a physician and Hoover Institution fellow at Stanford University, as well as a former FDA official, and Jeff Stier, an associate director of the American Council on Science and Health, "Pelosi has set up her own 'negotiating table'—nearly doubling the amount Washington would confiscate from the industry and planning vast new cuts in what Medicare would pay for drugs—a provision the industry was assured was off the other table. Give 'em a hand, they'll take an arm." But there's more. Pelosi's bill wanted to extract $20 billion more from medical-device manufacturers (those who provide Americans with insulin pumps and pacemakers) in "user fees"—a liberal's way to add more taxes. Miller and Stier accurately size up Pelosi's tactics: "House Speaker Nancy Pelosi's brand of politics might be dubbed the art of the execrable. Her health care juggernaut would not only create a massive entitlement program built on confiscatory taxation of businesses and individuals, but would also inhibit innovation by punishing industry more directly."[43]

One of the ways the Speaker tried to peddle her health-care bill was by asserting that it could in part be paid for through taxes on the wealthy. How she developed the income surcharge reveals how passing her agenda expeditiously was more important than any numbers related to the solvency of the plan. Initially the new taxes would strike adjusted gross incomes of $280,000 for individuals and $350,000 or more for families. Pelosi said, "I'd like it to go higher than it is." She wanted to raise the thresholds to $500,000 for individuals and $1 million for families so she could call it a "millionaire's tax." Pelosi explained, "When someone hears, '2,' they think, 'Oh, I could be there,' because they don't know the $280,000 is for one person. It sounds like you're in the neighborhood. So I just want to remove all doubt. You hear '$500,000 a year,' you think, 'My God, that's not me.'"[44] This was all part of the game plan. Liberals know that the middle class will be funding health care. But they tried to keep the middle class from knowing that. So they engaged in dialogue to leave the mistaken notion that average incomes wouldn't be touched by the overhaul. The bill signed into law did ensnare individuals making more than $200,000 and couples filing jointly earning $250,000. Beginning in 2013, they will be required to hand over an additional 3.8 percent Medicare tax on their investment income as well as having more of their salary confiscated for the Medicare payroll tax.[45]

Nancy Pelosi has charged insurance executives as well as anyone else who opposes her plan (all the enemy) with trying to act underhandedly. She said, "Facts mean nothing. Misrepresentation is the currency of their realm."[46]

Pelosi's deal, nonetheless, was initially advertised almost entirely with misrepresentations. While the final bill passed in 2010 didn't look exactly like this, the Speaker's goal with health care was explicit. First, she said that subsidies would be offered only to people whose employers didn't offer insurance or who worked for businesses employing 100 or fewer people. But according to *The Wall Street Journal*, this was nothing more than an initial "firewall" that would collapse when everyone else would want in on the great deal of "free" health care, thereby ensuring that the real taxpayer cost would skyrocket. Pelosi understood this. Then there is Medicaid and Medicare. Pelosi's end was to increase Medicaid and do away with private Medicare. *The Wall Street Journal* continues, "Mrs. Pelosi wants to steal $426 billion from future Medicare spending to 'pay for' universal coverage." Not only will Medicare's price controls be made tighter, but Medicare Advantage, a program offering private insurance choices, will be devastated. And concerning Medicaid, if all went according to schedule, within ten years, one fourth of the population would be enslaved to a program designed for the disabled and underprivileged. One of the most alarming strings in her web is the final government takeover of the insurance and health-care industries. Enthroned in Washington, the powerful new "health choices commissioner" would be busy determining what "essential benefits" all insurers would have to provide as first-dollar coverage. Moreover, private insurers would be told at what cost and to whom. The result? "Private" health insurance will be relegated to the history books. As *The Wall Street Journal* writes: "All of this is intentional, even if it isn't explicitly acknowledged. The overriding liberal ambition is to finish the work [that] began decades ago as the Great Society of converting health care into a government responsibility."[47] In the end, the government will run your doctor's office and your medicine cabinet. The bill the president signed in 2010 is just the first step. And in those first steps is coverage for 32 million uninsured, expansion of Medicaid, tax credits to purchase insurance in the new state-based exchanges for those who don't have access to coverage they can afford in the workplace, and fines for those who refuse to buy health insurance.[48]

Intrinsic in the Speaker's quest is her legacy. Surrounded by her boisterous Democratic colleagues after the bill garnered the needed votes for a majority in November 2009, "Pelosi grabbed the gavel and declared, 'the bill is passed.'" Just after she let the gavel fall, the Boss heralded her great achievement. She triumphantly compared the passage of the

Affordable Health Care for America Act to Social Security, in 1935, and Medicare, three decades later.[49] But the comparisons are less than honest. The previous massive overhauls were historic not only in their scope but in the bipartisan support they received. In 1935, the Social Security Act was not without controversy, but the final version of the bill passed the House by a vote 372-33, with 81 Republicans voting yea. It then breezed through the Senate, 77-6, with 16 Republicans voting to support the bill. And many in the GOP were also supportive of Medicare in 1965. This time the House vote was 307-116, with 70 Republicans for the conference report. The next day, 13 Republicans in the Senate threw their support to the final Medicare bill in a 70-24 vote.[50] The Pelosi-backed bill was shoved through, with 176 Republicans voting nay and one lone member of the GOP, Louisiana congressman Anh "Joseph" Cao, in support of the legislation.

Regardless, Pelosi's supporters were quick to praise their leader. Representative Jim McGovern (D-MA) said, "[Pelosi] really threaded the needle on this one." And California ally Congressman George Miller, one of the bill's engineers, claimed, "This is our moment to revolutionize health care in this country."[51] Pelosi was elated. She said, "Oh, what a night."[52] She had a bill.

Again, before the March 2010 vote, she proclaimed her moment in history. For her pre-celebratory walk to the Capitol, she was "wielding a sledgehammer-sized gavel" her colleague Representative John Dingell had loaned to her. Pelosi explained what the gavel meant: "A treasure in the Dingell family that was used in the enactment of the Medicare law. I will use it this evening when we cast a very successful vote for this important legislation."[53] This time the vote was 219-212, with every Republican voting no.[54] Still, her colleagues praised her once more. Representative Chris Van Hollen (D-MD) said, "[Pelosi] has eyes on the side of her head—she can see everything that's going on, 360-degree vision. She can see things coming before others can." Fellow California Democrat Zoe Lofgren has praised the Speaker on her ability to not stray from her focal point. "She's never distracted from where she's trying to take the country."[55]

Besides centralizing power, embedded within the health-care bill were clues to another intent of the takeover: impose a radical leftist agenda through legislation. First, there was the "pay or go to jail" provision. While thousands of dangerous criminals are roaming the streets, law-abiding citizens were going to join their ranks if they didn't purchase health insurance and pay the fine of approximately 2.5 percent of their income for not doing so. The nonpartisan Joint Committee on Taxation reported what was included in the 2009 House bill. Those who decided not to buy health insurance and pay the penalty would have been committing a misdemeanor and subjected to a fine of up to $25,000 and/or imprisonment of up to one year. "Willful evasion" would have made a citizen a felon punishable by a fine of up to $250,000 and/or imprisonment of up to five years.[56] Pelosi's plan was never about saving money. She would be willing to spend taxpayer dollars for the imprisonment of those who weren't dishing out money for her government-run plan. (There is one bright side. People who are incarcerated receive gratis health care.) The final bill that passed may not send you to jail, but it does include a key element of the Pelosi method: fail to purchase health insurance and you will receive a stiff fine.

If Pelosi is actually serious about controlling health-care costs, she would work to reduce medical malpractice lawsuits. In 2009, the nonpartisan Congressional Budget Office (CBO) concluded that if tort reform is implemented nationwide, there would be a $54 billion savings in government health-care outlays in the next ten years. James R. Copland, who directs the Manhattan Institute's Center for Legal Policy, says that both Harvard medical researchers and respected attorneys have proposed effective, innovative ideas. But innovative ideas won't benefit Nancy Pelosi. Trial lawyers, who make a lot of money in those malpractice lawsuits, are heavy funders of her machine (their PAC came in second for donations to Democratic congressional campaigns in the last election cycle), and she wants no part of any reform that benefits health-care workers instead of trial lawyers.[57] Pelosi always remembers who provides the oil to lubricate her machine.

Finally, the original draft of the bill was crafted to allow federal funds to be used for elective abortions. Those enrolled in the plan would be forced to collectively fund other women's abortions.[58] Pelosi was none too pleased when Representative Bart Stupak (D-MI) and his band of followers pestered her with their amendment banning the use of federal funds for abortion. At last, in March 2010, she dug in her heels, and it was the president who had to make a move. *Washington Post* reporter Vince Bzdek wrote, "[Pelosi] promised that there would be no health-care bill if it included the Stupak language. Instead, Obama issued a presidential order affirming the existing prohibition on federal abortion funding."[59]

Even though their strategy would prove differently, both Pelosi and the president maintained that they desired transparency while crafting their colossal health-care bill. When he was on the campaign trail in 2008, candidate Obama left citizens with the idea that they would be able to "pull up a chair" and enjoy watching the debate. He said, "we'll have [health-care reform] negotiations televised on C-SPAN, so the people can see who is making arguments on behalf of their constituents and who is making arguments on behalf of the drug companies or the insurance companies." But he changed his mind. And in early January 2010, Pelosi came out and said, with the support of the White House, that the House and Senate would devise the final bill "behind closed doors, according to an agreement by top Democrats."[60] The reason for their about-face was that both Pelosi and the president knew the American people would never buy into their deal.

So as the House and Senate were getting ready to cook up their final "gazillion-dollar health care bill" behind closed doors, C-SPAN's Brian Lamb urged the leaders to follow through on their word: allow the people to see what they are up to. Lamb's appeal, written at the end of December, was addressed to Nancy Pelosi, Harry Reid, John Boehner and Mitch McConnell. (Of course, the only two recipients who counted were Pelosi and Reid.) Lamb wrote:

> The C-SPAN networks will commit the necessary resources to covering all these sessions LIVE and in their entirety. . . . President Obama, Senate and House leaders, many of your rank-and-file members, and the nation's editorial pages have all talked about the value of transparent discussions on reforming the nation's health care system. . . . Now that the process moves to the critical stage of reconciliation between the Chambers, we respectfully request that you allow the public full access, through television, to legislation that will affect the lives of every single American.[61]

Pelosi defended her operation. "There has never been a more open process for any legislation," she told the press. Then she added, *"We will do what is necessary to pass the bill* [emphasis mine]."[62]

Pelosi's actions are all the more outrageous considering the speech she had given on the House floor on January 14, 2005. She accused Republicans of running "rough shod" over Democrats and "rigging the rules, negotiating for jobs, no reading of the bill," all of which she deemed an "absolute outrage." She went on to feign even more indignation because she claimed members "can't even see what they're voting on before they vote on it. And something like looking at your tax returns could be sneaked into the bill without any safeguards to protect you from that." She summed it all up by proclaiming this was an "abuse of power in this House, ignoring of the 3-day rule."[63] One can only wonder whether voters can take anything she says about ethics and the functioning of the House seriously.

Pelosi had claimed in 2009 that she wanted everyone involved in her health-care adventure. "Every single person in America is an expert on his or her health care. . . . We want this to work for the country. So we have to listen to everybody."[64] However, the Speaker's real motives became more transparent as the fallacy of the plan was revealed. The last thing she wanted to do was listen to everybody. That was quite apparent when protesters shook her up with their town hall meetings. She tried to quell the debate, saying at a weekly press conference: "I wish that we could all curb our enthusiasm in the statements that we make and understand that some of the ears that it's falling on are not as balanced as the person making the statement might assume."[65]

Madam Speaker insisted that her health-care reform was *for* the American people. Poll numbers indicated otherwise. The American public did not want the trillion-dollar deal. The results of a Rasmussen poll taken in August 2009 were clear: only 35 percent of voters were in support of the so-called public option, and 80 percent of those with health insurance at the time rated their coverage good or excellent. Furthermore, a mere 25 percent of voters polled agreed with her assessment of the insurance companies as "villains."[66]

While Pelosi made it plain who her enemies were, it is important to know her associates. A boss maintains control through strategically placed top lieutenants. In the spring of 2009, Pelosi gave Hoyer his marching orders: make sure the six committee and subcommittee chairmen who would have jurisdiction over the health-care legislation had their plan ready for committee action. The three key committee chairs who had command over health policy are close Pelosi allies: the embattled chairman of the Ways and Means Committee, Charlie Rangel (who finally stepped down in March 2010), Californian Henry Waxman of the House Energy and Commerce Committee, and confidant George Miller, chairman of the House Education and Labor Committee, who is also from California.[67] For Waxman to become chair of Energy and Commerce, the legendary John Dingell (D-MI), who has had his own battles with Pelosi over energy policy, had to be removed. Waxman defeated Dingell, 137-122. The vote was considered an upset, since it ignored the party's long-held principle of seniority. While Pelosi hadn't taken sides in the race, Rangel pointed the finger at her. He said, "I assume that not playing a role is playing a role."[68] But Pelosi needed Waxman, because his powerful committee would oversee not only health care but energy issues as well.

Now consider the backgrounds of the three deputies she had crafting the most intrusive, divisive legislation ever fashioned. First is Rangel. The Democrat from Harlem has been under investigation by the House Ethics Committee. His possible violations are manifold: failure to report rental income on his Dominican Republic villa or to pay taxes on it; not declaring at least $500,000 in assets on his 2007 congressional disclosure form, occupying four rent-stabilized apartments in a prestigious building for thousands of dollars per month below the current market value, which is a breach of the House's ban on gifts over $50; and using his Capitol Hill office to raise money for the Charles B. Rangel Center for Public Service from donors with business interests under his committee's consideration. Rangel chalked up his villa disclosure omissions to "unintentional bookkeeping errors."[69]

Rangel posed a quandary for Pelosi. The Congressional Black Caucus was expecting her to stand behind him. But Rangel's problems created tensions with the Speaker. He claimed that she was excluding his committee from involvement in health-care reform. And when she replaced his proposed income tax increase with her plan to hit higher incomes to raise money for their bill, she did so without consulting him. Rangel said, "She's never discussed it with me." Yet, publicly, both Pelosi and the president stood behind the powerful, liberal Rangel, with congratulatory words on his role in the health-care legislation. He said, "President called me and said I did a great job; Pelosi called me and said I did a great job. I'm doing a great job."[70]

Then there's Henry Waxman, who represents affluent voters in Beverly Hills as well as West Hollywood, Santa Monica and others. Waxman is considered one of the House's most prominent and liberal members, and he is positioned to exert considerable influence. From 1979 until 1994, he was chair of the Energy and Commerce Subcommittee on Health and the Environment. As early as the late 1970s, organized labor viewed Waxman as someone who could push for national health insurance.[71]

Pelosi's third lieutenant was George Miller, who represents California's Seventh District, just north of Berkeley, and is knotted to the philosophy of Phil Burton. Miller's father, who was the late chairman of the state senate Finance Committee, helped Burton during his early years in California politics. Waxman and Miller are both Burton protégés and Watergate babies who won their seats in 1974 on the tailwinds of Burton's exploitation of the scandal. Miller said of their election in 1974, "We had a real sense of urgency. We came here to take the Bastille."[72] Once in Washington, according to Burton biographer John Jacobs, Burton "took care of his California freshman." He made sure they immediately had seats on powerful committees. He found a place for Miller on his two committees, Interior and Education and Labor. And he snared a spot for Waxman on what was at the time the coveted Interstate and Foreign Commerce Committee. Waxman recalled, "It was a given that Phil Burton would get it for me. I never knew how difficult it could be to get on a committee. Now I know. . . . But he took care of me and George Miller and put us where we thought and he thought would be best."[73]

Moments before the vote on March 21, 2010, the Boss recognized these key players:

> We have also reached this historic moment because of the extraordinary leadership and hard work and dedication of all the Members of Congress, but I want to especially recognize our esteemed

Chairs—Mr. Waxman, Mr. Rangel, Mr. Levin, Mr. Miller, Mr. Spratt, Ms. Slaughter—for bringing this bill to the floor today. Let us acknowledge them.[74]

And it was only a few days later, with the ink barely dry on the passed legislation, that Representative Waxman took action against corporate America. Companies like AT&T, Verizon, Caterpillar, Deere, Valero Energy, AK Steel and 3M had the audacity to express the realistic concern that one of the tax provisions in the legislation was going to make the company's prescription drug coverage to its retired employees much costlier. In response, Waxman wrote a letter to several of the executives summoning them to Capitol Hill to explain themselves for saying that his new historic measure would incur hundreds of millions of dollars in health insurance expenses to their companies. Reporter Byron York wrote, "Waxman is also demanding that the executives give lawmakers internal company documents related to health care finances—a move one committee Republican describes as 'an attempt to intimidate and silence opponents of the Democrats' flawed health care reform legislation.' "[75]

Even though the public option was missing from the final bill, Speaker Pelosi is its champion. For her, it was a key component of her House bill, even though it didn't receive support from the majority of the American people. The medical treatment received by the beneficiaries of the public option, though, would in no way resemble the care Speaker Pelosi will be granted for the rest of her life. As a member of Congress, she will have superb care at her disposal. CBS News correspondent Sharyl Attkisson reports that the "generous" health plan that legislators have is "subsidized by millions of your tax dollars annually. The government doesn't even keep track [of] the total cost." Not only do members have five insurance plans to select from, but their premiums are almost the same as those for the average policy of the typical working-age household.

Nancy Pelosi doesn't have to worry about a coverage limit or any preexisting conditions. And when she's in Washington, she can receive care 24 hours a day, right in her office, from the clinic conveniently located inside the U.S. Capitol, the Attending Physician's Office. Then there's the Attending Physician benefit, which about half the members of Congress take advantage of, including Speaker Pelosi: for the paltry sum of $42 a month, she can just show up for some minor surgery, X-rays, physical therapy, drugs for emergencies and other requested specialists. If she needs a hospital, she will receive VIP treatment at Bethesda Naval Hospital while under the care of the best doctors, and at Walter Reed Army Medical Center, there is a place set aside for her and her colleagues at the elite Ward 72. If it's outpatient care Pelosi requires, it's gratis. The generous benefactor for all this exceptional care? The taxpayer.[76] So when Madam Speaker alleges that the health-care system is not fair, she is right. It's not fair that taxpayers should have to subject themselves to her plan, which limits choice, quality and access, when she has a "Cadillac" plan that the American people are footing the bill for.

South Carolina senator Lindsey Graham declared the public option unfair. "If we pass a law that says a public option will be made available, I think people like myself should get out of this plan [Congress's first-rate coverage] and go into the public option." But Senator Graham probably won't have that choice. Congress has made it clear that they aren't interested in a public option for themselves. According to Attkisson, "Congress has voted down all proposals that would switch them to a public option."[77]

In late 2009, *The Wall Street Journal* reported that Pelosi had told her Democratic colleagues that she was willing to take an enormous risk to push her health bill through. *She was prepared to take casualties in House seats in the 2010 midterm election.*[78] For a boss to take such risks, there must be great rewards. Indeed, her unyielding efforts became a race against unpopular opinion. After the Democrats' supermajority in the Senate vanished with the loss of the late senator Ted Kennedy's seat to Republican Scott Brown, Pelosi conceded that the Senate bill would not pass her House. She said, "I don't see the votes for [the Senate bill] at this time."[79]

But that didn't mean she wouldn't have the votes at another time. In fact, less than a week later, Pelosi made it clear she was again ready for battle. She promised she could rally the troops and collect enough votes to shove the Senate's bill through if the Senate did some fine-tuning in the reconciliation process. The speaker said, "Reconciliation resolving some of the issues: then we can pass this thing."[80] If one thing marks her career, it's her dogged persistence.

In spite of unpopular opinion and election losses, Waxman was still ready to go to work for Pelosi. He told reporters, "I think there's still the political will to do health reform. I think it's an essential for us to accomplish."[81]

After Brown's victory in Massachusetts, reports indicated that President Obama was considering a compromise with the Republicans. And both White House chief of staff Rahm Emanuel and Senate majority leader Harry Reid wanted to scale the measure back. Pelosi called it "kiddie care."[82] These guys didn't know how to get things done.

Pelosi admitted that some parts of her plan may have to be executed bit by bit. But the overall game plan was still the same. Near the end of January 2010 she said, "That doesn't mean that is a substitute for doing comprehensive. It means we will move on many fronts, any front we can. We will go through the gate. If the gate is closed, we will go over the fence. If the fence is too high, we will pole vault in. If that doesn't work, we will parachute in. But we are going to get health care reform passed for the American people for their own personal health and economic security [it's a crisis] and for the important role that it will play in reducing the deficit."[83] Did Pelosi miss the USA Today/Gallup poll just a week before she said this that made known the taxpayers' wishes? Fifty-five percent of Americans were in favor of Congress's "putting the brakes" on the present health-care reform endeavor.[84] Pelosi is the quintessence of a boss: she takes the answer no as just an inconvenience to deal with.

So she began strategizing how to deal with getting her bill passed. First she spent time "laying the groundwork" for a vote on the Senate bill in mid-March. But she indicated that she was considering other options. The maneuver she was thinking of is known as a "self-executing rule" or a "deem and pass." According to Washington Post reporters Lori Montgomery and Paul Kane, "Pelosi would rely on a procedural sleight of hand: The House would vote on a more popular package of fixes to the Senate bill; under the House rule for that vote, passage would signify that lawmakers 'deem' the health-care bill to be passed." It would have been a bold move, since the self-executing rule had never been used to pass such a significant bill. Nonetheless, the Speaker saw the advantage to such a tactic. It would give cover to lawmakers who were nervous about weighing in on the bill publicly. Pelosi told bloggers in a roundtable discussion that she liked the idea. She said, "It's more insider and process-oriented than most people want to know. But I like it because people don't have to vote on the Senate bill."[85]

Still, the Boss wasn't giving up on the vote count. In fact, she claimed she was trying to round up the votes with "a massive whip operation."[86]

The Speaker was sure that in the end she would pull it off. Just days before passage of the vast legislative undertaking, she informed reporters, "When we have a bill, then we will let you know about the votes. But when we bring the bill to the floor, we will have the votes."[87] And she did. As always, she found a way to burst through the gate.

8

THE BIG POWER GRAB: ENERGY

We will work together, holding hearings, developing
legislation, and tackling one of humanity's greatest
challenges yet—global warming.[1]

—Nancy Pelosi, 2007

For Madam Speaker, there is an even greater impending catas-
trophe hovering all around: global warming. And Nancy Pelosi knows
just whom to blame: people. She based her assessment on the findings
of a report by the Intergovernmental Panel on Climate Change (IPCC),
an arm of the United Nations, which confirmed, with a 90 percent cer-
tainty, that greenhouse gases emitted by human activities are the primary culprits of global warming. Moreover, she is convinced by the
study's conclusion that today's atmospheric level of carbon dioxide is,
by a long way, the highest in the past 650,000 years.[2] To counter all
those dirty carbon footprints from trampling Mother Earth, Pelosi
announced the 15 members of her new Select Committee on Energy
Independence and Global Warming, chaired by Representative Edward
J. Markey (D-MA), just two months after taking the gavel. She claimed,
"Global warming and energy independence are urgent issues that have
profound implications for our nation's economic competitiveness,
national security, environmental quality and public health."[3] She even
foresees that global warming will induce political volatility around the
world as refugees fleeing climate change move from nation to nation.[4]

Pelosi's legislative endeavors with energy parallel those regarding health care. She and her allies would eventually determine how much energy we get to consume by price, taxation on carbon footprints, and how much and what kinds of energy industry gets. Just imagine the Boss determining the fates of tens of thousands of people who work in energy and coal and other politically incorrect industries, as well as hundreds of millions of consumers.

In *Know Your Power*, Pelosi explains, "Since I've become Speaker, my flagship issue has been energy, security and addressing the global climate crisis." Pelosi feels that the eco-crusade, like health-care reform, has moral implications.[5] For her, it's not a policy question. There's no room for an honest disagreement about how to evaluate health care or the environment. No, the environment is a solemn "religious" issue. Disagree? Well, then, clearly you are a sinner.

In April 2007, she proclaimed that her environmental policies had been inspired by words in the Old Testament: "To minister to the needs of God's creation is an act of worship. To ignore those needs is to dishonor the God who made us." She then added, "We must move *quickly* [emphasis mine] to honor God's creation by reducing greenhouse gas pollution in the United States and around the world."[6]

Pelosi's response to the perceived crisis? Pass legislation that will deposit money in the government coffers, punish her enemies (this time big oil companies that make money and give more of it to Republican candidates) and base policy on shaky global warming studies, some of which have been under fire for authenticity.

The Boss's early moves, however, infuriated a few prominent House colleagues from both parties. First was the House's longest-serving member, John Dingell (D-MI), who has held a seat in Congress since 1955. He had chaired the Energy and Commerce Committee since 1981.[7] But the new global warming committee chaired by Markey, an environmental champion, was viewed by some as part of Pelosi's plan to grab power away from Dingell's committee, which had jurisdiction over global warming.[8]

A strong advocate of the auto industry and not green enough for the Speaker and her associates, Dingell was clearly irritated about the formation of the new committee. He said, "We should probably name it the Committee on World Travel and Junkets. We're just empowering a bunch of enthusiastic amateurs to go around and make speeches and make commitments that will be very difficult to honor. . . . They're going to get under the feet of and interfere with those who are trying to do a decent job of legislating."[9] And when the far-left *Grist* magazine asked Dingell if he thought the debate over global warming had been settled, he answered, "This country, this world, the [human] race of which you and I are a part, is great at having consensuses that are in great error."[10] However, with the election of Barack Obama, Pelosi and her allies saw opportunities for their climate change fantasies. So Dingell needed to go. He was booted out as Energy and Commerce chair by the election of Waxman in November 2008. Waxman's response? "Seniority is important, but it should not be a grant of property rights to be chairman for three decades or more."[11]

Like Dingell, Republican House minority leader John Boehner, a heavy smoker, lost one of his privileges: Pelosi brought an end to smoking in the House Speaker's Lobby in the Capitol.[12]

But the Boss had big plans for her whole House. "Newly elected Speaker Nancy Pelosi issued her edict: the House of Representatives must become carbon neutral by the end of this year and cut its carbon footprint in half within a decade." And to help her, taxpayers got to spend their money on a "Greening Czar." Chosen to spearhead her "Green the Capitol" initiative was Daniel P. Beard, whom Pelosi persuaded to come out of semiretirement to serve as a chief administrative officer (CAO) for the effort. He had at one time served on the staff of the House Appropriations and Natural Resources Committee.

Longworth House Office Building Café was one of the first stops on her journey to save the planet, and Beard moved fast. Within a year after Pelosi became Speaker, the cafeteria was transformed. Legislators now had their food served on compostable sugar cane plates and their drinks in cornstarch cups. On the menu were hormone-free burgers and fresh-made wraps and salads. The fruit was displayed on bamboo mats. The walls were safely covered with eco-friendly paint, and the Sustainable Forestry Institute had certified the wood trim. Another addition to the Capitol area was plenty of bike racks.[13] Exactly whom Madam Speaker expected to bike to their congressional office was not clear.

Then there was the matter of the carbon footprint. The House had

30,000 metric tons of greenhouse gases that had to be dealt with. So the House spent $89,000 in carbon offsets on the Chicago Climate Exchange (CCX).[14] The company advertises itself as operating "North America's only cap and trade system for all six greenhouse gases, with global affiliates and projects worldwide."[15] Richard Sandor, an economist who had left his position at the University of California at Berkeley for Wall Street, where he prospered in the junk bond market in the 1980s while with Drexel Burnham Lambert, and economist Dr. Michael Walsh launched the CCX. In 2003, they started the operation in earnest with more than $1 million of grant money they had received from the Joyce Foundation. At the time, Illinois state senator Barack Obama had a seat on the Joyce Foundation's board and was a player in the decision to fund CCX.[16]

The move to spend taxpayer dollars on carbon offsets brought out the critics. Even *The Washington Post* came out swinging. The *Post* reported that some of the money was being used on programs that were futile or had ended. Beard's response: "This is a fledgling market. Yes, it has problems, but it's the only market we have." The House had more plans, like purchasing wind power to offset all of its electricity.[17] Interestingly, in April 2009, Climate Exchange CEO Neil Eckert and the Speaker's son, Paul Pelosi, Jr., were speakers at the Milken Institute Global Conference. Climate Exchange PLC owns the CCX.

On Earth Day in April 2009, the Speaker kicked off the My Green Office program. And in January 2010, Nancy Pelosi said, "I'm pleased with the progress that Members have made to green their offices. It's critical for us to lead by example and show the American people that reducing our carbon footprint saves both energy and money." The goal is to have completed "green" consultations with all 7,000 Washington-based House employees by the end of 2010. What do the consultations include? According to a report released by the CAO, House staffers are being instructed in how to eliminate material, electric and pollutant waste within their offices. The report also stated that consultation sessions had taken place with the Speaker's five "green office representatives," who oversee the "greening" of Democratic leadership offices. And, at the time, the consultation with Steny Hoyer's staff was in progress, while John Boehner's office had not yet had any sessions.

As part of the program, House offices must now carry out a series of operational changes that include "using recycled paper, switching to compact fluorescent lightbulbs, converting to e-faxing, consolidating their servers, installing water filtration systems and optimizing their constituent mailing lists." But the changes have their challenges. For example, when staffers are busy at work and fail to move for hours, the motion-sensor lighting turns off. To get the lights back on, they have to wave their arms in the air.

The total savings from the Speaker's greening measure have not been identified. A CAO spokesman said it would be July 2010 before they had an assessment of the program's cost-effectiveness. As of early 2010, "the savings numbers are a moving target."[18] The bigger question is: how much will all these mandated measures cost the American taxpayer? Everyone wants a clean environment, but is this the best use of taxpayers' money in the midst of a recession and soaring unemployment?

To tout the accomplishments of Pelosi's Green the Capitol program, CAO Beard released a progress report in January 2010. The title? "Enabling a Green Workforce: Building a Culture of Sustainability in the House."[19] Sustainability? Undoubtedly, most citizens would argue they are more concerned about the sustainability of their jobs and incomes, safety from terrorist attacks, crumbling schools and protection from criminals.

When it came to energy policy, Pelosi had to quell an "intra-party feud" early on, in June 2007, between the powerful Dingell and other advocates of the coal and auto industries, and environmental activists, including Waxman and Markey. The tough greenhouse gas limits would hurt Dingell's Detroit. That is exactly why Pelosi had appointed Markey to head up her new committee. According to *San Francisco Chronicle* reporter Zachary Coile, she selected Markey, "whose unstated goal is to pressure Dingell, an ally of the auto industry, to act on climate change."[20] And her muscle was clear in the outcome of the fuel bill, in December 2007. Since 1984, Dingell had resisted a huge increase in fuel efficiency standards for cars. But Pelsoi held Dingell at bay while hoarding power. Dingell maintained that compromises had been struck on the bill. Pelosi, however, prevailed. The deal on the energy legislation provided for a bigger increase in fuel efficiency than the Democrat from Michigan had wanted. According to one of the provisions, fuel efficiency would be increased to an average of 35 miles per gallon by 2020. At first, when Dingell was asked if the House leaders, years his junior, were trying to marginalize him on the issue, he replied, "Let them try. They won't be able to do it."[21] But remember, he was dealing with the Boss. As events unfolded, Dingell reluctantly admitted, "If [Pelosi] wants it in the final package, it will probably be there." He still tried to feign an independent posture. "This is not a place where namby-pambies come down and are told what to do by speakers. My place is not to come down here and be a yes-man for Nancy Pelosi. . . . It's to see to it that the institution works." In the end, though, Dingell caved to Pelosi. "The speaker basically took him on and won," said environmental consultant Dan Becker.[22]

On greening issues, Pelosi is hard-line. She was a cosponsor of the Safe Climate Act of 2006, introduced by none other than Representative Waxman. Pelosi charged with blistering words:

> For decades, Big Oil and other polluting industries have undermined and obstructed the voices of scientists on global warming, just as Big Tobacco did for so many years on the issue of cigarettes, spreading doubt in the minds of Americans. The Bush Administration and the Republican leadership in Congress are willing partners in this dance of lies, muzzling government scientists or attacking their credibility when they refuse to remain silent. [As of early 2010, however, she was silent about the real Climategate.] But the scientific evidence of global warming is overwhelming, and growing each day with the release of new studies. The Arctic ice is melting, and Greenland's massive icecap is liquefying with unexpected speed. The oceans are warming, potentially generating stronger hurricanes, and becoming more acidic, threatening the building blocks of the marine food chain. The current heat waves across the United States and Europe, and the wildfires in the West, may be an unpleasant taste of what is to come.[23]

Pelosi also used a UN Intergovernmental Panel on Climate Change (IPCC) Working Group II report to try to stir up fear. "The new scientific report on global warming warns that global warming is already affecting the earth and that the effects are likely to be significant and widespread in this century, causing increased drought, drinking water shortages, and widespread extinction of species . . . *We must base our actions on the moral imperative and the scientific record, free of political interference in scientists' assessments of the effects of climate change on society and the environment* [emphasis mine]."[24]

The trouble is, much of the science about global warming has now been called into question. The Climategate scandal indicates that leading climate change scientists hid data that was inconsistent with their findings, that their data was at times deeply flawed, and that they conspired to prevent other academics from reviewing the data. Assertions that the Himalayan glaciers could melt by 2035, for example, were based on poor research and have been found to be untrue.[25] Claims of scientific rigor now appear to be a fraud: much of the science in the area was driven by an agenda rather than objective truth. But that hasn't led Pelosi to reconsider her views. Accepting that the science about climate change is mixed at best doesn't conform to her vision of a governmental superbody directing the lives of individuals in order to stave off an "emergency."

When the CLEAN Energy Act of 2007 passed the House on January 18 as part of the speaker's acclaimed "first 100 hours," Pelosi said, "We will promote homegrown alternatives, creating good-paying jobs while bolstering our national security, sending our energy dollars to the Midwest, not the Middle East." (After going through the Senate, the final bill, the Energy Independence and Security Act of 2007, was signed by President Bush on December 19.) House Democrats hailed its passage with the hope that it would sock Big Oil with massive tax increases.[26] The Boss either doesn't understand or is ignoring a basic and fundamental reality of economics: when you tax a business, they pass those costs on to consumers. So when Nancy Pelosi lands a blow to Big Oil's solar plexus, her punch merely ends up hitting the middle class in the gut.

Pelosi's drive to hammer Big Oil has a flip side: she has invested in green companies such as Clean Energy Fuels Corporation (CLNE). The Pelosis invested in oilman T. Boone Pickens's company, purchasing shares valued at $50,000 to $100,000 in an auction when Pickens publicly launched Clean Energy, in May 2007. In short, the Speaker stands to profit personally from the anti-oil, pro-green energy policies she has pushed as House speaker.[27]

In the summer of 2008, Republicans fought to have the moratorium on offshore oil and gas exploration lifted. Irritated, Pelosi lashed out saying. "I'm trying to save the planet; I'm trying to save the planet. I will not have this debate trivialized by [the Republicans'] excuse for their failed policy."[28] Pelosi was defending the congressional ban on offshore drilling that had been in effect since 1982.[29] This time, Big Oil was the Speaker's bull's-eye. It is independent and powerful. In short, it doesn't stand to benefit her. According to the Center for Responsive Politics, during the years Bush and Cheney occupied the White House, 80 percent of the oil and gas industry's contributions funded Republicans. And their contributions were hefty. They dispersed $82.1 million to federal candidates, parties and political action committees.[30] Like the circumstances for Big Tommy's ad tax in the 1950s, there's big money circulating that she and big government would like to get hold of. The oil companies are also a thorn in the side of one of Pelosi's constituencies: environmentalists.

Once more, the game was us versus them. Nancy Pelosi took on Big Oil in interviews in August 2008. She said that a vote in the House solely on offshore oil drilling was out of the question. She called it "a hoax on the American people." And the oil companies were the ones behind the scam. The Speaker said, "I can't allow a hoax to come to the floor."[31] Her choice of words was ironic, given the ruse of both her cap-and-trade legislation, based on questionable scientific findings, and the health-care reform bill she pushed through with backroom deals.

Pelosi said, "You want to drill? We want the royalties for the American people, and we want that to pay for renewable energy resources. We want to connect all that together." She went on to say that it was time to do away with "the failed energy policies supported by 'two oilmen in the White House.'" She deemed Big Oil selfish. They want to be able to drill and, according to Pelosi, "not pass their royalties to the taxpayer. They want us to subsidize the drilling." Instead, she said that energy alternatives like solar, wind, natural gas and oil released from the strategic energy supply should be required in any proposal.[32] The Speaker had more words for the oil industry as well as for Republicans and Democrats in the Senate who disclosed a measure that included permitting states to make the decision about drilling 50 miles or more from shore on the Outer Continental Shelf. She not only said she would prevent a vote on a bill allowing more offshore drilling, but she saw the measure as a "deceptive 'decoy.'" She told ABC's *This Week*, "I'm not giving the gavel away to a tactic . . . that supports the oil (companies), big oil at the cost and the expense of the consumer." Again, Pelosi ignored the polls. At the end of July 2008, the results of a *USA Today*/Gallup poll showed that, almost two-to-one, Americans would more likely lend their support to a candidate who favored expanded offshore drilling.[33]

Later that summer, however, with the reality of rising gas prices, Pelosi designed a legislative package that allowed for some offshore drilling along with $19 billion in tax incentives for alternative energy.[34] But her change of heart was startling, especially considering, as Manhattan Institute senior fellow Max Schulz wrote, "the speaker's belief that opening the outer continental shelf is a death knell for Mother Earth. . . ." Schulz said there were reasons to question her turnaround. Could it be she was offering some cover for Democrats in that year's upcoming election?[35] Just as recently as April 2010, the Speaker again expressed some support for a proposal to expand offshore drilling if cleaner energy programs were part of the deal. The plan would allow drilling off the Virginia coast, in the Gulf of Mexico if at least 125 miles from Florida's coastline and in areas of Alaska. California would be exempt, as well as Washington and Oregon. And Pelosi was ready for any criticism from environmentalists. She said, "It's about our national security to reduce our dependence on foreign oil. It's about our economy to create more jobs and [be] the leader in green jobs technology."[36] Could there be midterm election jitters?

In June 2009, with the oilmen out of the White House, Pelosi and the Democratic leaders were able to shove the "historic" cap-and-trade climate change bill, the American Clean Energy and Security Act, through their House. Pelosi, Representative Markey and House Energy and Commerce Committee chair Waxman were the three who released the draft of the legislation in April 2009. Markey said, "The planet is running a fever but there are no emergency rooms or plans so we have to act in a preventive way." And he was confident the proposed bill would create three to five million jobs for Americans. Waxman's words sounded just like Pelosi's: "This legislation will try to avert the terrible consequences of global warming . . . legislation that will renovate and transform our economy for many many new jobs to give our people the jobs they need to get out of this recession/depression."[37] But none of the three drafters explained how taxing people for their human activities could be tied to a job growth plan.

Still, the Boss was in complete control. She assigned authorship of the bill to Waxman's committee and then dodged House Ways and Means chair Charlie Rangel (D-NY) and his committee, allowing him only "cursory consideration" as she swept it to the House floor. Representative Rangel publicly complained that Pelosi had rammed the energy bill through the House, avoiding input from his committee. Undoubtedly, it was a bold move, since Rangel's committee was responsible for all the bill's tax provisions. Former powerful Ways and Means chair Dan Rostenkowski took notice of the Speaker's maneuvers. He said, "I can't believe that the Ways and Means Committee lets Nancy Pelosi determine what's in a bill."[38] It took months of negotiations before the more than 1,300-page bill narrowly passed, with a partisan vote of 219-212. Only eight Republicans voted for it, and 44 Democrats against.[39]

But Pelosi celebrated her victory. "We passed transformational legislation which takes us into the future," she said. Even Al Gore got involved in the deal cutting. House whip James Clyburn (D-SC) said, "Nancy Pelosi was the whip on this."[40] Her allies again cheered the Speaker's incredible machine skills—she had gotten the votes.

Pelosi had set the climate change bill up as one that would make us safer, keep us healthier and make us better people. Most of all, she said that it was "a moral issue for us to pass on God's beautiful creation to the next generation in a responsible way." But those who opposed the bill saw it as "economic suicide." They predicted it would prove to be the "most colossal mistake ever in the history of the United States Congress."[41]

New York Times reporter John Broder wrote, "The vote was the first time either house of Congress had approved a bill meant to curb the heat-trapping gases scientists have linked to climate change." Initially, in 2012, the cost of a permit to emit a ton of carbon dioxide will run about $13.[42] In reality, the legislation was a huge power grab. First, the bill was complex. But it was also full of regulatory mandates on industry, including a 17 percent reduction in greenhouse gas emissions by 2020, and an 83 percent cut by 2050. Moreover, within the next 11 years, 20 percent of electricity would come from renewable sources. There was a little mercy shown to petroleum refiners, farmers, electric utilities, coal plants, energy-intensive manufacturers and some other segments, which were guaranteed special protections during their switch to cleaner energy.

Those opposed to the bill saw it as more taxes on energy and higher prices for consumers. House minority leader John Boehner said, "This is the biggest job-killing bill that's ever been on the floor of the House of Representatives. Right here, this bill."[43] It was clearly a big-money deal in which legislation was passed based on the *threat* of the hotly debated "global warming" crisis. But that didn't stop Pelosi and her crew.

Not all Democrats were enthusiastic about the bill. Representative John Salazar (D-CO), who represents a low-income rural district that produces coal, understood the impact of the bill on his future. He said, "I'm in a tough spot. I really am. Either way I'm going to get creamed."[44] Undoubtedly, his lack of support would have repercussions with the Speaker.

Just a month before the passage of her historic legislation, Pelosi jetted off to China to talk nice with Chinese leaders she is usually dealing harshly with on human rights. This time Pelosi was there to discuss a safe environment as a basic human right. Speaking before an enthusiastic group of faculty and students, she said, "We are all in this together. The impact of climate change is a tremendous risk to the security and well-being of our countries." She went on to say that governments should look to science when making their decisions. But, she added, "[governments] also have to do it with openness, transparency, and accountability to the people. Everyone has to have their situation improved by it."[45]

In a speech in Beijing, Pelosi politicized the issue, calling climate change "a game changer in the U.S.-China relationship" and "an opportunity we cannot miss." (Maybe she was worried that the new, stricter U.S. standards would send more business China's way.) And during the same visit, at a U.S.-China Clean Energy Forum meeting, she said, "We are the biggest greenhouse gas emitters in the world. We have a responsibility to ourselves, to each other and to the world. We must work together."[46]

By "we" Pelosi does not mean that she is going to cut her own emissions, of course. She didn't take long to discover that being on the green diplomacy circuit creates opportunities to live quite comfortably. After all, you shouldn't have to scrimp when you are saving the planet. So when she took a House delegation to the much ballyhooed but failed Copenhagen Climate Summit in Denmark in December 2009, they lived quite well. There were five-star hotel rooms, and, according to CBS News correspondent Sharyl Attkisson, "Total hotel, meeting rooms and 'a couple' of $1,000-a-night hospitality suites topped $400,000." When Representative Waxman was questioned about his $2,200-a-day bill for room and food, he answered, "I can't believe that. I can't believe it, but I don't know." But Madam Speaker must have. She was the one who filed the group expense report. There were 64 people in the House delegation, and the Senate delegation counted 101 people, who mostly flew commercially. Still, some 320 nights were booked at Copenhagen's five-star Marriott.

And it was the Boss who'd decided who got to make the trip as part of her delegation. Among others, joining Representative Waxman were Charlie Rangel, Edward Markey, George Miller and Steny Hoyer. To get there, they fired up carbon-spewing jets—three military jets, to be precise: two 737s and a Gulfstream Five. The jets cost $168,000 just in flight time. Attkisson wrote of the overall large number of summit attendees, "They produced enough climate-stunting carbon dioxide to fill 10,000 Olympic swimming pools."[47]

Majken Friss Jorgensen, managing director of Copenhagen's largest limousine company, was surprised by the demand on her fleet for the summit. She said that on a regular day, she has 12 vehicles on the road. But when the "summit to save the world" opened, she was expected to have 200. She said, "We thought they were not going to have many cars, due to it being a climate convention. But it seems that somebody last week looked at the weather report." She estimated, the week before the summit, that there would be more than 1,200 limos on the streets.[48] Obviously, she didn't know much about the crowd in charge of hyping the climate change crisis. The airport was going to exceed its capacity to the point that some planes would have to park in Sweden. And the top hotels were also preparing for their guests. On the menus would be "scallops, foie gras and sculpted caviar wedges."[49] John Dingell may have had a point when he called Pelosi's new climate change committee the Committee on World Travel and Junkets.

In her design on the nation's energy policies, the Boss found a way to link the issue of global warming to, of all things, sexual discrimination. Speaking before a roundtable hosted by the Global Gender and Climate Alliance in Copenhagen, Pelosi blamed the United States for not taking the climate change crisis seriously enough. And just who had been positioned on the front line to struggle against global warming's pernicious plot? Women. Pelosi said, "Women have the most to gain and the most to lose in the climate crisis." She elaborated her bizarre claim:

> Changing agricultural conditions will hit women hardest. In most developing countries, women produce the vast majority of the household food supply. It is the world's grandmothers, mothers, and sisters in most countries who fetch water, gather wood and prepare meals. As resources become more scarce, so do opportunities for these women to attend school, tend crops, and lift themselves out of poverty.[50]

Climate change, it appears, is sexist.

Creating fear, distorting the truth and promoting drastic government solutions mean one thing: more power for the Boss. The result? More mandates, more taxes, less freedom and fewer choices—the oil that keeps Pelosi's machine humming. And for Madam Speaker, that works just fine.

9

FROM SHOE BOXES TO CORPORATE STOCKS

Nancy Pelosi would like us to believe that as Speaker, she leads the House of Representatives as a voice of ethical reform. Closer scrutiny of some of her financial transactions, however, shows otherwise. Big Tommy's ally Jack Pollack stored Election Day money in shoe boxes. Daughter Nancy, however, keeps her money in corporate stocks and high-priced real estate. Indeed, Nancy Pelosi has regularly leveraged her power as a political boss to enrich her family and friends.

Pelosi took charge of the Democratic congressional takeover in 2006 with promises of ethical reform and criticisms of a Republican "culture of corruption." When she took the gavel, on January 4, 2007, she announced in her acceptance speech a plan to "return this House to the American people" by "passing the toughest congressional ethics reform in history" within the first 100 hours of her speakership. "Let us join together in the first 100 hours," she proclaimed, "to make this Congress the most honest and open Congress in history."[1] Even before being elected Speaker, she swore that the first item on her agenda was to take on a major reform: ending the practice of allowing sponsors of earmarks to be anonymous. It was something that the Republicans had also promised but had failed to deliver. She told *USA Today*, "There has to be transparency. I'd just as soon do away with all [earmarks], but that probably isn't realistic."[2] True to her word, she and Appropriations Committee chairman David Obey led Congress to pass new rules in 2007 requiring that every bill be accompanied by both a list of the projects it contains and the names of the congressmen who requested each project. Furthermore, House members would have to certify that neither they nor their spouses would benefit financially from their earmarks.[3]

But then there was the matter of one of her own earmarks, which had the potential to enrich her family. In the words of the nonpartisan educational foundation Judicial Watch, Pelosi "snuck a $25 million gift to her husband, Paul Pelosi, in a $15 billion Water Resources Development Act."[4] On April 19, 2007, just three months after vowing to clean up Congress, the House passed the water resources bill. Her earmark, written during the first session of her speakership, called for renovations in the Embarcadero port area, in San Francisco, designed to further the neighborhood's comeback. As a result of Pelosi's $25 million project, the way would be cleared for cruise-ship-dock development. According to House financial disclosure documents, Paul Pelosi just so happens to be the owner of four commercial real estate properties near the Embarcadero—one located a mere 5,400 feet from the redevelopment site—that earn a combined rental income of more than $3 million. Renovation of the Embarcadero could possibly add to their value.[5]

By the time Republicans discovered and called in the apparent conflict of interest, it had already passed through the House as the Water Resources Development Act.[6] The incident did, however, land Pelosi a spot on Judicial Watch's 2007 list of Washington's "Ten Most Wanted Corrupt Politicians" (where, by the way, she would stay until 2009, for different reasons each year).[7] But Pelosi is proud of her accomplishment and boasts on her official website, "Under the leadership of Speaker Pelosi, the New Direction Congress has created unprecedented rules for transparency of WRDA [Water Resources Development Act] authorization requests by Members of Congress."[8]

But that was not her only major ethics flub at the beginning of her speakership. Pelosi has recognized, just like Big Tommy did, that maintaining and running an effective political machine means working with and backing people who don't stake much on ethics. Loyalty, it seems, is the character quality that really matters. In November 2006, Pelosi, then the Speaker-designate, set off a powder keg when she circulated a letter among House Democrats proclaiming her endorsement of John "Jack" Murtha in his bid for House majority leader.[9] In so doing, she broke a vow to stay neutral in the race.[10] The late Murtha, an ex-Marine and a 19-term representative from Pennsylvania's 12th Congressional District, was at the time the ranking Democrat on the Defense Subcommittee of the House Appropriations Committee. Over the years, Murtha had demonstrated that ethical scrapes were not something he appeared to be particularly worried about. He was involved in the FBI's Abscam bribery sting 26 years before his bid for majority leader.[11] Considered one of Congress's "kings of pork," he received almost $200 million—including another $800,000 in stimulus money in 2009—for the aptly named John Murtha Johnstown–Cambria County Airport, a Pennsylvania pork project that offers only three daily commercial flights and sees almost no customers. Steve Ellis, of Taxpayers for Common Sense, said, "It's practically a museum piece." And while the U.S. economy was on the brink, guess what the stimulus money was used for? The repaving of a crosswind runway that serves as a backup to the facility's main landing runway.[12]

Taxpayers for Common Sense reported that Murtha had requested more than $103 million in earmarks for his district in the 2006 defense spending bill alone. (Eventually, about $80 million of that got by President Bush's desk.) He was accused of exchanging federal money for campaign contributions, blocking ethics investigations and abusing his position as ranking member on the Appropriations Defense Subcommittee.[13] Beyond all of this, Murtha had dubious connections to defense executives and ex-military personnel found guilty of skimming money off government contracts. And he was tied to defense contractor Kuchera Industries and the now-defunct lobbying firm PMA Group, both of which are under federal investigation.[14]

And here was the Speaker of the House, Nancy Pelosi, on the eve of her great war on corruption, going well off the beaten path by putting her prestige on the line for Murtha, much to the befuddlement of those concerned about ethics in Washington. Melanie Sloan, the executive director of Democrat-leaning Citizens for Responsibility and Ethics in

Washington (CREW), captured the sentiments of many when she said, "Pelosi's endorsement suggests to me she was interested in the culture of corruption only as a campaign issue and has no real interest in true reform. It is shocking to me that someone with [Murtha's] ethics problems could be number two in the House leadership."[15] So what motivated Pelosi to make such a blatantly hypocritical move?

The pro-Murtha letter Pelosi circulated said that Murtha's early call for withdrawal from Iraq had motivated her to support him. But the reality is, Pelosi supported Murtha because he was useful to her.[16] The same way that Big Tommy had Jack Pollack, Pelosi had Murtha.

Pelosi and Murtha went way back. Wanting to win over Murtha, who represented a coal state, Pelosi made certain the black coal doll Big Tommy had kept as a keepsake from his fight for the union miners was visible whenever Murtha visited her office.[17] Murtha served as manager for her successful campaigns for House Democratic whip in 2001 and minority leader in 2002.[18] Their friendship, however, really began in earnest in 1989, when he sided with her over what to do with the Presidio, a contested San Francisco military base. Over the years they had worked together on many issues, including fund-raising and the war in Iraq.[19] And in 2004, Murtha's position on the Appropriations Defense Subcommittee allowed him to secure for her a pivotal victory in her fight for the Presidio.[20] By doing so, Murtha helped the Pelosi family protect their considerable financial interests. (More on this later.) Now it was time for Pelosi to return the favor.[21] Of course, it probably didn't hurt that Murtha's opponent in the majority leader race was Steny Hoyer, who'd challenged Pelosi unsuccessfully in 2001 for minority whip and with whom Pelosi had a strained relationship.[22] Maybe her reasons were a little too personal.

Murtha lost to Hoyer, even with the Speaker's weight behind him. But Pelosi would soon have another opportunity to show Murtha her loyalty when he became entangled in an investigation of the PMA Group. The PMA Group, which was founded by former House Appropriations Defense Subcommittee senior staffer Paul Magliocchetti, became one of Washington, D.C.'s most prominent defense-appropriations-focused lobbying firms. The firm, raided by the FBI in November of 2008, has in recent years distributed millions of dollars to legislators, mostly

House Democrats, in the form of campaign donations. It allegedly violated campaign finance laws by using "straw" donors to conceal the true source of their contributions (for example, by giving contributions through people listed as PMA Group lobbyists who were in fact never even employed by the firm). Murtha was the single largest recipient of contributions from the PMA Group, having accepted $2,378,552 from its clients and employees since 1998.[23] In return, Murtha and other lawmaking recipients rewarded PMA Group clients with millions of taxpayer dollars in earmarks, including more than $95 million in the 2006 defense appropriations bill alone.[24] Even after the investigations of PMA commenced, Murtha continued to earmark for the firm's former clients, requesting $16.2 million in earmarks for five clients in exchange for contributions to his PAC and campaign committee.[25] So how did Pelosi respond to this mockery of everything she'd campaigned on in 2006? Michael Steel, spokesman for House minority leader John Boehner, put it this way:

> The signs that Rep. Murtha may be hiding serious ethical problems are clearer every day, but Speaker Pelosi continues [to] turn a blind eye to the news about her hand-picked choice for House Majority Leader. Despite their campaign promises, the Democratic Leadership is still more interested in sweeping ethics problems under a rug than "draining the swamp."[26]

The Ethics Committee, not mentioning Murtha or any other specific lawmaker by name, revealed on June 11, 2009, that it was investigating "certain, specific allegations within the committee's jurisdiction" related to the PMA Group. By the end of 2009, the Office of Congressional Ethics had informed Murtha that it was no longer investigating the charges (though the Justice Department was looking into companies that have received his earmarks).[27] He retained his power in the House until his death, in February 2010.

Sadly, Pelosi's blind-eye favoritism toward Murtha is not an isolated occurrence. As Judicial Watch wrote in its 2008 list of Washington's "Ten Most Wanted Corrupt Politicians," "Speaker Pelosi has allowed corruption to run rampant in Congress and has ignored serious incidents of crooked behavior within her own party. . . . She continues to protect the worst of the worst of political corruption in the House of Representatives."[28] Consider Charles B. Rangel (D-NY), once House Ways and Means Committee chairman, who failed to disclose several hundreds of thousands of dollars in both assets and income on his financial disclosure forms for 2002 through 2006. According to records filed with the clerk of the House of Representatives, rental income received from a Harlem brownstone he sold in 2004 was a part of his lapse.[29] Strangely enough, in what Judicial Watch calls "clearly a publicity stunt," Rangel filed an ethics complaint against himself in 2008![30] The House Ethics Committee expanded the scope of the investigation that he had initiated, and his personal finances and fund-raising became the subject of two House ethics investigations. Republicans, including House minority leader John Boehner's staff, said that Rangel's inaccurate disclosure of assets and income, as well as the string of questions of ethics, merited his removal from the Ways and Means Committee chairmanship—a logical request, given that Ways and Means is the committee that oversees the tax code.[31] Pelosi, however, refused to ask him to step aside.

Pelosi and Rangel also go way back; he helped her jettison President George W. Bush's Social Security plan.[32] Pelosi and other Democratic leaders decided to let the 20-term representative retain his power as chief tax writer until he stepped down in March 2010.[33] And it was only when the House Ethics Committee admonished him for his lapses that Rangel gave up his gavel.

What makes these two cases even more self-condemning for Pelosi is that at the end of her acceptance speech for the speakership, she tagged to her pledge for ethics reform an equally daunting goal of pursuing bipartisan unity, saying: "Respectful of the vision of our Founders, the expectations of our people, and the great challenges that we face, we have an obligation to reach beyond partisanship to work for all Americans."[34] By campaigning on the Republicans' "culture of corruption" and then allowing that same kind of dishonesty to run rampant in her own House, she violates not only her pledge to ethics, but also her call for bipartisanship. Apparently, the Boss feels she has the discretion to suspend her standards when friends or prestige are involved, even when it means making a mockery of the House and her own party.

Similarly, Pelosi has attempted to sidestep federal laws enforced by the Federal Election Commission (FEC). For example, in 2002, she had two political action committees (PACs): the Team Majority and PAC to the Future. Federal law forbids PACs from contributing more than $5,000 per election to a single candidate or receiving more than $5,000 annually from a given donor. Federal law also stipulates that multiple PACs controlled by a single person are affiliated and need to abide by these restrictions as if they were one PAC; in other words, Pelosi's two PACs could not collectively give more than $5,000 per election to a given candidate or collectively receive more than $5,000 a year from a given donor. One might think that Pelosi, as a leading proponent of campaign finance reform, would use her two PACs correctly in accordance with these rules. But instead, she gave more than two dozen candidates the $5,000 maximum contribution from both Team Majority and PAC to the Future, violating federal law. Team Majority returned more than $100,000 it had collected beyond federal limits, earning her fund-raising committee a $21,000 fine in 2004.[35]

If any hope remains that Pelosi is in office just out of a sense of public service, a glance at the Speaker's own financial benefits derived from her office will dispel that notion. Like Big Tommy, she clearly enjoys the perks of the job. Pelosi established herself as a big spender during the first nine months of her speakership, in 2007, when she spent a little over $3 million—compared with her predecessor, Dennis Hastert (R-IL), who spent $1.8 million during the same period in 2006. In 2009, Pelosi dropped $30,610 of taxpayer money on food and beverage, $2,740 on bottled water and, between June and October alone, $2,993 on flowers. She also spent $5,000 on flowers as House minority leader in 2006. Granted, these expenses, though excessive, involve legitimate factors like schmoozing dignitaries and officials, as Pelosi's congressional offices are apt to remind critics. But what about a $10,000 contract she paid to have former Clinton White House speechwriter Heather Hurlburt write the speech she would deliver before the Israeli Knesset? Or the 51 workers on her payroll during the third quarter of 2006, compared with the 35 people Hastert employed?[36]

Then there are Pelosi's travel expenses, which seem more akin to the demands of a pop star than a public servant. Following the

September 11, 2001, attacks, Speaker Dennis Hastert was given access to a 12-seat commuter-style Air Force jet for travel between Washington, D.C., and his home district in Illinois. This post-9/11 security concession was a break from precedent; until then, the Speaker had always flown commercially between D.C. and his home district.[37] When Pelosi became Speaker, however, she decided that she didn't want a puny 12-seater; only a 42-seater would do.[38] How would she procure such an aircraft from the air force? Call Jack Murtha. A congressional source reported that Murtha had phoned administration officials to make sure Pelosi would get what she wanted. He allegedly accused Pentagon officials of sexism for resisting this request.[39] Murtha also warned them about leaking information that might reflect poorly on the Speaker; in his own words, "They're making a mistake when they leak it because she decides on [budget] allocations for them."[40] This is the bossism that Pelosi executes almost flawlessly.

The argument was that Pelosi needed a military plane for security reasons. The Pentagon, however, informed the Speaker on February 7, 2007, that they could not guarantee her access to the big jet (which could fly nonstop to California) that she asked for, though they could offer regular access to a smaller Air Force passenger jet. But the debate continued even after this, with government lawyers working to make her request fit with congressional travel rules and the Defense Department's policies.[41]

Having already effectively alienated House Republicans during her first month as Speaker, Pelosi would receive plenty of hard knocks for her travel request. When she appeared before the House Science Committee to parade her commitment to fight global warming, her Republican colleagues met her with prepared statistics about the carbon footprints of her hypothetical jet flights, along with criticism that she should lead by example and use a more eco-friendly, smaller plane. They even added an amendment satirizing her request to an environmental bill on the floor:

> The Congress also finds that in order to lessen United States dependence on foreign sources of petroleum, and decrease demand for petroleum in aircraft, such as passenger planes with 42 business-class seats capable of transcontinental flights, the nation must diversify its fuel supply for aircraft to include domestically produced alternative fuels.

This amendment forced a two-hour debate about Pelosi's jet request, and the bill passed—with the amendment—400 to 3.[42]

For sure, Pelosi had given her opponents much too good an opportunity to pass up. In fact, just the day before the amendment debacle, she appeared on television to defend her request for a big jet. At times she came off as petty, for example, claiming that former Defense secretary Donald H. Rumsfeld may have had a hand in leaking information concerning her request. The Speaker also said that she would just as soon fly commercially. "I don't even like having the security. I would rather travel on the plane with my friends to get some work done. I like my freedom, but there are certain sacrifices you have to make when you are speaker of the House," she explained. For good measure, she made a sexism charge, which had worked for her so often on her climb to the top: "I'm not saying that I am being discriminated against because I am a woman, I'm just saying as the first woman speaker, I have no intention of having less respect for the office I hold than all of the other speakers that have come before me."[43] (How denying her request for a plane more than three times the size of her predecessor's amounts to disrespect, she never went on to explain.)

The crash and burn of Pelosi's jet request was not enough to convert her into a gracious traveler. Since then, she has cultivated a reputation for exorbitant expenditures, unreasonable requests and last-minute changes and cancellations with those at the Pentagon who are required to meet her demands.[44] According to Judicial Watch, documents obtained from the air force through the Freedom of Information Act (FOIA) detail the Speaker's ridiculous use of taxpayer dollars while jet-setting on U.S. Air Force aircraft for congressional delegations (CODELs). Over just a two-year period, the air force was sent bills totaling $2,100,744.59. Pelosi's trips back to the Bay Area cost on average $28,210.51. And of the 103 Pelosi-led congressional delegations, almost a third of the trips included Pelosi family members. Of the two-year total amount, $101,429.14 was for in-flight expenses. Besides the food bills, there were substantial amounts of alcohol consumed. The cost of one trip from Washington to Baghdad in 2008, composed of congressional members and spouses, included tabs for "Johnny Walker Red scotch, Grey Goose vodka, E&J brandy, Baileys Irish Cream, Maker's Mark whiskey, Courvoisier cognac, Bacardi light rum, Jim Beam whiskey, Beefeater gin, Dewar's scotch, Bombay Sapphire gin, Jack Daniel's whiskey, Corona beer and several bottles of wine." Judicial Watch president Tom Fitton said, "Speaker Pelosi has a history of wasting taxpayer funds with her boorish demands for military travel. And these documents suggest the Speaker's congressional delegations are more about partying than anything else."[45]

Judicial Watch also obtained the flight-related correspondence between Pelosi's staff and the Pentagon, again through the FOIA. As Fitton puts it: "Taken together, these documents show that Speaker Pelosi treats the Air Force like her personal airline. Not only does Speaker Pelosi issue unreasonable requests for military travel, but her office seems unconcerned about wasting taxpayer money with last-minute cancellations and other demands." For example, she once requested an army escort and *three military planes* to fly her and other members of Congress to Cleveland, Ohio, to attend the funeral services of the late representative Stephanie Tubbs Jones. She even gave the escort a military-sounding name, calling it Operation Tribute.

On another occasion, she demanded that the military reroute her plane from San Francisco Airport to Travis Air Force Base, in nearby Fairfield, because she didn't want to spend an extra hour and a half in her limousine. It seems as if the young girl in Baltimore who claimed embarrassment at being dropped off at school by Big Tommy's limo has grown accustomed to the profligate use of taxpayer-funded private jets. Moreover, our military personnel have received less-than-cordial responses from Pelosi's intermediaries when silly requests have been denied. One message reads, "It is my understanding there are no G5s available for the House during the Memorial Day recess. This is totally unacceptable. . . . The Speaker will want to know where the planes are." Or: "This is not good news, and we will have some very disappointed folks, as well as a very upset [s]peaker."[46]

Not only does Nancy Pelosi work the system, she also finds inventive ways to turn something as innocent as a bus rehabilitation earmark into shameless profiteering, or worse.

It began with some conspicuous investments in Cisco Systems, the high-tech giant. Cisco Systems is a popular investment for members of

Congress. From at least 2004 through 2008 it remained one of the top four congressional investments for both chambers, holding the number two position in both 2004 and 2007. But in spite of the number of Cisco transactions that take place in Congress, the trend of Pelosi's Cisco transactions during those years raises some questions. Pelosi held between $15,001 and $50,000 in Cisco stock in 2004. She neither sold nor purchased any of that stock from 2004 through 2008, except for a group of four purchases made between November 7 and December 31, 2007. These purchases, however, expanded her Cisco holdings from less than $50,000 to a whopping $500,001 to $1,000,000—increasing to somewhere between 10 and 67 times the previous amount and making her and Senator John Kerry (D-MA) Congress's biggest holders of Cisco stock, according to most recent records. What makes this purchasing spree stand out—other than its sheer magnitude—is that Cisco stock was not seeing any kind of noteworthy increase in popularity in Congress in 2007. Furthermore, no other senator or representative enhanced their Cisco holdings in a way that remotely compared to Pelosi's increase.[47]

So why this sudden increase in Cisco stock? A partial explanation might be that Pelosi has pushed a tech policy that would benefit Cisco and other of her investments in the long run. Pelosi holds stock in a variety of high-tech and Internet-related companies, such as Apple, Microsoft and eBay, to name a few.[48] Her history with Silicon Valley has had its bumps, as when she spearheaded the attack against trade agreements with China and Central America, which are top priorities for tech companies dependent on exports. But in the fall of 2005, she abruptly took up the pro-tech banner when she met with her friend and ally John Chambers, Cisco's president and CEO, and others to develop a plan to expand the tech industry through, among other measures, federal funding for research and education. Touting a tech agenda has had its payoffs. In 2005, House Democrats used her plan to counter claims that they were antibusiness and to call in high-tech money for the 2006 election cycle, earning them $1.3 million from computer, Internet and software companies and their employees, up more than 50 percent from 2004, according to the Center for Responsive Politics. Pelosi took in $86,500 to her PAC from communications and technology industries in 2006, compared with $54,720 in 2004.

Pelosi's 12-page plan aimed to double the funding for the National Science Foundation and for broadband Internet access over five years, generate 100,000 engineers, mathematicians and scientists over four years, and permanently extend and increase the research and development tax credit.[49] Knowing that the House Democrats would back her in pursuing these kinds of major provisions, it is conceivable that Pelosi could have purchased Cisco stock with hopes that this and similar legislation would improve tech investments over time. But if Pelosi had made her 2007 investment because of some policy idea or pending legislation that would have significantly benefited Cisco, could this explain why her investment was such an outlier, and why the rest of Congress did not rush to buy Cisco stock with her?[50]

A more compelling explanation begins with Cisco's participation in the Clinton Global Initiative (CGI), on September 21, 2006. The CGI focuses on improving human life worldwide through practical, quickly implemented solutions and requires each participant to make a specific commitment to this end. Cisco responded by creating two initiatives to combat greenhouse emissions. One was an effort to reduce travel-related emissions at Cisco by reducing the need to travel for meetings through the development and use of high-definition virtual meeting technology (Cisco TelePresence). The other initiative was the Connected Urban Development initiative (CUD).[51]

The CUD is an effort to "reduce carbon emissions by introducing fundamental improvements in the efficiency of the urban infrastructure using information and communications technology."[52] This would reduce carbon emissions related to congestion and traffic delays. CUD established a partnership with the cities of Amsterdam, Seoul and San Francisco to pilot these technologies.[53]

It was with San Francisco that CUD partnered to create the Connected Bus, a green city bus that features free Wi-Fi and screens that can tell riders their current location, arrival time and the amount of greenhouse gases they are reducing by taking the bus. Complete with a picture of Mother Earth and an electronic display panel that shows green messages promoting carbon reduction, this bus is intended to increase bus use and thus reduce carbon emissions. Cisco officials, Ford and Mayor Gavin Newsom introduced the bus at CUD's Global

Conference 2008, cohosted by Cisco and the City and County of San Francisco. Chambers explained at the conference that the bus, and the CUD's dream, would begin with a few cities like San Francisco. But the goal was to see this approach extend to many other cities over time.[54] After all, the Clinton Global Initiative, from which the project was birthed, is exactly that—a "global initiative."

As Chambers sees it, "Corporate social responsibility is just plain good for business."[55] From this perspective, the unveiling of the bus looks a lot like the birth of a franchise—a new and profitable direction for Cisco. A document written specifically for the unveiling ceremony by the CUD and the San Francisco Municipal Transportation Agency lists the project's "success criteria." The very last criterion reads, "Transferable from demonstration pilot to project that could be installed throughout Muni fleet, funding permitted."[56]

Funding is where Pelosi enters the scene. On August 22, 2008, she announced a $980,000 Department of Transportation grant for the San Francisco Municipal Transportation Agency for "MUNI Bus Rehabilitation." This came from an earmark that she had attached to the 2008 Transportation and Housing & Urban Development Bill. She stated, "This grant will assist MUNI in meeting the transportation needs of residents and visitors. Funding will be used for the rehabilitation of approximately 10 percent of MUNI's bus fleet, extending the life of these vehicles, and ensuring reliable service." Her website's report of the announcement reads, "Pelosi has worked diligently to secure federal funding to assist the Municipal Transportation Agency in meeting San Francisco's transportation needs and will continue to work with city, state and federal officials and agencies to ensure that adequate resources are available."[57]

There is a glaring conflict of interest in that the Speaker secured earmarks helping to fund the Muni bus project just after becoming the owner of $500,000 to $1,000,000 in Cisco stock. Whether or not bus "rehabilitation" could entail purchasing more high-tech, efficiency-maximizing equipment from Cisco, having almost a million dollars thrown Muni's way would obviously give them a lot more financial freedom to produce more Cisco Connected Buses, either with earmarked funds or with their own cash freed up by Pelosi's earmark. And, outcomes aside, it's a little hard to assume that Pelosi's earmark was entirely selfless, based on the timing of her Cisco investment. The final commitment of all parties involved in the creation of the Muni bus occurred by September 17, 2007[58]—less than two months before Pelosi's first mega-purchase of Cisco stock.[59] In other words, it sure looks as if Pelosi became aware of Cisco's progress in trailblazing a new industry for improving transportation systems, and wanted a piece of the action and used her power to enhance her investment.

But the conflict of interest runs much deeper even than Pelosi's Cisco assets. It just so happens that one of the founding members of the CUD is none other than her son, Paul Pelosi, Jr.[60] How can one person squeeze profiteering and nepotism into something as benign as a bus rehabilitation earmark? To quote Chambers one last time, "It is hugely important to have supportive government."[61]

Pelosi's mixing of politics and personal profits was even more evident in her leadership role in a series of questionable real estate developments involving government funds and power surrounding the Presidio in San Francisco. One observer called them "the most corrupt legislative initiatives to pass successfully through San Francisco City government."[62]

The Presidio, which in Spanish means "garrison," was not only rich in history, but also one of the most stunning U.S. military bases in the world. A treasured part of San Francisco's heritage, it covers 1,488 acres—almost twice the size of New York's Central Park—and boasts breathtaking views of the Golden Gate Bridge and San Francisco Bay. It was a military post from 1776 to 1994, and from the 1950s to 1994 it was the headquarters for the Sixth United States Army. It served as home to some of the nation's most renowned military officials and was also the setting for glamorous military parties for more than a century. Beyond its aesthetic and historical value, it served as the fifth-largest employer in San Francisco.

By the early 1990s, however, it had become a major burden to taxpayers. When the bipartisan Base Closure and Realignment Commission recommended the closure or consolidation of many unneeded military bases around the country, the proud old base was put on the chopping block. The Cold War was over, and the threat of Pacific invasion had diminished, so there was now much less justification for the $50 million the Presidio cost the Defense Department to maintain each year.[63]

An initial report estimated that closing the Presidio could save taxpayers $74 million a year. Still, there were hurdles to overcome before it would be shut down. There was its rich 200-year history and the fond memories of many prestigious military leaders for whom it bore a sentimental attachment. And, on a more practical level, the closure of the Presidio would mean the loss of more than 5,000 jobs.[64]

Another sizable obstacle was Representative Nancy Pelosi, who had raised her family on Presidio Terrace, adjacent to the base's prized golf course.[65] She attempted to stop the closure of the base using a study that she and Representative Barbara Boxer had released in February 1989. This study concluded that closing the Presidio would carry with it a *cost* of $26 million per year, a sharp contrast to the previous estimate that the base's closure would *save* $74 million annually. Pelosi and Boxer's numbers received plenty of fanfare, but they failed to sway the Base Realignment and Closure Commission. Congress sided with the commission and designated the Presidio and 85 other military bases to be shut down.[66]

The numbers did, however, convince one member of the House Appropriations Committee. Jack Murtha's sympathy for Pelosi's cause would mark the beginning of their friendship. Murtha tried to block funding for the Presidio's closure. And while his actions could not ultimately prevent the base from closing,[67] he did offer Pelosi and Boxer some good advice: let the Department of Defense handle as many of the cleanup costs as possible.[68]

Ironically, Pelosi's first big break in the Presidio drama had a lot to do with legislation written into law years earlier by none other than the late Phil Burton, who just so happened to have been buried in the Presidio with his wife, Sala. The idea of the Presidio closing was not worth taking seriously in 1972. Nevertheless, in an act of remarkable foresight aimed at protecting the Pacific coast, Representative Burton created legislation that year that predetermined that the Presidio would become part of the Golden Gate National Recreation Area (GGNRA) should the military no longer need the base.[69] The result: the Presidio was transferred, upon closure, to the National Park Service.

This seemed like a great idea—after all, the Presidio, with its awe-inspiring natural beauty and more than a dozen rare or endangered plants, certainly deserved to be spared the industrialized fate awaiting other closed bases. But the Park Service soon discovered that in addition to the hang-up of having too many decidedly unparklike features (including its golf course, a bowling alley, two hospitals and lots of roads and buildings), the Presidio was far too costly for them to maintain on the federal budget. An early Park Service estimate predicted that running the Presidio would cost $45 million annually, more than Yosemite, Yellowstone and the Grand Canyon combined. They tried to take over the facility with the help of some extra congressional funding, but after a few years it had become painfully clear to them that Burton's good idea was not sustainable.[70]

Here's how Burton's law paved the way for Pelosi's intervention: the federal government, unable to maintain the Presidio through the National Park Service, wanted to sell it for development. On the other side of the fence were those in the community who wanted the government to pay the tens of millions needed to keep the park operating. So Pelosi proposed a compromise. With the backing of an assortment of businesspeople, environmentalists and nonprofit insiders, known as the Presidio Council, she authored a piece of legislation that proposed that the Presidio be handed over to a public-private partnership called the Presidio Trust.[71] The idea was that the Presidio Trust would receive more than $25 million a year in federal support to help it manage the national park until it could attain self-sufficiency. The trust, with its mission of "promoting environmental and social causes and the arts," would have discretion over development plans for the land.[72] The Presidio Trust did not become a reality until it was pushed through Congress in 1996 (following a failed attempt in 1994).[73] Pelosi thanked friends and colleagues Barbara Boxer, Dianne Feinstein, George Miller, Ralph Regula and, of course, "our early champion" Jack Murtha for being "instrumental in its passage."[74] There was a noteworthy catch for the Presidio Trust, though: according to Pelosi's legislation, if the park did not wean itself off federal tax dollars by 2013, it would lose its national park status and be sold to developers.[75]

Pelosi made use of her expert political maneuvering to designate the Presidio to her Presidio Trust, going to extreme measures like personally visiting each Republican on the House Resources Committee and inviting them for a visit to receive a personal tour through the Presidio. The persistent lobbying efforts she used to secure her Presidio Trust legislation drew praise from both parties. But why all this work? What was her interest in the Presidio? Pelosi biographer Marc Sandalow writes in *Madam Speaker* that Pelosi "was driven by her determination to forever preserve such a unique setting as a park," in line with Burton's original vision of preserving the Pacific coast.

That might be true to her environmentalism, but there was more to it than that.

To call the Presidio prime real estate would not do it justice. It was a developer's dream. A conservative estimate by *Forbes* magazine put the value of the Presidio at $4 billion.[76] Therefore, both of the two popularly voiced options for use of the land—strict environmental preservation and low-income housing—would have wasted its real estate potential. In fact, turning the land into low-income housing would run the risk of depressing property values in surrounding wealthy neighborhoods. What makes this analysis particularly interesting is that the Pelosis actually own several real estate investments near the Presidio, including a building only two blocks away on Broadway and another on Point Lobos. Noticeably, Pelosi had a personal stake in the land's development.[77]

So her Presidio Trust's development plan was designed to enhance the property's potential. Under a 1998 draft of the Presidio Trust's development plan, for example, the Presidio would be transformed into a "city within a city," featuring restaurants, bed-and-breakfast inns, a movie theater, a conference center, 4,800 daytime office jobs, and 1,600 units of market-rate housing. And through all of this, the Presidio would retain its place in the National Park System and its $25 million plus from the federal government! A cozy arrangement.

Several movements Pelosi had traditionally supported opposed the plan. On the one hand, religious leaders and city officials (including Mayor Willie Brown) argued that the trust was not doing enough to meet the city's need for low-income housing. A group called Religious Witness for Homeless People went so far as to sponsor a June 1998 ballot initiative (Measure L) demanding that the Presidio set aside more space for low-income housing. Pelosi was against the measure.[78] On the other hand, environmentalists complained that endangered wildlife habitats and historic resources needed greater protection. Critics charged that the development plan violated the Park Service's general management strategy, which called for protecting the Presidio's forests, meadows and wetlands.[79] In the end, the environmentalists proved easier to buy off. In exchange for their support, they were given choice leases on commercial real estate that would become some of San Francisco's most expensive and desirable. In fact, the Presidio would grow to become a sort of progressive Disneyland, with 8 percent of its more than three million square feet of office space rented to international and environmental groups by 1998,[80] including former Soviet dictator Mikhail Gorbachev.[81] Indeed, when the Gorbachev Foundation set up shop in the early nineties, Pelosi welcomed the Communist to San Francisco.

So when it came to real estate redevelopment that affected Pelosi's own property values and those of her rich friends and supporters, "the people" who would have benefited from affordable housing lost out.

There were even more shenanigans involving the 936-acre Hunters Point Shipyard. Hunters Point was the largest tract of undeveloped land in San Francisco and one of the choicest real estate properties within the Presidio. However, it was also a federal Superfund site containing all sorts of contaminates, including hazardous materials, bioaccumulative toxic substances, PCBs, acids, total petroleum hydrocarbons, pesticides and toxic metals, to name but a few.[82]

Pelosi worked for more than 15 years to designate 75 acres of the shipyard, Parcel A, to become the first tract of the Presidio to be transferred to the care of San Francisco. In 1989, seven years before Congress passed the legislation creating the Presidio Trust, Pelosi took it upon herself to secure report language in the 1990 Defense Authorization Act urging the navy to formulate a plan for future use of the shipyard by March 1990. She followed this up in 1990 with another addition to the Defense Authorization Act, the Pelosi Amendment, which authorized the transfer of Hunters Point Shipyard to the city.[83] There would follow more than 14 years of back-and-forth negotiations and approximately $350 million worth of navy-funded environmental investigation and cleanup of the shipyard before Parcel A would finally go to San Francisco.[84] Not that Pelosi would let the federal appropriations stop there, of course. For example, in 2008 she added earmarks to the defense budget totaling $9.3 million for Hunters Point and $4 million for the Presidio Trust. She tacked another $11.05 million for Hunters Point and the Presidio onto the defense budget in 2009.[85]

But it is important to take a step back and note that just a few weeks before the navy signed the land away, it wrote Mayor Newsom a letter expressing doubts about going ahead with a symbolic, prescheduled agreement that Pelosi had already announced.[86] She responded by calling on her by now old friend Jack Murtha to—as she put it—"assist" in "this last round of negotiation."[87] Murtha pressured navy officials to sign the Hunters Point Shipyard Conveyance Agreement, telling them "he wanted a binding agreement signed 'by Wednesday.'"[88]

The Radiological Affairs Support Office had raised new concerns about Parcel A's safety for residential developments because of a recent, enormous investigation into the use of radioactive materials at the shipyard from 1939 to 2003. Investigators found hundreds of buildings contaminated with radiation, as well as the entire storm, drain, and sanitary sewer systems, dry docks and even the ground itself (Hunters Point had been the site of the Naval Radiological Defense Laboratory).[89] Nevertheless, navy assistant secretary H. T. Johnson[90] signed the shipyard over to San Francisco on March 31, 2004. Apparently, Murtha was more persuasive than the findings of the radiological investigation. At the announcement of the signing, Pelosi thanked her "good friend" John Murtha (to whom she would return the favor with her endorsement of him in the 2007 House majority leader race) and said of the agreement, "This is a crucial agreement for the Bayview Hunters Point community, which establishes important environmental protections." Newsom sealed the Hunters Point deal in an official ceremony in January 2005, signing the Hunters Point Shipyard redevelopment measures into law and accepting the transfer of Parcel A of Hunters Point in exchange for—I kid you not—one dollar.[91]

The 75-acre tract Pelosi had won for San Francisco was a developer's dream, but the developer selected for the job turned it into a nightmare. As is often the case with boss politics, it all started with a little nepotism. Gavin Newsom signed over commercial development rights to the limited-liability, Miami-based *Fortune* 500 developer Lennar/BVHP as part of the Hunters Point Shipyard Conveyance

Agreement. Laurence Pelosi, Nancy's nephew and Newsom's cousin and former mayoral campaign treasurer, was Lennar's vice president of acquisitions.

A consultant for the San Francisco Redevelopment Agency had recommended awarding the development rights to an Ohio-based company called Forest City. But that would not do. Lennar called on some politically connected friends, and a parade of their supporters weighed in on their behalf to the Redevelopment Agency. Many of them were friends of Mayor Willie Brown and—you guessed it—Aunt Nancy. (It should be noted that Brown also had deep ties to Lennar; his former head of economic development was Kofi Bonner, president of Lennar Urban for Northern California, who had also previously worked for the Redevelopment Agency.) The Redevelopment Agency commissioners, all mayoral appointees, went with Lennar. For those who have any doubt about whether Laurence Pelosi's ties to relatives Newsom and Nancy Pelosi were advantageous to Lennar, note that he resigned from the company in May 2004, just before the shipyard legislation was up for approval. He went off to work for Morgan Stanley and joined the board of directors of San Francisco Planning and Urban Research (SPUR).[92]

So how did Lennar handle the job? Their website claims, "Our Lennar Associates are committed to always doing the right thing for the right reason, and approaching each day with the highest of *Integrity*" (their emphasis).[93] To put it lightly, this is a very generous assessment of Lennar/BVHP's egregious environmental negligence. Before developing the Presidio, the company had already caused asbestos problems in California's El Dorado as a result of dynamiting. Their irresponsibility in El Dorado had resulted in a $350,000 settlement in 2006 (for which they negotiated to have one of their contractors held solely responsible). Sadly, evidence from its work at Hunters Point would suggest that Lennar had not learned from its mistakes.

The April 2000 environmental impact report for the shipyard reuse clearly warned, "Because asbestos-containing serpentinite rock occurs at Hunters Point Shipyard, construction-related excavation activities could cause chrysotile asbestos associated with serpentinite to become airborne, creating a potentially significant impact to public health and safety." The necessity of stringent asbestos monitoring was equally clear. Within a quarter mile of Parcel A are located the Milton Meyer Recreation Center, the Hunters Point Boys and Girls Club, and the Muhammad University of Islam, a small, year-round private school, operated by the Nation of Islam, just on the other side of a chain-link fence from Parcel A. Children are especially vulnerable to asbestos hazards, and state asbestos laws require increased asbestos monitoring for sites close to schools. But in spite of all of this, Lennar's environmental consulting group CH2M Hill, didn't bother to include any air monitoring whatsoever in its original plan for Parcel A.

The air district corrected this negligence by imposing its own, strict plan, which Lennar agreed to implement in the summer of 2005, beginning ten months prior to construction. The plan required precautions like sweeping and watering the construction sites, maintaining certain air-monitoring requirements and making sure that vehicle tires were washed before drivers exited.

One way that Lennar fell short of the plan was in its watering requirements. Justifying its actions, the president of Lennar Urban for Northern California, Kofi Bonner, told the Redevelopment Agency, "Given the hilly terrain, it can only be watered enough so as not to create difficult conditions for the workers going up and down the site." But far more serious was Lennar's disregard for the air district's asbestos-monitoring requirements. The developers actually went 13 months— including three months of massive earth-moving operations next to the school—with no data to show how much asbestos the nearby students were being exposed to. Lennar's executives eventually alerted the air district in August of 2006 and replaced CH2M Hill, though they contested aspects of the violated safety requirements instead of apologizing. They also chose not to release their other two subcontractors and, as critics have testified at agency meetings, did not do enough to keep them in check when violations continued.

The air district issued Lennar a notice of violation in September 2006 for the period July 14, 2005, through August 3, 2006.[94] Lennar's violations, which included intentionally concealing the danger of being exposed to toxic dust laden with high levels of asbestos beyond allowable amounts, were potentially criminal in scope and stature. Lennar entered into a settlement agreement with the Bay Area Air Quality

Management District (BAAQMD) in August 2008 under which Lennar paid $515,000 in civil penalties, and the air district agreed not to seek criminal or civil penalties for Lennar's violations related to their actions documented in 2006.[95]

But this agreement was not the only legal attempt to punish Lennar. On March 17, 2007, attorney Angela Alioto sued Lennar in superior court on behalf of three of the corporation's former executives.[96] Allegations included racial discrimination against the executives, as well as unlawful retaliation against them for raising questions about the dust problems at the construction site.[97] More notably, the case also involved allegations of "environmental racism."[98] (Bayview–Hunters Point is San Francisco's last black neighborhood).[99] Lennar, having tried unsuccessfully to get the case dismissed, settled it outside of court in January 2008 for an unknown amount. Later, in June 2009, another suit was filed against Lennar on behalf of more than a dozen local school children, for failing "on many occasions" to stop work when asbestos levels far surpassed the cutoff threshold.[100]

Lennar has also received plenty of flak from community activists. Bayview–Hunters Point has endured 20 years of disproportionately high rates of asthma. An increase, however, in complaints of respiratory ailments following Lennar's monitoring failures has compelled some, like community leader Minister Christopher Muhammad, to go on the offensive. As minister of Muhammad University of Islam (the school across the fence from the site mentioned earlier), he had complained to the Redevelopment Agency in November 2006 concerning the dust problems at the school. (Lennar vice president Paul Menaker was said to have dismissed the grievances and called the minister a "shakedown artist.")[101] In 2007, Muhammad reported that children were complaining about breathing problems and tear-swollen eyes "everyday [sic] practically for over a four-month period." He said, "You can't hardly knock on a door in Bayview–Hunters Point where you can't find a person that's been ill-affected by that shipyard." Even four-month-olds have been diagnosed with asbestos-related respiratory problems, the minister reported. Of his congresswoman, he said, "Quite frankly, this looks bad to talk about human rights around the world, and right in your back yard there's a dirty little secret that you don't want to talk about."[102]

In spite of the great outcry against the development project, a pending federal EPA report has declared the Hunters Point Shipyard development project environmentally safe and having effective safeguards for minimizing asbestos exposure. Other reports have shared this conclusion, though some project critics remain skeptical—for example, because the report did not involve screening individual residents for asbestos-related symptoms.[103] While the project's actual environmental safety has infinite importance to the Bayview–Hunters Point residents and to the health of that community, it has far less relevance as a measure of the overall corruption of the development project. Either way, Lennar ignored monitoring requirements, citizens lived in fear, and their environmentally friendly, pro-housing representative was the one who subjected them to this fate.

10

HOLY NANCY

[My parents] didn't raise me to be the speaker. They raised me to be holy.

—Nancy Pelosi[1]

Compared with her liberal compatriots, Nancy Pelosi's brand of religiosity can seem downright laudatory. As leftist activist and rabbi Michael Lerner admits in his book *The Left Hand of God: Taking Back Our Country from the Religious Right*, "Many on the Left, to be blunt, hate and fear religion."[2] Lerner's admission is backed up by examples too numerous to catalog; however, a few notable mentions from leading national liberal commentators underscore the left's antipathy to faith and those who worship God. Indeed, the snarky and often hostile language liberals use against religion in general and Christian voters in particular can be jaw-dropping. To wit: the day after President George W. Bush's reelection, liberal *New York Times* columnist Maureen Dowd explained that Bush's victory was the result of religious zealots brainlessly voting on the basis of "fear, intolerance, ignorance" and a deep desire for "religious rule." As Dowd graciously taught her readers, George W. Bush "ran a jihad in America so he can fight one in Iraq—drawing a devoted flock of evangelicals, or 'values voters,' as they call themselves, to the polls by opposing abortion, suffocating stem cell research and supporting a constitutional amendment against gay marriage."[3]

Dowd's derision toward Christian Evangelicals, however, is mild when compared with the likes of Robert Reich, Labor secretary under former president Bill Clinton. According to Reich, one of the greatest dangers America will face in the 21st century, besides terrorism, is men, women and children who worship God:

> The great conflict of the 21st century may be between the West and terrorism. But terrorism is a tactic, not a belief. The underlying battle will be between modern civilization and anti-modernist fanatics; between those who believe in the primacy of the individual and those who believe that human beings owe blind allegiance to a higher authority; between those who give priority to life in this world and those who believe that human life is no more than preparation for an existence beyond life; between those who believe that truth is revealed solely through scripture and religious dogma, and those who rely primarily on science, reason, and logic. Terrorism will disrupt and destroy lives. But terrorism is not the only danger we face.[4]

Clearly, Speaker Nancy Pelosi, a self-described practicing Catholic and graduate of Trinity College (now Trinity Washington University), a Catholic institution, is nowhere near as hostile toward religion or those who practice their faith as many of her fellow leftists. To her credit, Nancy Pelosi speaks proudly of the Christian heritage Big Tommy and Big Nancy imparted to her.

"They'd be proud," Pelosi says of her parents, "but they didn't raise me to be the speaker. They raised me to be holy; they raised me to care about other people. They told us that you shouldn't pray to win an election; that really wasn't appropriate."[5]

Pelosi's friend Sally Hambrecht agrees with the Speaker's espousal of her deep Catholic heritage and faith. Hambrecht describes the Speaker's church attendance as rock solid and unwavering. "Every Sunday she goes to Mass," says Hambrecht. "And it doesn't matter where she is; she finds a way to go. And it's just part of her makeup."[6]

When the *National Catholic Reporter*, a major Catholic publication, asked Pelosi if she considers herself a "conservative Catholic," Pelosi said she did:

> I think so. I was raised, as I say, in a very strict upbringing in a Catholic home where we respected people, were observant,

were practicing Catholics and the fundamental belief was that God gave us all a free will and we were accountable for that, each of us. Each person had that accountability, so it wasn't for us to make judgments about how people saw their responsibility and that it wasn't for politicians to make decisions about how people led their personal lives; certainly, to high moral standards, but when it got into decisions about privacy and all the rest, that was something that individuals had to answer to God for, and not to politicians.[7]

Yet despite her strong religious upbringing and consistent church attendance each Sunday, Nancy Pelosi has proved herself to be unusually adept at performing theological gymnastics when it comes to policy issues that are in direct conflict with her Christian faith. As Pelosi has herself conceded, she finds herself on a collision course with the Catholic Church on a host of issues and stances:

I have some concerns about the church's position respecting a woman's right to choose. I have some concerns about the church's position on gay rights. I am a practicing Catholic, although they're probably not too happy about that. But it is my faith. I practically mourn this difference of opinion because I feel what I was raised to believe is consistent with what I profess, and that is that we are all endowed with a free will and a responsibility to answer for our actions. And that women should have that opportunity to exercise their free will.[8]

Pelosi's confrontations with the Catholic Church over her radical proabortion policy positions and the Church's long-standing pro-life stance have been both consistent and public. For her part, the Speaker didn't help matters when, in 2008, she sparked an uproar by claiming that "doctors of the church" were in disagreement over when exactly life begins, adding that abortion "continues to be an issue of controversy" in the Catholic Church.[9] The response from many Catholic leaders was loud and vociferous. A number of U.S. bishops publicly scolded Pelosi by pointing out that the Catholic Church's opposition to abortion dates all the way back to the first century. In an article in *Christianity Today* titled "Pope Gives Pelosi a Stern Reprimand," religion reporters Paul

Virgo and Kevin Eckstrom reported that the wording of a Vatican statement "suggests she [Pelosi] received another reprimand from the pope over her support for abortion."[10] Indeed, the statement, which was issued after a meeting between Pelosi and His Holiness Pope Benedict XVI in 2009, read: "His Holiness took the opportunity to speak of the requirements of the natural moral law and the Church's consistent teaching on the dignity of human life from conception to natural death which enjoin all Catholics, and especially legislators, jurists and those responsible for the common good of society, to work in cooperation with all men and women of good will in creating a just system of laws capable of protecting human life at all stages of its development."[11]

The Holy See's disapproval was unequivocal. Interestingly, following her meeting with the pope, Pelosi's public statement sidestepped the "papal lecture" she received regarding natural moral law. Instead, Pelosi said she and her husband, Paul, praised the Church's leadership in combating poverty, hunger and global warming.[12]

Pelosi says she has grown accustomed to sharp disagreements over abortion with those she respects and loves, including members of her own family. "I come myself from a family that does not share my views on choice," says Pelosi.[13] "I try to abide by all the teachings of the church in relationship to family," Pelosi told the *National Catholic Reporter*.[14]

But the rift between Speaker Pelosi and the Catholic Church over abortion didn't close following her papal visit. It widened. So at odds are her policy stands with Catholic teachings that Pelosi has received stern reprimands from her own archbishop. Part of the Boss's problem involves her bizarre twisting of well-established theological tenets of Catholicism. For example, Pelosi, a mother of five, has repeatedly used the doctrine of free will as a justification for mothers to destroy their unborn children. On January 13, 2010, Archbishop George Niederauer confronted the Speaker's theological contortions head-on. Archbishop Niederauer said that Pelosi's decision to support abortion by citing her free will "is entirely incompatible with Catholic teaching." As the archbishop explained, "Embodied in that statement are some fundamental misconceptions about Catholic teaching on human freedom." He also pointed out that "it is entirely incompatible with Catholic teaching to conclude that our freedom of will justifies choices that are radically contrary to the Gospel—racism, infidelity, abortion, theft. Freedom of will is the capacity to act with moral responsibility; it is not the ability to determine arbitrarily what constitutes moral right."[15]

The Boss's views, not surprisingly, lack warmth and compliance. In an interview between the Speaker and liberal journalist Eleanor Clift, Speaker Pelosi did her usual two-step, wherein she invoked her traditional mother/family values shield while simultaneously pushing back against Catholic teaching.

> I had five children in six years. The day I brought my fifth baby home, that week my daughter turned 6. So I appreciate and value all that they [the Church] want to talk about in terms of family and the rest. When I speak to my archbishop in San Francisco and his role is to try to change my mind on the subject, well then he is exercising his pastoral duty to me as one of his flock. When they call me on the phone here to talk about, or come to see me about an issue, that's a different story. Then they are advocates, and I am a public official, and I have a different responsibility.[16]

Pelosi's abortion-based clash with Archbishop George Niederauer is indicative of the left's reliance on arguments rooted in moral relativism. Moral relativism—the belief that morality is entirely subjective and contingent on the ethical preferences of each individual—is the pasture on which most of the left's sacred cows graze. Seen through this rhetorical lens, liberals contend that there are really no black-and-white moral absolutes. Instead, say liberals, decisions are just that—gray options among a host of many. Such arguments, however, unravel precisely because they turn in on themselves; it's hard to claim that an opponent's position is "immoral" when you yourself do not believe in a black-and-white code of right and wrong. But that's not how Pelosi sees herself or her positions. In her world, the Boss's policy stands are entirely compatible with Catholic teachings. How? Because she is doing the Lord's work and stands on the side of the angels. Indeed, Nancy Pelosi views her political profession and involvement as a holy act of worship. "Love of country, deep love of the Catholic church, and love of family were all the values I was raised in," says Pelosi. "I don't like to have religion and politics come too closely together, but I will say that

I am motivated by the Gospel of Matthew, as many people in politics are. I find it an inspiration."[17]

The Boss wants to have it both ways. On the one hand, she says she doesn't want religion and politics to commingle. On the other hand, says Pelosi, she believes politics is a vehicle through which she can carry out her religious convictions. She wistfully recalls her "upbringing—working on the side of the angels with my parents—to help people, again according to [the] Gospel of Matthew, and the idea . . . [that we] look upon God's creation as an act of worship. To ignore the needs of God's creation is to dishonor the God that made them. And that we have that responsibility, all of us."[18]

Not much separation of church and state there, what with the "working on the side of the angels" and all.

Yet Pelosi's self-imposed separation of church and state not only stands in contrast to her own upbringing; it also stands in sharp contrast to the way she raised her five children. In fact, Pelosi quite literally fused faith and politics by having her children sing common Christian songs, altering the lyrics to include political campaigning. "Our daughter Christine remembers leafleting with me when she was a toddler," writes Pelosi. "When they were older and capable of doing more, they helped with the mailings. Our cheerful assembly line often sang while they worked. One of their favorites was a spirited rendition of 'He's Got the Whole World in His Hands.' They changed the words to describe the task they were doing: 'He's got the stuffers and the sealers in his hands . . .'"[19]

Pelosi's insistence that she prefers to decouple religion and politics is similarly undermined by her own invocation of religious rhetoric in her public statements. When it's convenient or politically advantageous for her to do so, the Boss sprinkles her speeches with religious flourishes or allusions. "Pelosi has strongly encouraged other Democrats in the House to speak up about their faith, as well," writes Pelosi biographer Vincent Bzdek, "although an aide said she has cautioned against invocations of faith from those who aren't truly faithful. Authenticity is what she's looking for."[20]

For example, in her statements in support of embryonic stem cell research, ironically, Nancy Pelosi invoked religiosity in championing a policy that her church staunchly opposes. "The National Institutes of Health and Science hold the biblical power of a cure for us," said Pelosi.[21] Nothing like a person opposed to inserting religion into politics . . . inserting religion into politics.

Or consider Pelosi's statement shortly after she became Speaker-nominee. When her archrival, Representative Steny Hoyer, beat out her ally and friend Representative John Murtha for the House majority leader spot, here's what the non-publicly religious Speaker Pelosi had to say: "I look forward to working with him in a unified way. We've had our debates; we've had our disagreements in that room. And now, that is over. As I said to my colleagues, as we say in church, let there be peace on Earth and let it begin with us."[22]

Others have noted this trend in Pelosi's rhetoric. Pelosi biographer Vincent Bzdek analyzed myriad speeches by the congresswoman. He concluded that "sifting back through recent speeches, it's remarkable how often Pelosi cites direct passages from the Bible as specific calls for action on a wide range of issues." From calls for health care to the environment to relief for Hurricane Katrina to even immigration, on each issue, the Boss didn't fail to miss a chance to invoke the Almighty as support for her political designs and ideological causes.[23]

To be sure, tweaking the lyrics of religious songs for one's children to enjoy and peppering speeches and public statements with religious references for political ends can be dismissed as lacking in lasting impact. But the Boss is smart. She understands what Big Tommy taught her to understand: politics is a game of numbers and coalitions. She is also aware of the so-called God gap that exists between the Democratic Party and the Republican Party. "The God gap" is the term used by pollsters and pundits to denote the large variance between political identification and regular church attendance. As former president Bill Clinton's pollster, Stanley Greenberg, has explained, "the Faithful" (Greenberg's name for white Christians) represent a strong and potentially powerful voting bloc whose actions stand to seriously thwart the left's radical agenda. According to Greenberg, this voting bloc comprises nearly one out of every five Americans. "White evangelicals vote for the Republicans, as if it were an article of their faith," writes Greenberg. His data reveal that more than 70 percent of these voters break for the Republican Party, "giving the Republicans nearly a 50-point margin (72 percent, compared to the few 'lost souls,' the 23 percent who align with the Democrats)."[24]

Whatever the electoral ramifications of Pelosi's use of religion in her political tactics, far more troubling is her contention—similar to the late U.S. senator Ted Kennedy's—that a sort of "heaven on earth" is possible if only lawmakers would act progressively in passing laws that recalibrate and equalize existing inequalities or injustices that result from humans' sinful nature. "The respect that we have for the individual because of the spark of divinity that we all carry serves me well in politics," says Pelosi.[25] In this way, a sort of "societal salvation" becomes possible for those willing to join with the people "working on the side of the angels" (aka leftists). By crafting legislation that draws attention to the poor and underrepresented, the Boss believes she is doing her saintly work. The imposition of the liberal agenda on Americans, therefore, is akin to her path to heaven. The problem is this: Pelosi's "salvation" means taxpayers' "damnation." For Pelosi, fusing belief and politics propels and emboldens her to foist her liberal agenda on the American taxpayer. "Seventeen centuries ago," says Pelosi, "St. Augustine said any government that is not formed to promote justice is a bunch of thieves. In order to do the job, you have to have a belief. It's what drives your engine, what you keep coming back to."[26]

A prime example of this can be seen in Pelosi's handling of the debacle that became President Barack Obama's attempts at a government takeover of health care. When opposition arose surrounding provisions within the bill that would have created a pathway for taxpayer-funded abortions, Pelosi went to work on a Catholic cardinal:

> I talked to one of the cardinals. I said to him that I believe that what we are doing honors the principles we talked about: we want to pass a health-care bill, we want it to be abortion neutral, and we want it to [have] no federal funding [for abortion], which is the law. And we believe that our language does that. They said, 'We believe that it does not.' I said, let's sit down at the table and our lawyers can compare language. That's what the meeting was about—to make our case. Clearly, the people at that table were not willing to accept what we know to be a fact.[27]

Of course, as usual, Pelosi's spin didn't add up. The "fact" was that the bill *did* provide for taxpayer monies to extend federal monies for elective abortions. So much so, in fact, that in November 2009, 12 pro-life Democrats (yes, there are that many pro-life Democrats in the U.S. House of Representatives), led by Representative Bart Stupak, threatened to vote against the bill if the proabortion language was not removed.

But abortion has not been Pelosi's only conflict with her church's teachings. As she makes clear, the Speaker holds myriad beefs with the Catholic Church. The San Francisco congresswoman supports gay marriage. Her church opposes it on the grounds that marriage is a God-ordained holy institution intended for one man and one woman. Pelosi strongly supports federal funding for embryonic stem cell research. Her church opposes embryonic stem cell research, arguing that creating life only to destroy it is a sin and violates God's commands to protect, not threaten, innocent life. And finally, the Boss says she opposes efforts to thwart female priests. "I have always thought that there should have been a stronger role for women in the church."[28]

In traditional cutthroat Pelosi fashion, the Boss has not idly sat back and allowed the Church's public condemnations to go unchecked. When efforts were made by some bishops to ban proabortion Catholic law-makers from being able to receive communion at Mass, House minority leader Nancy Pelosi linked arms with 47 other Catholic Democratic House members in signing and sending a letter to Cardinal Theodore McCarrick of Washington condemning such efforts as "deeply hurtful" and "counterproductive." The issue gathered steam during the 2004 presidential election when Archbishop Raymond Burke of St. Louis told Senator John Kerry, the Democratic presidential nominee, that he would not be able to receive Communion in Missouri. Similarly, Bishop Michael Sheridan of Colorado Springs told Catholics who vote for elected officials who support gay marriage, stem cell research, abortion, or physician-assisted suicide that they should go to confession prior to receiving the sacrament. These decisions so angered Catholic congress-man Bart Stupak (D-MI) that he threatened to take away the bishop's IRS tax-exempt status on the grounds that the bishop was making a par-tisan claim, thus violating his church's standing as a nonpolitical entity.

"I truly resent [his action]," said Representative Stupak. "Who does he think he is?"[29]

The Boss, however, doesn't waste her time worrying about whether she will be barred from receiving Communion. In typical Pelosi fashion, she's already devised a fallback strategy:

> If I was going to receive Communion, in my district in California, in my archdiocese . . . I never knew if this was the day it would be withheld. And that's a hard way to go to church. Fortunately, I'm invited—I have a big family—I go to a lot of weddings, I'm in a different church every week. I'm a moving target. I travel, so I'm not exactly a target in terms of always being in the same church.[30]

Perhaps conservatives should find a shred of solace in Nancy Pelosi's public religious persona. Amid all the contradictions inherent in her policy positions and public declarations of religious faith, Pelosi still finds it favorable and indeed necessary to invoke the Almighty to justify her policy agenda. To be sure, this is hypocritical, as the Speaker rails against mixing politics and religion even as she mixes politics and religion. But the fact that a savvy political boss like Pelosi feels the need to do so says something about the nation as a whole and about voters in particular. Far from the left's utopian vision of a "post-religious" nation, America, it seems, still likes its political leaders to have a soul—and to be unafraid to speak freely and candidly about how their religious beliefs and values animate their words and deeds.

But regardless, a power broker like Nancy Pelosi can sniff out and leverage power—religious or otherwise—a parish away. She was preternaturally wired to do so. "I'm going to be a priest when I grow up," she used to tell her mother repeatedly. Around the age of nine or ten, Big Nancy regretted having to explain to Little Nancy that women couldn't be Catholic priests.

"Well, then," replied Little Nancy, "I'll go into politics instead."[31]

11

PELOSI'S PLANET

"The United States has no greater ally in NATO than Italy."
At least, that's what Speaker Pelosi thinks when it comes to geopolitics.
(You might have trouble finding anyone who would agree with her.) She
actually said this on February 13, 2009, just before she and seven other
members of Congress embarked on a trip to visit U. S. troops stationed
in that country. Once they were on Italian soil, Gianfranco Fini, president of the Italian Chamber of Deputies, welcomed Pelosi's delegation
and even gave her a "very special and very personal" gift: the baptismal
certificate of her grandfather, who was born in Abruzzo. It was only one
year later, on February 4, 2010, that Pelosi repeated her pro-Italy claim
when she appeared in front of the press with President Fini at the U.S.
Capitol: "Italy has no better friend and the United States has no better
friend in NATO than Italy."[1]

Likely all 28 NATO members would find this surprising (maybe
even amusing)—especially the United Kingdom, Canada and, of
course, Italy! Perhaps Madam Speaker might have assessed our NATO
allies more accurately if her grandfather had been born in Greenwich
or Liverpool.

Speaker Pelosi's foreign policy, like her hyperbolic praise for her family's nation of origin, is just another indicator of her underlying double standards and subjectivity. Pelosi views foreign policy as an extension of domestic politics. And that leads to, let us say, contradictory attitudes toward matters such as human rights, not to mention other international topics.

Many of Pelosi's human rights–oriented foreign policy positions coincide with the demographics of her home district, but oddly enough end at that district's border. For example, when members of Congress drafted a symbolic resolution in 2007 that would affirm the 1915 massacre of Armenians by Ottoman Turks as genocide, Pelosi vowed to push it to a vote, even though President Bush had warned that it would harm U.S. relations with NATO ally Turkey. "She feels morally committed to this issue," said her close ally Representative John Murtha. It probably didn't hurt that Pelosi, like several other California members of Congress who have pressed for similar proposals for years, comes from a district that is home to many Armenian Americans. In response, Turkey did strongly protest the genocide resolution, even implying that it would end logistical support for the U.S. war in Iraq. And when Democratic support of the resolution lessened in the face of Turkey's criticism, Pelosi reneged on her promise to bring it to vote. Pelosi's blunder on the Armenia resolution provoked much criticism; even Murtha said that she'd "misjudged the resolution."[2] But to the Boss it made sense. She was protecting her power base instead of looking at the larger issue of America's relations with an important NATO ally. Consider what Pelosi's move would have been if her district were home to many Turkish Americans.

On a much larger scale, and of more fundamental importance to America, the Speaker takes a radical stance on the issue of immigration and relations with our neighbor to the south. Her voting record makes her position on immigration clear, having earned her a 0 percent rating from the U.S. Border Control (USBC) in 2006 and a 0 percent rating from the Federation for American Immigration Reform (FAIR). Pelosi favors loose borders and liberal standards once illegals are here.[3] Though she has said that securing U.S. borders is a top priority,[4] she opposed legislation in 2006 that would prohibit the use of U.S. funds to update the Mexican government on the movements of the Minuteman Project, a group of volunteers who patrol the Mexican border. That same year, Pelosi was also against a plan to improve the security of our borders through, among other things, the construction of more than 700 miles of fencing.[5]

Indeed, some of Pelosi's positions are specifically designed to *help* illegal immigrants, like her advocacy of lowering public college tuition for illegal aliens, her efforts to preserve health programs for illegal immigrants in spite of the high cost for taxpayers and her promise to do away with legislation protecting employers from lawsuits for requiring English at work. In 2009, Nancy Pelosi accepted an invitation from Representative Luis Gutierrez (D-IL) to speak on the immigration issue in San Francisco's Mission District (part of her home district). She and Representative Gutierrez stood before a lively crowd that was chanting, "*Si se puede*," or "Yes we can." Inside St. Anthony's Church, she voiced her radical stance before hundreds of families, mostly Hispanic and some here illegally. Pelosi denounced the Immigration and Customs Enforcement agents for doing their job. The Speaker called for an end to raids and deportations that separate parents from their children, asking her audience, "Who in this country would not want to change a policy of kicking in doors in the middle of the night and sending a parent away from their families?" While few would argue in favor of kicking in doors in the middle of the night, she also stated, "Taking parents from their children . . . that's un-American" and "It must be stopped. . . . What value system is that? I think it's un-American. I think it's un-American." Moreover, she praised immigrant families—whether they arrived two days ago or centuries earlier—"that opportunity, that determination, that hope has made America more American." She called her audience "very, very patriotic" for coming out to the event, which was one stop in a cross-country "Family Unity" tour spearheaded by the Congressional Hispanic Caucus leadership.[6] But some of her colleagues were not impressed by her rallying cry. Iowa's representative Steve King, the highest-ranking Republican on the House Immigration Subcommittee, responded to Pelosi's remarks:

> It is no surprise that Speaker Pelosi believes our current immigration laws are "un-American." Her liberal San Francisco values

do not reflect the views of the overwhelming majority of Americans who support enforcement of our immigration laws, border security and no amnesty for illegal immigrants. Enforcement actions against employers hiring illegal workers are a step in the right direction, especially in these trying economic times. The Pew Hispanic Center estimates 7 million jobs in this country are held by illegal immigrants. I would suggest it is un-American to allow illegal immigrants to hold jobs while so many American citizens are out of work.[7]

But at least Pelosi's audience liked her speech.

The Boss's personal stake in immigration is at least twofold. First of all, there's the uncharacteristically large immigrant influence in her district. According to the 2000 U.S. census, Pelosi's district was 36.7 percent foreign-born, 16 percent Hispanic and 46 percent speaking a language other than English.[8] Maybe Pelosi would rather secure her reelection than our borders. Second, the Pelosis have a history of reaping financial benefits from cheap immigrant labor. Some of her largest investments, like the restaurant chain Piatti and the exclusive Napa Valley hotel and resort Auberge du Soleil, are nonunion, employing immigrant labor. The Pelosis have even hired harvesting firms that do not have contracts with the United Farm Workers (UFW) to pick their vineyard in Napa Valley.[9]

Another large segment of Pelosi's constituency is Chinese Americans, who make up nearly 20 percent of San Francisco's population, according to the 2000 U.S. census. And once again it was none other than Pelosi's mentor Phil Burton who was the first political candidate to take notice of the city's Chinese community, in 1956, when he protested mass subpoenas that had been issued on their family associations in a crackdown on immigration fraud. David Lee, executive director of the nonprofit Chinese American Voters Education Committee, said Burton needed their votes to beat his Republican opponent. Burton's actions earned him the Chinese community's support.[10]

Pelosi has her own legacy of taking up human rights causes relevant to her Chinese constituents. In fact, when it comes to human rights violations, few legislators have played hardball with the Chinese as Pelosi has.[11] She is the former chair of the bipartisan Congressional Working

Group on China, and it was after the massacre of pro-democracy demonstrators in Beijing's Tiananmen Square, in 1989, that Pelosi began paying close attention to human rights in China.[12] She and a delegation of around 20 other members of Congress would personally visit the site of the atrocity two years later and unfurl a banner that read, "To those who died for democracy in China." Almost at once, Pelosi and her group were surrounded by police and plainclothes Chinese officials, who roughed up some of her colleagues and detained the press who were with them. Pelosi said, "I started running."[13] Although she was expelled from China, she believed she had made her point."[14]

In 2008, she became the first foreign politician to meet with the Dalai Lama, the exiled Tibetan spiritual leader, after China violently crushed protests in Tibet. She condemned China's crackdown, urging world leaders, including President Bush, not to attend the opening ceremony of the 2008 Beijing Olympics.[15]

Calling her opposition to China "bold" would be a serious understatement. For example, when she met former Chinese president Jiang Zemin for the first time, in 1997 (during his initial visit to the United States), she greeted him with a letter demanding the release of political prisoners and criticized him for his country's rights violations.[16] She would repeat the gesture in 2009, sending President Hu Jintao a letter requesting the release of ten "prisoners of conscience," including pro-democracy activists and pro-Tibetan advocates.[17] The Speaker's fiercely combative policy against China provoked China's state news agency, Xinhua, to say that Pelosi "is detested by the Chinese people" and to call her "disgusting."[18] "This isn't only a China issue," Pelosi once said in an interview. "It's about human rights wherever they are." Indeed, Pelosi has argued that in order for the United States to be a standard-bearer for democracy in other countries, it must promote freedom in China as well.[19] But what about other countries facing human rights issues?

It turns out that Pelosi isn't always as zealous when it comes to opposing the evils of nations that are not represented in her home district. Take Cuba, for example. Radio Martí, an initiative of the Reagan administration to provide news to the people of Cuba, was created in 1983, and just seven years later, TV Martí was launched.[20] Radio and TV Martí, like Voice of America, provide news information to people living in a closed society where there is no independent media. But in 1998, Pelosi voted to eliminate funding for TV Martí broadcasts to Havana, and in 2004 she cast her vote to end Radio Martí broadcasts as well.[21] On the other hand, in November 2009 the Speaker voiced her support for ending the travel ban to Cuba. She said, "I've always been a supporter of lifting the travel ban to Cuba . . . I don't know when that would be coming to the floor."[22] Moreover, she has time after time voted against imposing a tougher trade embargo against the Castro regime, an interesting position given that she has repeatedly opposed extending normal trade relations to China.[23] Would she still vehemently oppose Communist China and favor Communist Cuba if she were a representative from Miami?

On matters of the geopolitical sphere, Little Nancy did not follow her father. Big Tommy never would have tolerated any Communist regime. Furthermore, for him, there was an unambiguous distinction between his New Deal liberalism and leftist beliefs based on socialism. When accused of "socialistic" thinking like that in the Soviet Union of the 1950s, Tommy took offense. Pelosi biographer Marc Sandalow writes, "[Big Tommy] was a fierce anti-Communist. Communism was particularly reviled by the Catholic Church, and D'Alesandro railed against what he sometimes called the 'evil doctrine of Communism' and other times simply 'ungodly Communism.'"[24]

While it's one thing to be soft on an oppressive regime by voting in its favor, it is something else entirely to break ranks and travel halfway around the world to offer it credibility. In 2007, Pelosi became the most senior American leader to visit Syria since relations had deteriorated between the two countries four years earlier. Pelosi's office claimed that it was just taking the lead from the Iraq Study Group's recommendations to engage Middle East governments, including Syria, in discussions of issues of security. Syria, a brutally ruled nation that has backed terrorists and supported the destruction of Israel, has consistently been viewed by a broad coalition of foreign policy thinkers on both sides of the political aisle as a pariah regime. But Pelosi cast all that aside and suddenly assumed the role of peacemaker, whether diplomats wanted her to or not. Before returning home from Damascus, she announced that she had informed President Assad that Israel was ready to negotiate with Syria. (This came as a surprise to many around the world, but likely none more so than the Israelis themselves.) Israeli prime minister Ehud Olmert's office responded by underlining preconditions for negotiation, like the cessation of Syria's "support for terrorist groups." Vice President Cheney claimed it was apparent that Olmert had not actually authorized Pelosi's message. "The president is the one who conducts foreign policy, not the speaker of the House," Cheney added during an interview. Regardless, Pelosi called her visit an "excellent idea"[25] and her talks with Assad "very productive," in terms of the "path to peace."[26]

Others, however, were less enthused. President Bush said her trip sent "mixed signals" that "lead the Assad government to believe they are part of the mainstream of the international community, when in fact they are a state sponsor of terror."[27] Cheney said, "I think it is, in fact, bad behavior on her part," and, "Fortunately I think the various parties involved recognize she doesn't speak for the United States in those circumstances, she doesn't represent the administration."[28] Farid Ghadry, president of the Reform Party of Syria, wrote in the *Washington Times* about how Pelosi's presence had helped legitimize Assad's regime and "thoroughly dampened any confidence by the Syrian people that they could count on the West and the United States in particular." He goes on to write,

> [Assad's] regime was able to frame Mrs. Pelosi's visit in the most beneficial and helpful manner possible. By projecting the image of the West "needing" Mr. Assad, his hand in the region was strengthened regardless of the international momentum that had been steadily built up against him since the assassination of former Lebanese Prime Minister Rafiq Hariri.[29]

In explaining her staunch opposition to the war in Iraq, Pelosi has justified herself on the basis of her decade-long tenure on the Intelligence Committee.[30] When she left her position as the ranking Democrat on that committee in 2003 to become the House Democratic leader, she took with her the title of longest-serving member of that committee in the history of the House. Even after leaving that post, she was still one of the eight lawmakers with the highest clearances to access classified information.[31] But if her record-long tenure gave her any expertise or clout, it also became a liability to her image as a human rights advocate and a moral opponent of the war.

The release of 2002 and 2005 Justice Department memos in April 2009 revealed much that had been hidden about the use of "enhanced interrogation techniques" against alleged Al Qaeda operatives during the first years following the 9/11 terrorist attacks.[32] The most extreme of these techniques was waterboarding, a form of simulated drowning that involves raising the feet above the head, covering the mouth and nose with a cloth and pouring water over the face. It was revealed that this technique had been used on three individuals; one of these three, Abu Zubaydah, was subjected to waterboarding at least 83 times in August 2002.

When the news was made public, a heated debate erupted. Pelosi professed to be outraged. She condemned the technique as torture and deemed it a moral blot on the Bush administration and America. But then it was leaked that Pelosi had known that the techniques were being used. The Speaker responded by saying that the claim was a lie. However, documents demonstrated that the Central Intelligence Agency (CIA) had indeed briefed Pelosi and three other members of Congress on the "use of" harsh interrogation techniques. The briefing was held on September 4, 2002, and involved a virtual tour—lasting more than an hour—of the CIA's overseas detention sites as well as the techniques interrogators had devised to extract information from terror suspects. Two officials present at the briefing recall that waterboarding was one of the techniques described, and neither Pelosi nor her three colleagues expressed objections to waterboarding or any of the other techniques. In fact, the concern that was expressed was whether enough was being done. According to a U.S. official who observed the exchange, "The briefer was specifically asked if the methods were tough enough." Congressman Porter Goss, the chair of the House Intelligence Committee at the time, and one of the other members present at the briefing, claims, "Among those briefed, there was a pretty full understanding of what the CIA was doing," and "the reaction in the room was not just approval, but encouragement."

The ambiguous 2002 briefing was the only enhanced interrogation briefing Pelosi attended. Almost seven years later, however, the truth finally caught up with the Boss. She told reporters on April 23, 2009, "We were not—I repeat—were not told that waterboarding or any of these other enhanced interrogation methods were used. What they did tell us is that they had some . . . Office of [Legal] Counsel opinions, that they could be used, but not that they would." But in February 2003, only five months after Pelosi's briefing, one of her top aides, Michael Sheehy, attended a CIA briefing in which it was explicitly spelled out that harsh techniques, including waterboarding, were being used on Abu Zubaydah. Moreover, those present at this briefing received a thorough description of precisely how the waterboard was used. Another attendee of the briefing was Representative Jane Harman (D-CA), ranking minority member of the House Intelligence Committee, who wrote the CIA's general counsel a letter just a few days later, on February 10, 2003, questioning the interrogation techniques—the only known formal objection raised by a lawmaker during 2002 or 2003, the years terrorists were subjected to waterboarding. It was in December 2007, seven months after four senators had submitted their own written objections to the then-retired techniques, that Pelosi acknowledged in a statement that she was aware of Harman's letter and "concurred" with it. But it wasn't until May 14, 2009, during a tense press conference, that the speaker came clean and admitted she had learned from Sheehy in early 2003 that the CIA had subjected suspects to waterboarding.[33]

The memos released in April 2009 unleashed an uproar against Pelosi and her party.[34] But Nancy Pelosi, like a tough political boss, knew how to handle the allegations. At first she fiercely denied the charges leveled at her, and then she accused the CIA of lying to her. Next the Speaker turned her guns on her Republican colleagues. At a weekly news conference in July 2009, she went so far as to say, "Our success is driving the Republicans to distraction. Any excuse will do."[35] Obviously, Pelosi had a lot to lose. Making her acceptance—if not support—of the interrogation techniques even more shocking was her outspoken criticism of the Bush administration's treatment of detainees as early as 2004, "saying the specter of torture had damaged the nation's reputation and put military forces at risk."[36]

While supporting harsh interrogations might contradict Pelosi's proclaimed positions, it would fall nicely in line with her father's example. "Enhanced interrogation" techniques were standard operating procedure at the cop shop in Big Tommy's Baltimore, to combat organized crime and street criminals. And his mark on the Speaker was apparent when she confronted the waterboarding furor. Big Tommy's advice, as he once told Dan Gifford? "When accused, deny everything, admit nothing, and make counter-accusations."[37]

As if the evidence were not already stacked high against Pelosi, she brushed off yet another major opportunity to show her alleged compassion for the detainees at Guantánamo Bay in January 2009. President Obama had signed an executive order that called for shutting down the prison within the year. But when it came to the 245 Guantánamo prisoners who were going to be tried in military commissions, where would they go? Representative Bill Young (R-FL) suggested they could go to "the Rock," also known as Alcatraz, the famous prison located in San Francisco Bay, which had been shut down in 1963.[38] Alcatraz is on an island where the prisoners could enjoy the legal oversight that comes with being held in the United States, and the detainees would still be at a safe distance from American citizens. It also happens to be in Speaker Pelosi's district. Certainly some potential visitors would rethink their travel plans to a city holding accused terrorists, even if at a "safe distance."

When asked whether Representative Young's idea was a serious proposal, Pelosi answered, "It is—no." She said of Young, "Perhaps he's not visited Alcatraz. Alcatraz is a tourist attraction. It's a prison that is now sort of like a—it's a national park."[39] However, if Alcatraz were on an island in the Gulf of Mexico or off the coast of the Carolinas, the speaker may have considered it a possible solution for housing the prisoners. But not to worry. The Boss was impressed with President Obama's plan to use an entire year to study each detainee's case. Pelosi told ABC's *This Week*, "What the president put forth was very wise. He said he's going to close Guantánamo, take the time to do it. You can't just go down there today and say, 'Everybody out,' and lock the door. They're going to review the cases, narrow it down and then go from there. . . . It's brilliant." So much for her alleged interest in the well-being of 245 prisoners, the good name of a nation tarnished by Guantánamo's war crimes, or the preservation of justice.[40]

Perhaps some more compassionate member of Congress will one day graciously offer to shelter these abused prisoners in his or her home district. After all, in a world where Italy is America's greatest NATO ally, anything is possible.

12

INCIVILITY AND HYPOCRISY UNLEASHED

[The Republican-run House] is the most corrupt Congress in history.[1]

—Nancy Pelosi

Incivility among members of Congress is nothing new. Perhaps the most famous and extreme example occurred in 1856, when pro-slavery congressman Preston Brooks of South Carolina beat Massachusetts abolitionist senator Charles Sumner with his walking cane in the Senate chamber. Sumner's injuries were so severe that they prevented him from continuing his work in the Senate for more than three years.

While no one has resorted to physical violence on the House floor during Nancy Pelosi's tenure as Speaker, her pledges of civility can only be construed as sheer hypocrisy in light of the harsh rhetoric and verbal volleys she and her Democratic allies have unleashed on her political opponents. The day before Democrats took back control of the House of Representatives, in November 2006, Nancy Pelosi informed her colleagues that the words "civility, honesty and fiscal responsibility" would characterize their new majority.[2] But leading the charge in civility has proved to be a challenge for the Speaker. In fact, just a few weeks before the 2006 election, CBS's Lesley Stahl questioned Pelosi about the sincerity of her civility charge in an interview on *60 Minutes*. Pelosi had called the Republicans, among other names, "immoral" and "corrupt." Stahl said, "I mean, you're one of the reasons we have to restore civility in the first place."

Unbending, Pelosi answered, "Well actually, when I called them those names, I was being gentle. There are much worse things I could've said about them."[3]

Indeed, from a young age Pelosi has been a strident partisan, taking personal offense at those with political views different from her own. When she was a little girl, she accompanied her parents to a polling place where a Republican poll worker gave the mayor's young daughter a small toy elephant. (A toy for a kid—how nice.) But Little Nancy was repulsed and gave it back. "He thinks I don't know what this is," Pelosi recalled. "I was *offended* [emphasis mine]."[4] Pelosi proudly recounted this story about the stuffed pachyderm later in life—offering it as a demonstration of her character. She also recounted how, a few decades later, she refused much more than a small toy. She turned down a rental transaction on a house when she discovered that the owners were Republicans.

Most people would judge these incidents as examples of petty behavior. But for Pelosi they are signs of purity. She no doubt learned this hyper-partisanship to some degree from her mother. When Ronald Reagan ran for reelection in 1984, he traveled to Baltimore to attend an event. When an aide to the president called to extend an invitation to former mayor D'Alesandro, Big Nancy answered the phone. She scoffed at the offer, saying, "After what he has done to poor people, he should not come near our house."[5]

Even longtime family friends were not exempt from Big Nancy's fury for party disloyalty. Maryland governor William Donald Schaefer had been invited by the D'Alesandro matriarch to join her at her table for a spaghetti dinner at St. Leo's in Little Italy in the summer of 1992. But just days after he received his invitation, Governor Schaefer made "the colossal political blunder." He endorsed George H. W. Bush for president. The very next day he received a letter from Big Nancy. Not only was he disinvited, but he was a "traitor to his party." Schaefer said, "And, she never talked to me again the rest of her life."[6]

Pelosi credits her parents with teaching her and her brothers "to be compassionate and to be aware of the world around us."[7] But compassion apparently only extends to those who agree with her, or those who are part of her machine.

So the Speaker's many calls for civility and bipartisanship must have been directed at herself as well as her colleagues. Days before taking the gavel, she said Democrats would lead the nation in a "new direction that restores civility and bipartisanship."[8] If remarks she made about President Bush while she was the House minority leader were considered, that "new direction" would be 180 degrees from where she had been.

When Pelosi disagrees with you, it is not simply a difference of opinion, but an indictment of your character and competence. Otherwise you would agree with her. Consider a May 2004 interview with the *San Francisco Chronicle* concerning President Bush and Iraq:

> Not to get personal about it, but the president's capacity to lead has never been there. In order to lead you have to have judgment. In order to have judgment you have to have knowledge and experience. He has none.
>
> Bush is an incompetent leader. In fact, he's not a leader. He's a person who has no judgment, no experience, and no knowledge on the subjects that he has to decide upon.[9]

In her weekly press briefing that same week, she said, "I think the time has come to speak very frankly about the lack of leadership in the White House, the lack of judgment. So the emperor has no clothes. When are people going to face reality?" And in a speech to newspaper editors that spring, she similarly said, "The president's resolve may be firm, but his judgment is not sound. It is ironic that in a nation obsessed with reality television, we have a president who is increasingly divorced from reality."

She went further in the *Chronicle* interview, becoming more personal. "They [the Bush Administration] are so pathetic; they are so in denial about their own ineffectiveness." She added, "George Bush is in over his head," and, "It's hopeless for George Bush. He has made it hopeless. In the private sector he would have been long gone. . . . He simply doesn't have the capacity to lead us to a resolution in Iraq. We need a new commander in chief."[10]

To be sure, the body count in Iraq was rising more rapidly than anyone would have liked at that time, and the future Speaker had said at the outset of the war, "I consider it one of the great disappointments of my public life that I could not use my influence to stop this war."[11] Her criticisms, however, are not so much based on policy as they are an indictment of the *person*, in this case President Bush. "Incompetent," "pathetic," "hopeless," "no judgment," "no knowledge," "in over his head"—those are harsh words for a wartime president. Many would even call them unpatriotic.

But it was an election year. Assessing Bush's chances of being returned to office, Pelosi said in the same *Chronicle* interview, "He's gone. He's so gone."[12] Perhaps she was the one divorced from reality. Bush was reelected.

During the CBS interview in 2006, Stahl asked Pelosi about those harsh words for President Bush:

> "It sounds personal," Stahl remarks.
> "This isn't personal," Pelosi says.
> "He's 'incompetent,' he's. . . ." Stahl continues.
> "Well, I think he is," Pelosi states.
> "Well, that's personal," Stahl points out.
> "Well, I'm sorry, that's his problem," Pelosi replies.
> "How does this raise the level of civility?" Stahl asks.
> "Well, this is a—well—we're in a political debate here. We didn't come here to have a tea party together, and toss a coin to see who would win on an issue," Pelosi says. "I have very thick skin, I don't care what they say about me."[13]

Pelosi must have forgotten the advice of her brother, Little Tommy, whom she calls her biggest political influence. "He always advises me to put myself in my opponents' shoes and understand their point of view. He also says not to take politics personally and never let friendship leave your voice."[14]

While Pelosi's words about the president were *personal*, Bush used humor to point out *policy* differences with the Democratic leader. During the midterm elections of 2006, the president often used this line: "The top Democrat leader in the House made an interesting declaration. She said, 'We love tax cuts.' Given her record, she must be a secret admirer."[15] Those elections swept Democrats back into the majority and Pelosi into the Speaker's chair.

Nonetheless, Bush wasted no time demonstrating civility toward

Pelosi, hosting her at a White House lunch two days after the election. Even the menu, which included pasta salad and a chocolate dessert, was selected in an effort to please her. Both Pelosi and Bush indicated that they would put the past behind them and work together. And the president noted in a deferential manner her rise as the first woman to become Speaker: "As the father of young women . . . I think it's important," he said. "We won't agree on every issue, but we do agree that we love America equally, that we're concerned about the future of this country, and that we will do our very best to address big problems."

Pelosi agreed, "We have our differences and we will debate them, and that is what our founders intended. But we will do so in a way that gets results for the American people."[16]

It was not the first time Bush had reached out to Pelosi. During his first month in office, he took questions from congressional Democrats at a retreat. Pelosi asked with forceful words why he had cut off funding for international family planning. Some conservatives in attendance called her language disrespectful. However, the president called Pelosi afterward, telling her she was always welcome to question him. "He respected their difference of opinion and had no problem with her vocal challenge."[17]

There were other moments of civility offered to Pelosi *from* Republicans. As new minority leader John Boehner handed her the gavel when she was sworn in as Speaker, he did so with the words "today marks an occasion that I think the Founding Fathers would view approvingly. And my fellow Americans, whether you're a Republican, a Democrat, or an Independent, today is a cause for celebration."[18] A few weeks later, Bush again affirmed Pelosi's political success in the opening words of his State of the Union address. After Speaker Pelosi introduced him, he responded:

> And tonight, I have a high privilege and distinct honor of my own—as the first President to begin the State of the Union message with these words: Madam Speaker. In his day, the late Congressman Thomas D'Alesandro, Jr., from Baltimore, Maryland, saw Presidents Roosevelt and Truman at this rostrum. But nothing could compare with the sight of his only daughter, Nancy, presiding tonight as Speaker of the House of Representatives. Congratulations, Madam Speaker.[19]

Pelosi wrote in her book *Know Your Power*, "I knew that President Bush had a great deal of respect for the office of the Speaker, because I could see at our leadership meetings how he treated Dennis Hastert when he was Speaker. And it was interesting to me that when I became Speaker, I received the same level of respect from the President."[20] Perhaps it was so "interesting" to her because of the incivility she had shown him in the past.

However, she, too, struck a conciliatory note in her swearing in speech. She said, "Respectful of the vision of our founders, the expectations of our people, and the great challenges we face, we have an obligation to reach beyond partisanship to serve all Americans. Let us all stand together to move our country forward, seeking common ground for the common good. We are from different parties but we serve one country."[21]

Nice words. It just didn't happen.

The next year, when Republican presidential nominee John McCain chose Sarah Palin as his running mate, Pelosi was asked for her opinion of the pick. She compared Palin to Bush, saying, "I have a very high standard for president of the United States. I guess George Bush has proven that anybody can do it, but can they do it well? I think he has not. I think he has done great harm and damage to our country." Echoing her theme of poor judgment, she said that's what McCain had exercised when choosing Palin. "We're talking about a heartbeat away from the president. He knows better."

As for Palin herself, Pelosi said she didn't feel that the Alaska governor had the "credentials and the depth" needed to be president. She expressed doubt that Palin's résumé had adequately prepared her to take over the job of president if necessary.[22] In her role as Speaker, Pelosi is only one more heartbeat removed from assuming the presidency than the vice president. Yet, it's worth noting, her résumé prior to serving in Congress included mostly raising money for candidates, while Palin had spent years governing in executive positions that required her to relate to members of both parties.

The Speaker has selected, targeted vitriol aimed at Republicans. In October 2004, when the Ethics Committee admonished Majority Leader Tom DeLay (R-TX), Pelosi was quick to respond, saying, the next day, "Mr. DeLay has proven himself to be ethically unfit to lead the party. The burden falls upon his fellow House Republicans. Republicans must answer: Do they want an ethically unfit person to be their majority leader or do they want to remove the ethical cloud that hangs over the Capitol?"[23]

However, when that very committee denounced Charlie Rangel's actions in almost the exact same fashion in February 2010, Pelosi's guns fell silent. Some of her first words concerning her good friend and political ally were "We'll just see what happens next." The Ethics Committee concluded that on at least three occasions Rangel's aides had tried to inform him that there were corporate sponsors for his trips to Antigua in 2007 and St. Maarten in 2008. Rangel himself said that the report "exonerates me," since it cited no evidence that he was aware of the corporate sponsorship.[24] He eventually stepped down, but there is no evidence that Pelosi pushed him.

During the uncertain days of the looming financial crisis in September 2008, Pelosi discussed negotiations for a Wall Street bailout between the parties in Congress. Although she said they were nearing a deal with the Republicans, she couldn't resist putting her knife in their collective back and turning it by gratuitously calling them "unpatriotic" for delaying negotiations.[25] Her tenure as Speaker has meant the passage of spending bills that have doubled our national debt in a few short years. However, in 2006 she labeled the proposed Republican budget "unpatriotic" because she felt it was not fiscally responsible.[26]

In fact, "unpatriotic" and "un-American" are two of her favorite descriptions for those who don't agree with her. In a *USA Today* editorial cowritten with Majority Leader Steny Hoyer in August 2009, at the height of the congressional town hall protests over proposed healthcare reform legislation, they wrote, "These disruptions are occurring because opponents are afraid not just of differing views—but of the facts themselves. Drowning out opposing views is simply un-American." They went on, "It is now evident that an ugly campaign is underway not merely to misrepresent the health insurance reform legislation, but to disrupt public meetings and prevent members of Congress and constituents from conducting a civil dialogue."[27]

However, Pelosi herself had written about the need for "disruptions" on this very issue. In *Know Your Power*, she writes, "That is the tradition of our country. Our Founders were disrupters—magnificent disrupters. Martin Luther King, Jr., was a disrupter, as were the suffragettes. It is the American way. The change that resulted from these leaders has made our country greater. How can we follow their lead?"[28] It seems you are allowed to follow their lead only if you follow her.

It is important to note that she also tried to liken these American citizens—especially seniors, who were concerned, even scared, about having their decision-making power about their health care taken away from them by the government—to those responsible for the violence in Pelosi's hometown more than 30 years earlier. A month after her words appeared in *USA Today*, she said in an emotional news conference, her voice breaking, "I have some concerns about some of the language being used, because I saw this myself in the late '70s in San Francisco; this kind of rhetoric was very frightening, and it created a climate where violence took place."[29] What was she referring to? The most notable violent episodes involving San Franciscans during that period were the murders of key political leaders in 1978. First, Congressman Leo Ryan, who was at the time representing Northern California's 11th District, and four others were shot and killed by Peoples Temple leader Jim Jones's gunmen at a jungle airstrip near Jonestown, Guyana. Jones's tie to San Francisco politics was that he had been appointed to chair the city's Housing Authority in 1976 by Democratic mayor George Moscone. The next violent act, just days later, was the murder of both Mayor Moscone and Harvey Milk, an openly gay member of the San Francisco Board of Supervisors, by former disgruntled board member Dan White.[30] White killed Moscone and Milk not because of dangerous rhetoric but because of his own mental instability. How on earth could this in any way be compared to hardworking Americans meeting to debate their personal rights concerning the proposed health-care takeover?

The comparison was beyond the pale. Voices raised at town hall meetings do not equal weapons drawn by disturbed people. So rather than quell resistance to her plan by leading an issues-focused debate (she knew she could not win), she made every effort to create a climate of fear by demonizing those who opposed her. Pelosi not only labeled these protests "un-American," but she tried to drown out any "opposing views." Yet plainly she doesn't mind disruptions by those who share her views. When antiwar protesters interrupted a town hall meeting in San Francisco in January 2006, she said, "It's always exciting. This is democracy in action. I'm energized by it, frankly."[31] In 2007, she told a group protesting against the Iraq war to "just go for it, I respect your enthusiasm."[32]

This flies in the face of Pelosi's numerous commitments to ensure that every American's voice is heard. She called the Capitol "the most beautiful building in the world because of what it represents: the voice of the people."[33] After describing the Speaker of the House she most admires, Tip O'Neill, as being able to work with President Reagan in a bipartisan way, she said, "I know that America can achieve true greatness when we work together to make certain that every voice in America is a voice that will be heard."[34] What the Speaker left unsaid is that she means every voice that echoes her own.

Pelosi has compared her role as mom to her job in politics. Surely she wouldn't have let her own children get away with reproachful name-calling, as members of her caucus have used while she has been Speaker. Minnesota Democrat Keith Ellison said Dick Cheney's actions as vice president were "the very definition of totalitarianism, authoritarianism, and dictatorship."[35] In 2007, he also compared President Bush's reaction to the September 11 attacks to Hitler's when a fire was staged in the Reichstag. Ellison said, "It's almost like the Reichstag fire, kind of reminds me of that. After the Reichstag was burned, they blamed the communists for it and it put the leader of that country in a position where he could basically have authority to do whatever he wanted." He later backed away from his statements, saying that, "In hindsight, I wouldn't have used that reference point."[36] There is no evidence that Pelosi was front and center in denouncing such an outrageous charge.

In August 2009, Pelosi's resolve to pass her health-care bill remained firm. But the public was learning more about what she had planned, and it was becoming more difficult for her allies to defend the proposed legislation. So, like Pelosi, they knew their best line of defense was to engage in personal attacks. Not only was the number of citizens attending town hall meetings escalating, but so was their anger. In response, Representative Brian Baird (D-WA) chose to conduct "telephone town hall" meetings rather than show up in person where he said, "extremists" would have "the chance to shout and make YouTube videos." Baird said, "What we're seeing right now is close to Brown Shirt tactics. I mean that very seriously."[37] Representative Baron Hill (D-IN) also chose not to encounter his constituents personally at the meetings. He explained, "I'm trying to control the event. What I don't want to do is create an opportunity for the people who are political terrorists to blow up the meeting and not try to answer thoughtful questions."[38] The "political terrorists" to whom he referred were Americans concerned about skyrocketing health-care costs and possible rationing of care. About those same town hall protests, senior Democratic member John Dingell of Michigan said the last time he had confronted such opposition was when he had voted for a civil rights bill. "At that time, we had a lot of Ku Klux Klan folks and white supremacists and folks in white sheets and other things running around causing trouble."[39]

Pelosi's California colleague, Democrat Pete Stark, is no stranger to less-than-civil language. At a September 2009 town hall meeting in his district, Stark fielded a question from an elderly constituent who concluded his remarks with the words "Mr. Congressman, don't pee on my leg and tell me it's raining." Stark's response? "I wouldn't dignify you by peeing on your leg, it wouldn't be worth wasting the urine." Later in the meeting, he responded to another constituent who suggested the congressman was lying: "Whether you think I'm a liar or not, I still want to get your input—and I'll make up how I'm gonna lie about it after I get it."[40]

In a House floor speech in 2007, Stark reacted to President Bush's support for hundreds of billions of dollars in spending on the Iraq war while vetoing $35 billion for a children's health insurance program. He said, "You're going to spend it to blow up innocent people if we can get enough kids to grow old enough for you to send to Iraq to get their heads blown off for the president's amusement." To her credit, the Speaker did distance herself—mildly—from those remarks, saying, "While members of Congress are passionate about their views, what Congressman Stark said during the debate was inappropriate and distracted from the seriousness of the subject at hand—providing health care for America's children."[41]

In another moment on the House floor, Speaker Pelosi's face registered visible shock at South Carolina Republican representative Joe Wilson's outburst of "You lie!" during President Obama's address on health care to a joint session of Congress in September 2009. But in great contrast, she was apparently unfazed by the fiery remarks of Representative Alan Grayson (D-FL) on the House floor just weeks later. Complete with visual aids, he outlined his view of the Republicans' health-care plan: "1. Don't get sick. 2. If you do get sick. 3. Die quickly."

Understandably, there were calls on all sides for both men to apologize. Wilson wasted no time in calling the White House to apologize to the president. Grayson took to the House floor to extend his apologies, too, but not to Republicans. He apologized to the dead, citing a Harvard study that estimates mortality rates based on poor access to health insurance. Representative Tom Price (R-GA) filed a privileged resolution on Grayson, calling on him to formally apologize. Hoyer filed one calling for Wilson to be reprimanded. Grayson said on CNN that he had "no intention of apologizing," describing his Republican colleagues as "foot-dragging, knuckle-dragging Neanderthals who think they can dictate policy to America by being stubborn."

When Pelosi weighed in on both incidents, she said the Republicans were holding the Democrats to a higher standard than themselves, referring to Wilson's refusal to make an apology to the House. (He felt that since he had expressed regret to the president, who had accepted his apology, that was as far as he needed to go.) She said, "There's no more reason for Mr. Grayson to apologize than for . . . In other words, if anyone is going to apologize, everyone should apologize."[42]

Yes, Madam Speaker. Exactly.

One wonders what she meant when she said at the White House lunch with President Bush almost three years earlier that under her leadership the House would debate differences as the founders had intended. Is this what they had in mind?

O'Neill may be the Speaker Pelosi most admires, but she has not followed his lead in civility. John Farrell, author of *Tip O'Neill and the Democratic Century*, wrote about the relationship between O'Neill and Reagan: "Tip had an ability to maintain friendship and civility while they were savaging each other. There was something about those earlier generations of politicians' ability to compartmentalize."[43] Not only was Pelosi not able to "compartmentalize" her relationship with President Bush, but the friendship is missing from her voice when she speaks about Republican colleagues and even the American people.

In her now famous teary news conference in September 2009, Pelosi said, "Our country is based on people being able to say what they believe, but I also believe they must take responsibility for any incitement they may cause."[44] Reflecting on those remarks later, she said, "in all of these debates, we have to talk about ideas, and where we go from there, and not characterize or personalize experiences."[45] The Speaker should heed her own words and call on her Democratic members to do the same. Perhaps then the restoration of civility would have a fighting chance.

EPILOGUE

Nancy Pelosi rose to power not on the basis of ideas but by pulling the master levers of a fine-tuned machine—raising money, demanding loyalty, and enforcing uncompromising discipline when necessary. Both liberals and conservatives misunderstand her by believing that she is motivated solely by ideology. Far from it. Certainly Pelosi's record spells out a worldview that is consistently left of the American public. In fact, when she took charge of her party, in 2002, as House Democratic leader, her job was to direct her wayward party back to its liberal base, "providing the voters with a clear idea of what Democrats would do differently if they were in charge," says reporter Mary Lynn F. Jones.[1] On the basis of ideology, Pelosi would be a natural choice, given her leftist views.

But there is something more worrying and more potent than her extreme agenda: the well-engineered boss politics she has imposed into the legislative process. Certainly politics can be a dirty business. No one expects government or politicians to carry on like Jimmy Stewart in *Mr. Smith Goes to Washington*, but a system based on hypocrisy, patronage and unrestrained behavior can have devastating effects on a country. Political machines running at high speed, lubricated with coercion, corruption and shenanigans, burden the electorate with ridiculous mandates, unfair taxes and restriction of freedom.

Political machines never bring out the best in the human spirit. By design, they are highly beneficial to a few at the expense of the many citizens and taxpayers who are expected to sacrifice their independence for the operation. Think of it this way: a political machine is like a car made to take *them* where *they* want to go. And who pays for all the gasoline and upkeep? The taxpayers. And since the car is for the benefit of the bosses and their allies, they have neither an incentive to drive safely nor cause to worry about the gas mileage.

The end result in a free society is axiomatic: the implosion of a machine operating on gears in overdrive is unstoppable. Backroom deals are difficult to keep secret with 24-hour cable television, the Internet, talk radio and an informed electorate. Sometimes bosses get desperate, as was evidenced by the Speaker's reactions to the town hall meetings. Things were getting out of control. According to social critic Camille Paglia, "a sputtering, rattled Pelosi struggled to deal with the nationwide insurgency of town hall protesters—reputable, concerned citizens whom she outrageously tried to tar as Nazis."[2]

Big Tommy's political career fell to pieces amid charges of scandal and patronage. Some of his largesse was stolen when civil service jobs, based on merit, increased in number. And television provided a way for voters to become acquainted with other candidates. Finally, those denied any of the largesse got angry and challenged him. These were all big hitches in Tommy's sputtering operation. When power is foiled and largesse pilfered, the machine breaks up. As journalist Mark Bowden wrote, "A boss with no patronage is no boss."[3]

When the Republicans, led by Newt Gingrich, took over the House in 1994 with their Contract with America in hand, Michael Barone, author of the *Almanac of American Politics*, called it "the collapse of the House that Phil Burton built."[4] By the mid-nineties the consequences of Burton's outrageous deal making were plain. For example, his Supplemental Security Income (SSI) program had spiraled out of control. There were 6.3 million beneficiaries, who were costing taxpayers $25 billion a year. Some of the money was going to support the habits of 250,000 drug and/or alcohol addicts. And then there were the 700,000 newly arrived immigrants who were benefiting from Burton's government program.[5] When the corruption and excesses of government spending were exposed, the electorate rebelled. Unbridled programs never turn out well. They create a dependence on government, subsidize destructive behaviors and bankrupt the treasury. As Ronald Reagan said in 1964, "A government bureau is the nearest thing to eternal life we'll ever see on this earth."[6]

Former Speaker Newt Gingrich says it's now time for Republicans to show some of their own political savvy. He believes it would benefit them to work with the Democrats on noncontroversial measures so the voters would see them willing to get something done with "huge bipartisan majorities." But Pelosi is the catch. Gingrich says, "We could get clever and work with her. . . . And I think people should work with her. . . . But at that point it becomes a huge problem because nobody trusts her, they distrust her ideology and distrust her because she has run over them so hard."[7]

Even some of the Speaker's troops are getting tired out. It is becoming more difficult for conservative congressional members to go home. In July 2009, when members returned to their districts, there were more than just Fourth of July fireworks going off. Many constituents were angry about the outcome of the energy vote. And things became even more explosive in August, when health reform was on the agenda.[8] Some members of Congress are "bristling over the 'Pelosi style.'" One House Democrat who is close to Pelosi said, "She doesn't delegate. It's her biggest flaw. She has to have her hand in every decision."[9] And even some of her usually friendly liberal base is not pleased with the concessions she's made to the moderates.

But Pelosi is confident of her course. Soon after becoming her party's leader, in 2002, Pelosi distinguished herself from then–majority leader Tom DeLay (R-TX), who was called "the Hammer." She made it clear what her style would look like. She said that she didn't believe she needed to start out pounding a sledgehammer to get people to go along with her positions. Even so, she would be ready to do so. Instead, she was willing to begin with a feather but, if necessary, would resort to using a steamroller.[10] Recently, there have been scant feathers but plenty of steamrollers.

Her adviser and confidant John Burton agrees with her direction: "She has the guts. I've got absolute faith in her. I've got friends in office that I love and occasionally I've had to call [them] up on certain votes and ask, 'What the hell were you thinking voting like that?' Never, ever, ever had to think about making that call to Nancy Pelosi. . . . Nothing like her in the whole world."[11]

There is evidence, however, of machine fatigue. Pelosi has over-reached, and the cracks are becoming visible. The Speaker can try to fine-tune by replacing people, make modifications by trying new tactics and engaging in dishonest spin, and throw lots of money at attempted repairs through legislative bills. But it won't work. The engine is running rough, the spark plugs are misfiring and the fan belt is loose. Eventually, the most well-oiled machine falls apart.

Bosses hold tight, though. In February 2010, Pelosi said in an interview with CNN's *State of the Union*, "I'm not yielding one grain of sand; we're fighting for every seat." But that may not be possible, and the "bullet in the head" may become the standard, leaving the Speaker to decide whom to help and whom to leave behind.[12]

The day after Pelosi became Speaker, in January 2007, she returned to Baltimore in a nine-car entourage with a police escort. Honors were the order of the occasion. Next to a statue of Big Tommy was now a plaque honoring his daughter's remarkable and hard-fought triumph. The city also acknowledged its hometown girl by dedicating the street she grew up on in Little Italy to her. The 200 block of Albemarle Street had a new name: Via Nancy D'Alesandro Pelosi. Mayor Martin O'Malley said, "This is where it all started."

Pelosi said, "Every step I took to the speakership began in this neighborhood."[13] But is the House that Nancy Pelosi built ready to collapse?

ACKNOWLEDGMENTS

Few endeavors are one person's alone. And that was certainly true with this project.

First I commend Sentinel and Adrian Zackheim for considering me for this undertaking. Thank you to David Moldawer who understood the project and was instrumental in the early vision. Jillian Gray has been the ideal editor: encouraging, insightful, and always keeping me on the right track. Much appreciation is also extended to my agents, Lynn Chu and Glen Hartley, who believed I could meet the deadline.

During this dash, I was surrounded by talented professionals who assisted me in research, offered valuable ideas, and were willing to make those minor tweaks that make a huge difference. On this front, thanks are due to Wynton Hall, Jonathan Nicholson, Lori Hutto, and Rhonda Adair.

Dan Gifford was helpful as he talked to me about his experiences in Baltimore years ago delivering envelopes among the powers that be, including Thomas D'Alesandro, Jr. For this book I relied on well over a hundred sources. As much as possible, I tried to use those that covered the political spectrum and that were as accurate as I could judge them to be. There were two in particular that were informative. I found Marc

Sandalow's *Madam Speaker* to be well researched and complete from his years of experience as a journalist writing about Nancy Pelosi for the *San Francisco Chronicle*. Vincent Bzdek's *Woman of the House* was quite helpful as well. Certainly, the authors won't agree with some of my conclusions. And, of course, sources aren't always completely precise. So please forgive me for any errors. I do believe the portrayal, as a whole, is accurate.

I am also appreciative of Ed Hague, who helped modernize my computer abilities, and moved me from a virus-filled computer to an Apple in an instant, since that's all I had.

Friendship is a treasured ally during a project like this. And fortunately, some of my friends have remarkable spouses too. Thank you is really inadequate for what the friendships of Becky and David Healy, Elizabeth and Richard Albertson, Jill and Bill Mattox, Sally Jo and Anthony Roorda, Sharon and John Steigner, Lorri and Mike Short, and Kimberly and Jeremy Cohen have meant during this past year. And there are many more amazing friends and valuable mentors who called to check in with me when I didn't emerge for weeks. I am grateful to Karla Enwright, who often wanted to spend some time with my children just when I needed the help and to my Aunt Naomi who would call to see if I was taking care of myself.

I began this book just a few months after my mother passed away, and I am blessed with not only friends but also a family who has encouraged me. Thank you to my aunts and uncles, dozens of cousins, in-laws, and my brother Rich. Most important are my children and husband. Jack and Hannah are not only my brightest "stars," but also the two who make me laugh just when I need to. Most of all, thank you to Peter, who not only provided great professional advice and some fabulous ideas, but who has been with me through almost everything. I am grateful for you.

As always, the author alone is responsible for the contents of this book.

NOTES

Prologue: The Titanium Queen

1. David Rogers, "Pelosi: 'I'm Trying to Save the Planet'," Politico, July 29, 2008. Online and available at http://www.politico.com/news/stories/0708/12122.html.

2. Vanessa Grigoriadis, "Why Is Nancy Pelosi Always Smiling?" *New York*, November 9, 2009.

3. Katherine Skiba, "Nancy Pelosi's House: After Her Historic First Term as Speaker, Tough Challenges Ahead," *U.S. News & World Report*, January 5, 2009. Online and available at http://www.usnews.com/articles/news/politics/2009/01/05/nancy-pelosis-house-after-her-historic-first-term-as-speaker-tough-challenges-ahead.html.

4. David Rogers, "Nancy Pelosi's Lesson: 'You Can't Always Get What You Want'," Politico, October 30, 2009. Online and available at http://www.politico.com/news/stories/1009/28919.html.

5. Grigoriadis, "Why Is Nancy Pelosi Always Smiling?"

6. Skiba, "Nancy Pelosi's House."

7. John Bresnahan and Jonathan Allen. "Nancy Pelosi's Brutal Reality Check," Politico, March 1, 2010. Online and available at http://www.politico.com/news/stories/0210/33670.html.

8. Skiba, "Nancy Pelosi's House."

9. Ibid.

10. Camille Paglia, "Pelosi's Victory for Women: Sure, Her Healthcare Bill Is a Mess, but Her Gritty Maneuvering Shows Her Mettle," Salon.com, November 10, 2009. Online and available at http://www.salon.com/news/opinion/camille_paglia/2009/11/10/pelosi/index.html.

11. Karen Breslau, Eleanor Clift, and Daren Briscoe, "Rolling with Pelosi: The GOP Says She's a Loony Lefty, and She Is, In Fact, Unabashedly Liberal. But She's Also

a Pol, and May Just Become Madam Speaker," *Newsweek*, October 23, 2006. Online and available at http://www.newsweek.com/id/72464.

12. Holly Bailey, "More Poll Numbers That Should Have the Dems Seriously Nervous," Newsweek Blog, September 23, 2009. Online and available at http://blog .newsweek.com/blogs/thegaggle/archive/2009/09/23/more-poll-numbers-that-should-have-the-dems-seriously-nervous.aspx.

13. Grigoriadis, "Why Is Nancy Pelosi Always Smiling?"

14. Brian Montopoli, "Poll: Low Favorability Ratings for Pelosi, Reid," Political Hotsheet, CBS News, March 22, 2010. Online and available at http://www.cbsnews .com/8301-503544_162-20000937-503544.html.

15. Leah Garchik, "Celebrating 'Most Powerful Italian Since Caesar'," *San Francisco Chronicle*, January 5, 2007. Online and available at http://articles.sfgate.com/2007-01-05/news/17226666_1_french-toast-first-woman-speaker-inauguration.

16. Edward Epstein, "Stronger Than Ever After 20 Years: Pelosi Marks Milestone, Having Risen from Quiet Obscurity to Become House's Leading Voice," *San Francisco Chronicle*, June 10, 2007.

17. Rogers, "Nancy Pelosi's Lesson."

18. David Firestone, "Woman in the News; Getting Closer to the Top, and Smiling All the Way," *The New York Times*, November 10, 2002.

19. Marc Sandalow, *Madam Speaker: Nancy Pelosi's Life, Times, and Rise to Power* (New York: Modern Times, 2008), 58.

20. Erica Werner and the Associated Press, "New House Speaker Shows She's Boss," *The Washington Post*, January 22, 2007.

21. Eve Fairbanks, "Nancy Pelosi: The Extreme Moderate: Despite Shrill GOP Warnings, the Speaker of the House Has Proved Politically Pragmatic Thus Far," *Los Angeles Times*, April 15, 2007. Online and available at http://www.latimes.com/news/ opinion/commentary/la-op-fairbanks15apr15,0,2160743.story.

22. Kim Hart and Jordan Fabian, "Pelosi: GOP Has Had Its Day; Confident Dems Can Pull Together on Health Bill," *The Hill*, February 28, 2010. Online and available at http://thehill.com/homenews/house/84089-pelosi-gop-has-had-its-day-217-healthcare-votes-in-sight.

23. Karen Tumulty, "Person of the Year 2009: Runners-Up: Nancy Pelosi," *Time*, December 16, 2009. Online and available at http://www.time.com/time/specials/ packages/article/0,28804,1946375_1947252_1947257-1,00.html.

24. Carolyn Lochhead, "Obama on Pelosi: She's Tough," Politics Blog, *San Francisco Chronicle*, January 14, 2010. Online and available at http://www.sfgate.com/cgi-bin/ blogs/nov05election/detail?entry_id=55307.

25. Joshua Green, "The Amazing Money Machine: How Silicon Valley Made Barack Obama This Year's Hottest Start-up," *The Atlantic*, June 2008. Online and available at http://www.theatlantic.com/doc/200806/obama-finance.

26. Sandalow, *Madam Speaker*, 60.

27. Lynne Duke, "Pride of Baltimore: Nancy Pelosi Learned Her Politics at the Elbow of Her Father the Mayor," *The Washington Post*, November 10, 2006.

28. Rich Lowry, "Lovin' Nancy: The Pelosi Honeymoon Begins. But It's Not Too Late to Call Off the Marriage!" NationalReviewOnline, October 27, 2006. Online and available at: http://article.nationalreview.com/295578/lovin-nancy/rich-lowry.

29. Rogers, "Pelosi: 'I'm Trying to Save the Planet'."

30. Juliet Eilperin, *Fight Club Politics: How Partisanship Is Poisoning the House of Representatives* (Lanham, Md: Rowman & Littlefield, 2006), 37–39.

31. "Boss Tweed," ECONOMICexpert.com. Online and available at http://www.economicexpert.com/a/Boss:Tweed.htm.

32. Rupert Cornwell, "Nancy Pelosi: Madam Speaker?: The First Woman to Lead Either Party in Either Chamber on Capitol Hill Has Broken through a Marble Ceiling," *The Independent*, November 4, 2006.

33. Bresnahan and Allen, "Nancy Pelosi's Brutal Reality Check."

34. "Text of Nancy Pelosi's Speech," *San Francisco Chronicle*, January 4, 2007. Online and available at http://www.sfgate.com/cgi-bin/article.cgi?f=/c/a/2007/01/04/BAG5ANCTQ27.DTL&type=politics.

35. Werner, "New House Speaker Shows She's Boss."

36. Epstein, "Stronger Than Ever After 20 Years."

37. Jackie Calmes and David Rogers, "Rumsfeld's Ouster Transforms Iraq Debate; Bush, Pelosi Face Challenge: How Much Compromising Can Each Stand to Do?" *The Wall Street Journal*, November 9, 2006.

38. Sandalow, *Madam Speaker*, 11.

Chapter One: Big Tommy

1. Thomas D'Alesandro, Jr., oral history, Maryland Historical Society. Interviewed by Francis Colletta, March 3, 1973. Quoted in Sandalow, *Madam Speaker*, 24.

2. Fred Hobson, *Mencken: A Life* (New York: Random House, 1994), quoted in Vincent Bzdek, *Woman of the House: The Rise of Nancy Pelosi* (New York: Palgrave Macmillan, 2008), 14.

3. Mark Bowden, "Bossin' Around: A History of How Things Got Done in Baltimore," *City Paper*, June 29, 1979.

4. Salvatore LaGumina, "Political Dynasties: Italian American Style," *Ambassador*, Volume 16, Issue 4 (Winter 2005).

5. Bowden, "Bossin' Around."

6. Joe Feuerherd, "Roots in Faith, Family and Party Guide Pelosi's Move to Power," *National Catholic Reporter*, January 24, 2003. Online and available at http://natcath.org/NCR_Online/archives2/2003a/012403/012403a.htm.

7. Bowden, "Bossin' Around."

8. Mark Z. Barabak, "Triumph of the 'Airhead'; Foes Say New House Minority Leader Nancy Pelosi Is a Lightweight. What They Should Know Is That the 'Liberal Dilettante' Is Actually a Savvy Daughter of Baltimore Machine Politics," *Los Angeles Times Magazine*, January 26, 2003.

9. Ibid.

10. Lee Bernstein, *The Greatest Menace: Organized Crime in Cold War America* (Amherst, Mass.: University of Massachusetts Press, 2002), 36.

11. Bowden, "Bossin' Around."

12. Ibid.

13. Gilbert Sandler, *The Neighborhood: The Story of Baltimore's Little Italy* (Baltimore: Bodine & Associates, Inc., 1974), 23–24.

14. Michael Olesker, *Journeys to the Heart of Baltimore* (Baltimore: The Johns Hopkins University Press, 2001), 32–33.

15. Olesker, *Journeys to the Heart of Baltimore*, 33.

16. Ibid., 33–34.

17. Ibid., 80.

18. Bzdek, *Woman of the House*, 21–22.

19. Olesker, *Journeys to the Heart of Baltimore*, 37–38.

20. Sandalow, *Madam Speaker*, 17.

21. Feuerherd, "Roots in Faith."

22. Bzdek, *Woman of the House*, 21.

23. Bowden, "Bossin' Around."

24. Olesker, *Journeys to the Heart of Baltimore*, 35.

25. LaGumina, "Political Dynasties: Italian American Style."

26. Feuerherd, "Roots in Faith."

27. "Form 'Crusaders' Branch,'" *The New York Times*, April 30, 1930.

28. Sandalow, *Madam Speaker*, 19.

29. Ibid.

30. Bowden, "Bossin' Around."

31. Sandler, *The Neighborhood*, 35.

32. Ibid., 37.

33. Mark Halperin, "Transcript: Pelosi Press Conference," March 19, 2010, The Page, *Time*, March 19, 2010. Online and available at http://thepage.time.com/transcript-pelosi-press-conference-march-19-2010/.

34. Sandler, *The Neighborhood*, 37–39.

35. Kenneth D. Durr, *Behind the Backlash: White Working-Class Politics in Baltimore, 1940–1980* (Chapel Hill, N.C.: University of North Carolina Press, 2003), 14.

36. Keith Richburg, "NY-20 Recount Takes a Turn for the Absurd," Capitol Briefing, *The Washington Post*, April 15, 2009. Online and available at http://voices.washingtonpost.com/capitol-briefing/2009/04/ny-20_recount_takes_a_turn_for.html.

37. Bowden, "Bossin' Around."

38. Bzdek, *Woman of the House*, 20–21.

39. Nancy Pelosi with Amy Hill Hearth, *Know Your Power: A Message to America's Daughters* (New York: Anchor Books, 2009), 82.

40. Olesker, *Journeys to the Heart of Baltimore*, 97.

41. Bzdek, *Woman of the House*, 23.

42. Bowden, "Bossin' Around."

43. Olesker, *Journeys to the Heart of Baltimore*, 141.

44. Bowden, "Bossin' Around."

45. "The History of Pimlico Race Course," Preakness.com. Online and available at http://Preakness.com/pimlicoHistory.

46. Bowden, "Bossin' Around."

47. Durr, *Behind the Backlash*, 54, 56.

48. Brennen Jensen, "Pins and Needles," *City Paper*, October 7, 1998. Online and available at http://citypaper.com/news/story.asp?id=3691.

49. Sandalow, *Madam Speaker*, 13.

50. Durr, *Behind the Backlash*, 20; and CIO Political Action Committee (PAC) Collection, Papers, 1943–1960s. Online and available at http://reuther.wayne.edu/files/LR000647.pdf.

51. Erin McCormick and Marc Sandalow, "Pelosi Mines 'California Gold' for Dems Nationwide/Personal Skills, Wide Network of Wealthy Donors Help Party's House Leader Gather Millions," *San Francisco Chronicle*, April 3, 2006. Online and available at http://articles.sfgate.com/2006-04-03/news/17292378_1_paul-pelosi-campaing-finance-democratic-party.

52. Durr, *Behind the Backlash*, 62.

53. Feuerherd, "Roots in Faith."

54. Durr, *Behind the Backlash*, 62.

55. Olesker, *Journeys to the Heart of Baltimore*, 89–90.

56. Ibid., 90.

57. Durr, *Behind the Backlash*, 62.

58. Bowden, "Bossin' Around."

59. "Cities: The Little World of Tommy," *Time*, unattributed, April 26, 1954.

60. "D'Alesandro Son Charged; Grand Jury Urges Prosecution for Perjury in Rape Trial," *The New York Times*, December 12, 1953.

61. "Political Notes: 21 in a Row," *Time*, unattributed, March 14, 1955.

62. "Cities: The Little World of Tommy," *Time*.

63. Bzdek, *Woman of the House*, 25.

64. "Political Notes: 21 in a Row," *Time*.

65. Bowden, "Bossin' Around."

66. Ibid.

67. "Baltimore Mayor Runs for Senator; D'Alesandro Gets Backing of Democratic Chiefs and Quits Governor Race," *The New York Times*, January 12, 1958.

68. Bowden, "Bossin' Around."

69. "Baltimore Mayor Loses in Primary; D'Alesandro's Bid for 4th Term Fails as Grady Rolls Up Substantial Vote," *The New York Times*, March 4, 1959.

70. Bowden, "Bossin' Around."

71. "Baltimore Mayor Loses in Primary," *The New York Times*.

72. "Baltimore Mayor Here; Back from Europe, He Learns of Unpleasantness at Home," *The New York Times*, August 5, 1953.

73. Peter Braestrup, "Chief of Renewal Reported Picked; D'Alesandro, Ex-Baltimore Mayor, Kennedy's Choice Over Weaver's Objections," *The New York Times*, February 18, 1961.

74. "Ex-Post Office Aide Indicted in Bribery," *The New York Times*, May 29, 1969.

75. "Builder in Baltimore Gets Sentence in Labor Case," *The New York Times*, May 30, 1969.

76. Ibid.

77. "Jury Studies Bribery Reports; Long and Brewster Mentioned," *The New York Times*, August 31, 1969.

78. Bowden, "Bossin' Around."

79. La Gumina, "Political Dynasties"; Barabak, "Triumph of the 'Airhead'."

Chapter Two: Basic Training

1. Sandalow, *Madam Speaker*, 13.

2. "Tommy D'Alesandro Announces Another Sure Vote—It's a Girl," *Baltimore Sun*, March 27, 1940; Sandalow, *Madam Speaker*, 11–12.

3. Olesker, *Journeys to the Heart of Baltimore*, 12–13.

4. "D'Alesandro Greeted as Tommy on Initial Visit to President," *Baltimore Sun*, November 22, 1939.

5. Pelosi and Hearth, *Know Your Power*, 10.

6. Sandler, *The Neighborhood*, 33–34; Pelosi and Hearth, *Know Your Power*, 11.

7. Sandalow, *Madam Speaker*, 16.

8. Elaine S. Povich, *Nancy Pelosi: A Biography* (Westport, Conn.: Greenwood Press, 2008), 1–2.

9. Sandalow, *Madam Speaker*, 13.

10. Bzdek, *Woman of the House*, 19.

11. Povich, *Nancy Pelosi*, 4.

12. Barabak, "Triumph of the 'Airhead'."

13. Pelosi/Hearth, *Know Your Power*, 12.

14. Sandalow, *Madam Speaker*, 24.

15. Rogers, "Nancy Pelosi's Lesson."

16. Johanna Neuman, "Hard Work, Political Roots Fuel Pelosi's Rise," *Los Angeles Times*, November 10, 2002.

17. Barabak, "Triumph of the 'Airhead'."

18. Duke, "Pride of Baltimore."

19. Pelosi and Hearth, *Know Your Power*, 21.

20. Feuerherd, "Roots in Faith."

21. Bzdek, *Woman of the House*, 20.

22. Sandalow, *Madam Speaker*, 24.

23. Povich, *Nancy Pelosi*, 4.

24. Bzdek, *Woman of the House*, 28.

25. Marc Sandalow and Erin McCormick, "Pelosi's Goal: Democrats Back on Top/Minority Leader Practices Hardball Politics to Position Her Party for Midterm Election," *San Francisco Chronicle*, April 2, 2006. Online and available at http://articles.sfgate.com/2006-04-02/news/17289305_1_pelosi-house-democratic-caucus-michigan-house.

26. Povich, *Nancy Pelosi*, 4.

27. Pelosi and Hearth, *Know Your Power*, 22–23.

28. Sandalow and McCormick, "Pelosi's Goal: Democrats Back on Top."

29. Ibid.

30. Pelosi/Hearth, *Know Your Power*, 81.

31. Bzdek, *Woman of the House*, 21.

32. "Tommy D'Alesandro Announces Another Sure Vote—It's a Girl," *Baltimore Sun*.

33. Pelosi and Hearth, *Know Your Power*, 14.

34. Povich, *Nancy Pelosi*, 6.

35. Ellen Gamerman, "Child of Politics, All Grown Up; Pelosi: The Woman Who Is About to Become House Minority Leader Distills Her Baltimore Father's Savvy and Her Mother's Steely Will," *Baltimore Sun*, November 14, 2002.

36. Pelosi/Hearth, *Know Your Power*, 13.

37. Bzdek, *Woman of the House*, 27.

38. Edward Epstein, "Pelosi: Lifetime Commitment to Politics, Democrats," *San Francisco Chronicle*, November 8, 2006. Online and available at http://articles.sfgate.com/2006-11-08/news/17318700_1_rep-sala-burton-phil-burton-special-election

39. Bzdek, *Woman of the House*, 27–28.

40. Ibid., 27; Olesker, *Journeys to the Heart of Baltimore*, 98.

41. Neuman, "Hard Work, Political Roots Fuel Pelosi's Rise."

42. Ibid.

43. Olesker, *Journeys to the Heart of Baltimore*, 97.

44. Bzdek, *Woman of the House*, 27.

45. Olesker, *Journeys to the Heart of Baltimore*, 96.

46. Bzdek, *Woman of the House*, 27.

47. Olesker, *Journeys to the Heart of Baltimore*, 13, 98.

48. Gamerman, "Child of Politics, All Grown Up."

49. Neuman, "Hard Work, Political Roots Fuel Pelosi's Rise."

50. Barabak, "Triumph of the 'Airhead.'"

51. Rafael Medoff, "Pelosi's Father Defied FDR on the Holocaust," *The Jewish News Weekly of Northern California*, December 1, 2006, Volume 110, Issue 47.

52. Sandalow, *Madam Speaker*, 29, 24.

53. "City Employees Discuss Strike: $5,000 for Mayor, but Not 50¢ for Workers," *Afro-American*, November 24, 1951.

54. "Congress Job Is a Tough One, D'Alesandro Wryly Concludes," *Baltimore Sun*, June 18, 1939.

55. David Cort, "The Scandalous Ad-Tax," *The Nation*, January 18, 1958.

56. Ibid.

57. "Thomas J. D'Alesandro, Jr., Father of Speaker Pelosi," A Langsdale Library Special Collection.

58. Epstein, "Stronger Than Ever After 20 Years."

59. Bzdek, *Woman of the House*, 23.

60. Wolfgang Saxon, "T. D'Alesandro Jr., a Baltimore Mayor, Dies," *The New York Times*, August 24, 1987.

61. "Cities: The Little World of Tommy," *Time*, unattributed, April 26, 1954; Bzdek, *Woman of the House*, 25.

62. "Baltimore Mayor Lashes at 'Greed'; D'Alesandro Levels Charges at the American League for Denying Browns' Move," *The New York Times*, March 21, 1953.

63. Thomas B. Edsall, "The Unraveling Begins?" *The New York Times*, November 18, 2006.

64. Povich, *Nancy Pelosi*, 2.

65. Sandalow, *Madam Speaker*, 22.

66. Ibid., 23.

67. Bzdek, *Woman of the House*, 25.

68. Sandalow, *Madam Speaker*, 116.

69. Pelosi/Hearth, *Know Your Power*, 101.

70. Barabak, "Triumph of the 'Airhead'."

71. Olesker, *Journeys to the Heart of Baltimore*, 65.

72. Duke, "Pride of Baltimore."

73. Olesker, *Journeys to the Heart of Baltimore*, 79.

74. Durr, *Behind the Backlash*, 14.

75. Ibid., 56.

76. Olesker, *Journeys to the Heart of Baltimore*, 79.

77. Ibid., 88.

78. "The Jacksons Abroad: On Tour of Southern Italy," *Afro-American*, October 13, 1951.

79. "You Can't Slow Down, Thurgood," *Afro-American*, January 25, 1958.

80. "Why Not Benedict Arnold?" *Afro-American*, May 15, 1948.

81. Mae Medders, "Party Bosses Ignore Tan Unit at Confab; Break with D'Alesandro Seen As Result of 'Slap in Face,'" *Afro-American*, June 14, 1952.

82. "About Politics and Some Politicians," *Afro-American*, February 28, 1959.

83. Bowden, "Bossin' Around."

84. Olesker, *Journeys to the Heart of Baltimore*, 79.

85. Bowden, "Bossin' Around."

86. George Collins, "Balto. Mayor Asks 'Open City'," *Afro-American*, November 2, 1963.

87. Durr, *Behind the Backlash*, 62.

88. Olesker, *Journeys to the Heart of Baltimore*, 263–65.

89. Ibid., 37.

90. Bowden, "Bossin' Around."

Chapter Three: On the Move

1. Perry Bacon, Jr., "Don't Mess with Nancy Pelosi," *Time*, August 27, 2006. Online and available at http://www.time.com/time/magazine/article/0,9171,1376213,00.html.

2. Jerry Roberts, "'Rabid' Demo Pelosi Tries for GOP Votes," *San Francisco Chronicle*, April 4, 1987.

3. Bzdek, *Woman of the House*, 92.

4. Sandalow, *Madam Speaker*, 28.

5. Bzdek, *Woman of the House*, 92.

6. Pelosi and Hearth, *Know Your Power*, 83.

7. Duke, "Pride of Baltimore."

8. Povich, *Nancy Pelosi*, 5–6.

9. Pelosi and Hearth, *Know Your Power*, 27.

10. Ibid., 28–29.

11. Sandalow, *Madam Speaker*, 36.

12. Pelosi and Hearth, *Know Your Power*, 30.

13. Pelosi and Hearth, *Know Your Power*, 35–36; Povich, *Nancy Pelosi*, 12.

14. Sandalow, *Madam Speaker*, 37; Jerry Roberts, "Washington Insider Wants to Put Her Connections to Work for S.F.," *San Francisco Chronicle*, March 23, 1987.

15. Sandalow, *Madam Speaker*, 38.

16. Povich, *Nancy Pelosi*, 13

17. "Miss D'Alesandro Is Future Bride of Paul F. Pelosi," *The New York Times*, June 1, 1963.

18. Pelosi and Hearth, *Know Your Power*, 39–40.

19. Epstein, "Pelosi: Lifetime Commitment to Politics."

20. Pelosi and Hearth, *Know Your Power*, 41–42.

21. Epstein, "Pelosi: Lifetime Commitment."

22. Christine Pelosi, *Campaign Boot Camp: Basic Training for Future Leaders* (Sausalito, Calif.: PoliPointPress, LLC, 2007), 1.

23. Barabak, "Triumph of the 'Airhead'."

24. Christine Pelosi, *Campaign Boot Camp*, 1.

25. Pelosi and Hearth, *Know Your Power*, 45–46.

26. Ian Talley, "Pelosi Investment Shows Unlikely Energy Alliance," *The Wall Street Journal*, August 23, 2008.

27. Sandalow, *Madam Speaker*, 48–49.

28. Bzdek, *Woman of the House*, 83.

29. Ibid., 73–74.

30. Sandalow, *Madam Speaker*, 48.

31. Neuman, "Hard Work, Political Roots Fuel Pelosi's Rise."

32. Bzdek, *Woman of the House*, 85.

33. "Pelosi's Hometown Circle," *San Francisco Chronicle*, January 25, 2004. Online and available at http://www.sfgate.com/cgi-bin/article.cgi?f=/c/a/2004/01/25/ING5V4D1HG1.DTL.

34. Sandalow, *Madam Speaker*, 51.

35. Pelosi/Hearth, *Know Your Power*, 48–50.

36. Sandalow, *Madam Speaker*, 45.

37. Phillip Matier and Andrew Ross, "Feinstein's $16.5 Million View in Pacific Heights," *San Francisco Chronicle*, January 29, 2006.

38. Barabak, "Triumph of the 'Airhead'."

39. John Wildermuth, "Pelosi's Husband Prefers a Low Profile/Successful Investor Has Taken Care to Avoid Causing Controversy," *San Francisco Chronicle*, January 1, 2007. Online and available at http://articles.sfgate.com/2007-01-01/news/17226205_1_paul-pelosi-political-career-speaker.

40. Michael Crowley, "Follow the Leader," *The New Republic*, November 25, 2002. Online and available at http://www.tnr.com/article/follow-the-leader.

41. McCormick and Sandalow, "Pelosi Mines 'California Gold'."

42. McCormick and Sandalow, "Pelosi Mines 'California Gold,'"; "Pelosi's Hometown Circle, *San Francisco Chronicle*.

43. John Bresnahan, "Pelosi's Plan: Wine, Dine Big Donors," Politico, August 6, 2009. Online and available at http://news.yahoo.com/s/politico/20090806/pl_politico/25859.

44. Harold Meyerson, "Sala's Choice: Nancy Pelosi Carries On a Powerful Legacy," *The Washington Post*, January 3, 2007.

45. Bzdek, *Woman of the House*, 72.

46. Gamerman, "Child of Politics, All Grown Up."

47. Daniel Schorn, "Nancy Pelosi: Two Heartbeats Away: Lesley Stahl Profiles the Woman Who Could Become the Next Speaker of the House," October 22, 2006. Online and available at http://www.cbsnews.com/stories/2006/10/20/60minutes/main2111089.shtml.

48. Susan Easton, "A Tale of Two Speakers," *Human Events*, May 26, 2009.

49. Pelosi/Hearth, *Know Your Power*, 53–54.

50. The Leakey Foundation, eNewsletter. Online and available at http://leakeyfoundation.org/index.php/the-foundation/Mission.html.

51. John Jacobs, *A Rage for Justice: The Passion and Politics of Phillip Burton* (Berkeley, Calif.: University of California Press, 1995), 172.

52. Pelosi/Hearth, *Know Your Power*, 55–56.

53. "Pelosi's Hometown Circle," *San Francisco Chronicle*.

54. Sandalow, *Madam Speaker*, 55.

55. Pelosi/Hearth, *Know Your Power*, 62–63.

56. Sandalow, *Madam Speaker*, 55–56.

57. Bzdek, *Woman of the House*, 74.

58. Povich, *Nancy Pelosi*, 22.

59. Neuman, "Hard Work, Political Roots Fuel Pelosi's Rise."

60. Sandalow, *Madam Speaker*, 56.

61. Pelosi/Hearth, *Know Your Power*, 64–65.

62. Neuman, "Hard Work, Political Roots Fuel Pelosi's Rise."

63. Barabak, "Triumph of the 'Airhead'."

64. Sandalow, *Madam Speaker*, 67–68.

65. Sandalow, *Madam Speaker*, 68, 70; Jacobs, *A Rage for Justice*, 415.

66. Sandalow, *Madam Speaker*, 66–67, 69.

67. Barabak, "Triumph of the 'Airhead'."

68. Roberts, "Washington Insider Wants to Put Her Connections to Work for S.F."

69. Pelosi/Hearth, *Know Your Power*, 66.

70. Povich, *Nancy Pelosi*, 24.

71. Alexandra Pelosi, *Sneaking into the Flying Circus: How the Media Turn Our Presidential Campaigns into Freak Shows* (New York: Free Press, 2005), 257.

72. Pelosi/Hearth, *Know Your Power*, 66.

73. Sandalow, *Madam Speaker*, 77.

74. Crowley, "Follow the Leader."

75. Povich, *Nancy Pelosi*, 24–25.

76. Sandalow, *Madam Speaker*, 77–78.

77. Dan Balz, "Pelosi Blasts Rival: DNC Candidate Decries Labor's Tactics," *The Washington Post*, January 29, 1985.

78. Sandalow, *Madam Speaker*, 80–81.

79. A. Mellinkoff, "Nancy Pelosi and the Democratic Future," *San Francisco Chronicle*, January 8, 1985.

80. Povich, *Nancy Pelosi*, 26.

81. Roberts, "'Rabid' Demo Pelosi Tries for GOP Votes."

82. Povich, *Nancy Pelosi*, 26

83. Epstein, "Pelosi: Lifetime Commitment to Politics, Democrats."

84. Povich, *Nancy Pelosi*, 30.

85. Epstein, "Pelosi: Lifetime Commitment to Politics, Democrats."

86. Sandalow, *Madam Speaker*, 91.

87. Neuman, "Hard Work, Political Roots Fuel Pelosi's Rise."

88. Bzdek, *Woman of the House*, 87.

89. Sandalow, *Madam Speaker*, 96.

90. Bzdek, *Woman of the House*, 86–87.

91. Sandalow, *Madam Speaker*, 93–94.

92. Wildermuth, "Pelosi's Husband Prefers a Low Profile."

93. Pelosi/Hearth, *Know Your Power*, 74.

94. Clint Reilly, "Nancy Pelosi: 'A Voice That Will Be Heard'," *News & Views From 465 California Street*, March, 11, 2008. Online and available at http://clintreilly.com/nancy-pelosi.

95. Sandalow, *Madam Speaker*, 96–97.

96. Reilly, "Nancy Pelosi: 'A Voice That Will Be Heard'."

97. Marshall Ganz, "Distributed Leadership in the Obama Campaign," About the Lecture, *MIT World*, March 19, 2009. Online and available at http://mitworld.mit.edu/video/662.

98. Pelosi/Hearth, *Know Your Power*, 77–78.

99. Christine Pelosi, *Campaign Boot Camp*, 53.

100. Sandalow, *Madam Speaker*, 97–99.

101. Ibid., 107–8.

102. Roberts, "'Rabid' Demo Pelosi Tries for GOP Votes."

103. Barabak, "Triumph of the 'Airhead'."

104. Neuman, "Hard Work, Political Roots Fuel Pelosi's Rise."

105. Crowley, "Follow the Leader."

106. Sandalow, *Madam Speaker*, 104, 109.

107. Associated Press, "Pelosi Wins Nomination for California House Seat," *The Washington Post*, April 9, 1987.

108. Sandalow, *Madam Speaker*, 111.

109. Povich, *Nancy Pelosi*, 35.

110. "Nude Ban Stirs Revolt," *The New York Times*, December 3, 1955.

111. Jeffrey Lord, "When Nancy Met Harry," *The American Spectator*, October 5, 2006. Online and available at http://spectator.org/archives/2006/10/05/when-nancy-met-harry.

112. Roberts, "Washington Insider Wants to Put Her Connections to Work for S.F."

Chapter Four: Launching a Heat-Seeking Liberal Missile

1. Tumulty, "Person of the Year 2009."
2. Sandalow, *Madam Speaker*, 195.
3. Jacobs, *A Rage for Justice*, xxv.
4. Ibid., 169.
5. Ibid., xxv.
6. Ibid., xxii.
7. Bzdek, *Woman of the House*, 89.
8. Barabak, "Triumph of the 'Airhead'."
9. Cornwell, "Nancy Pelosi: Madam Speaker?"
10. Sandalow, *Madam Speaker*, 49.
11. Bzdek, *Woman of the House*, 86.
12. Jacobs, *A Rage for Justice*, xx.
13. Ibid., 3.
14. Ibid., xxi.
15. Ibid., 91.
16. Meyerson, "Sala's Choice."
17. Jacobs, *A Rage for Justice*, 46, 44.
18. Jacobs, *A Rage for Justice*, 163.
19. Povich, *Nancy Pelosi*, 29.
20. Bzdek, *Woman of the House*, p. 84.
21. Sandalow, *Madam Speaker*, 54.
22. Meyerson, "Sala's Choice."
23. Jacobs, *A Rage for Justice*, 41.
24. Grigoriadis, "Why Is Nancy Pelosi Always Smiling?"
25. Jacobs, *A Rage for Justice*, xxii.
26. Bzdek, *Woman of the House*, 84–85.
27. Jacobs, *A Rage for Justice*, 117–20.
28. Epstein, "Stronger Than Ever After 20 Years: Pelosi Marks Milestone, Having Risen from Quiet Obscurity to Become House's Leading Voice," *San Francisco Chronicle*, June 10, 2007.
29. David Frum, *How We Got Here: The 70's: The Decade That Brought You Modern Life (For Better or Worse)* (New York: Basic Books, 2000), 278–79.
30. Jacobs, *A Rage for Justice*, xix.
31. Richard E. Cohen, "Pelosi's Bill: How She Did It," *National Journal*, November 14, 2009.
32. Grigoriadis, "Why Is Nancy Pelosi Always Smiling?"
33. Glenn Thrush, "Nancy Pelosi on Being Unpopular: 'I Don't Care'," Politico, July 27, 2009. Online and available at http://www.politico.com/news/stories/0709/25445.html.
34. Feuerherd, "Roots in Faith."
35. Jacobs, *A Rage for Justice*, 24, 68–70.
36. Ibid., 252.
37. Ibid., 259.
38. Pelosi and Hearth, *Know Your Power*, 116.
39. Bzdek, *Woman of the House*, 82, 85.

40. Jacobs, *A Rage for Justice*, 180.

41. Ibid., 185–87.

42. Ibid., 189.

43. Ibid., 206.

44. Ibid., 199.

45. Sandalow, *Madam Speaker*, 122–23.

46. Bzdek, *Woman of the House*, 81.

47. Ibid., 85.

48. Jacobs, *A Rage for Justice*, 100.

49. Sala Galante Burton, Representative, 1983-1987, Democrat from California, *Women in Congress*. Online and available at http://womenincongress.house.gov/member-profiles/profile.html?intID=29.

50. Jacobs, *A Rage for Justice*, 28.

51. Bzdek, *Woman of the House*, 80.

52. Ibid., 81, 84.

53. Pelosi/Hearth, *Know Your Power*, 164.

54. Jacobs, *A Rage for Justice*, 230–31.

55. Sandalow, *Madam Speaker*, 195.

56. Zachary Coile, "Pelosi Seeks Input from Diverse Array of Confidants," *San Francisco Chronicle*, December 19, 2006. Online and available at http://articles.sfgate.com/2006-12-19/news/17326085_1_rep-nancy-pelosi-silicon-valley-new-staffers.

57. Clint Reilly, "John L. Burton," *News & Views from 465 California Street*, January 1, 2008. Online and available at http://www.clintreilly.com/john-l-burton/.

58. Robert Salladay and Greg Lucas, "Our Man in Sacramento: John Burton is Pushy, Profane, Pugnacious—and Powerful," *San Francisco Chronicle*, September 1, 2002.

59. Peter Hecht, "Veteran Pol Burton Vows to Lead Democratic Future," Capitol Alert, *Sacramento Bee*, April 25, 2009. Online and available at http://www.sacbee.com/static/weblogs/capitolalertlatest/2009/04/veteran-pol-bur.html.

60. Jacobs, *A Rage for Justice*, 94.

61. Ibid., 121.

62. Marshall Kilduff and Phil Tracy, "Inside Peoples Temple," *San Francisco Chronicle*, August 1, 1977.

63. B. Drummond Ayres, Jr., "It's Official: Willie Brown Runs for Mayor," *The New York Times*, June 4, 1995.

64. Lance Williams and Chuck Finnie, "Mayor's Patronage Army: Brown Fattens Payroll with Loyalists, Colleagues, Friends," *San Francisco Chronicle*, April 30, 2001. Online and available at http://articles.sfgate.com/2001-04-30/news/17595568_1_city-hall-civil-service-patronage.

65. Coile, "Pelosi Seeks Input."

66. Gamerman, "Child of Politics, All Grown Up."

67. Jacobs, *A Rage for Justice*, xxi.

68. Ibid., 260.

Chapter Five: From the Whip to the Gavel

1. Crowley, "Follow the Leader."

2. Sandalow, *Madam Speaker*, 123.

3. Ibid., 91.

4. Crowley, "Follow the Leader."

5. Pelosi/Hearth, *Know Your Power*, 87.

6. Bzdek, *Woman of the House*, 94.

7. The FAIR Foundation, "Our Government's Bio-Medical Research Allocations."

8. Pelosi/Hearth, *Know Your Power*, 88–89.

9. Centers for Disease Control, "Heart Disease and Stroke Prevention: Addressing the Nation's Leading Killers: At a Glance 2010." Online and available at http://www.cdc.gov/chronicdisease/resources/publications/AAG/dhdsp.htm#aag.

10. Pelosi and Hearth, *Know Your Power*, 91.

11. Ibid.

12. Sandalow, *Madam Speaker*, 101.

13. Ibid., 127.

14. Ibid., 129.

15. Ibid.

16. Sandalow, *Madam Speaker*, 126, 131.

17. Bill Ghent, "A Leader on Our Side: The Selection of House Minority Leader Nancy Pelosi Ensures Gay Rights Will Stay on the Agenda," *The Advocate*, December 24, 2002.

18. Bzdek, *Woman of the House*, 94.

19. Alan Miller, "It's Trendy to Resent California: Analysts Say There's a Growing Backlash in Congress Against the Golden State," *Los Angeles Times*, August 28, 1990.

20. Povich, *Nancy Pelosi*, 47.

21. Larry Liebert, "Nancy P. Has Finally Arrived on Capitol Hill," *San Francisco Chronicle*, December 13, 1990.

22. Sandalow, *Madam Speaker*, 160.

23. Povich, *Nancy Pelosi*, 47.

24. Bzdek, *Woman of the House*, 95.

25. Edward Epstein, "Campaign 2006: Eighth Congressional District/3 Challengers Fight for Pelosi Seat/Only in S.F. Would Minority Leader Be Criticized as Too Moderate," *San Francisco Chronicle*, October 20, 2006. Online and available at http://articles.sfgate.com/2006-10-20/bay-area/17317847_1_leader-pelosi-rep-nancy-pelosi-house-democrats.

26. Crowley, "Follow the Leader."

27. Nancy Pelosi, "Congresswoman Nancy Pelosi: Unilateral Use of Force Will Be Harmful to the War on Terrorism," U.S. House of Representatives, October 10, 2002. Online and available at http://www.house.gov/pelosi/UnilateralUseofForce101002.htm.

28. Pelosi/Hearth, *Know Your Power*, 95.

29. Ibid., 92.

30. McCormick and Sandalow, "Pelosi Mines 'California Gold'."

31. Barabak, "Triumph of the 'Airhead'."

32. Bzdek, *Woman of the House*, 129–30.

33. Neuman, "Hard Work, Political Roots Fuel Pelosi's Rise."

34. Bzdek, *Woman of the House*, 130.

35. Eleanor Clift, "Capitol Letter: Old Boys' Club," *Newsweek*, July 26, 2001. Online and available at http://www.newsweek.com/id/78539?tid=relatedcl.

36. Ibid.

37. Bzdek, *Woman of the House*, 97.

38. Mike Soraghan, "Seeds of Pelosi's Rise Planted in the 1990s," *The Hill*, September 28, 2009. Online and available at http://thehill.com/special-reports/the-hills-15th-anniversary/60633-seeds-of-pelosis-rise-planted-in-the-1990s.

39. Bzdek, *Woman of the House*, 71.

40. Zachary Roth, "The Establishmentarian: Democrats Have Won Control of the House, and Steny Hoyer Has Tom Delay's Old Job. Some Things Will Change. Some Won't," *Washington Monthly*, November 2006.

41. Ibid.

42. Bzdek, *Woman of the House*, 133.

43. Sandalow, *Madam Speaker*, 190–93.

44. McCormick and Sandalow, "Pelosi Mines 'California Gold'."

45. Adam Clymer, "A New Vote Counter: Nancy Patricia Pelosi," *The New York Times*, October 11, 2001.

46. McCormick and Sandalow, "Pelosi Mines 'California Gold'."

47. Crowley, "Follow the Leader."

48. Sandalow, *Madam Speaker*, 193.

49. Michael Crowley, "Follow the Leader."

50. Sandalow, *Madam Speaker*, 199.

51. Ibid.

52. Clymer, "A New Vote Counter: Nancy Patricia Pelosi."

53. Marc Sandalow, "House Democrats Pick S.F.'s Pelosi for Minority Whip/First Woman to Hold No. 2 Post Could Be on Track for Speaker," *San Francisco Chronicle*, October 10, 2001. Online and available at http://articles.sfgate.com/2001-10-10/news/17620886_1_pelosi-black-leather-whip-house-democrats.

54. Sandalow, *Madam Speaker*, 201.

55. Sandalow, "House Democrats Pick S.F.'s Pelosi."

56. Barabak, "Triumph of the 'Airhead'."

57. Sandalow and McCormick, "Pelosi's Goal: Democrats Back on Top."

58. Neuman, "Hard Work, Political Roots Fuel Pelosi's Rise."

59. Sandalow, *Madam Speaker*, 220.

60. Bzdek, *Woman of the House*, 149–50.

61. Marc Sandalow, "Politics: Democratic Party; Savvy, Cash Clinched Job for Pelosi; Tightly Orchestrated Campaign Followed Lucrative Fund Raising," *San Francisco Chronicle*, November 17, 2002.

Chapter Six: Pounding the Gavel

1. Bacon, "Don't Mess with Nancy Pelosi."

2. Salena Zito, "Mom's Duties Prime Nancy Pelosi for Leadership," *Pittsburgh Tribune-Review*, April 26, 2009. Online and available at http://www.pittsburghlive.com/x/pittsburghtrib/news/pittsburgh/s_622362.html.

3. Steve Kornacki, "Rahm Emanuel Still Makes Nancy Pelosi Nervous," *The New York Observer*, December 17, 2008. Online and available at http://www.observer.com/2008/politics/rahm-emanuel-still-makes-nancy-pelosi-nervous.

4. Bzdek, *Woman of the House*, 151.

5. Grigoriadis, "Why Is Nancy Pelosi Always Smiling?"

6. Bzdek, *Woman of the House*, 151.

7. Bacon, "Don't Mess with Nancy Pelosi."

8. Rogers, "Nancy Pelosi's Lesson."

9. Grigoriadis, "Why Is Nancy Pelosi Always Smiling?"

10. Bzdek, *Woman of the House*, 152.

11. Ibid.

12. John Bresnahan, "Brian Wolff: Staffer and Pelosi Make Perfect Pair," Politico, June 3, 2008; Pelosi and Hearth, *Know Your Power*, 105.

13. Pelosi and Hearth, *Know Your Power*, 112–13.

14. Ibid., 113–16.

15. Ibid., 116–17.

16. Ibid., 117–18.

17. Lord, "When Nancy Met Harry." Also see Jeffrey Lord, "Pelosi to Polanski to Jennings: Why Sean Hannity Is Right," *The American Spectator*, October 6, 2009. Online and available at http://spectator.org/archives/2009/10/06/pelosi-to-polanski-to-jennings.

18. Ibid.

19. Congresswoman Nancy Pelosi, "Statement Celebrating San Francisco Lesbian, Gay, Bisexual and Transgender Pride and in Honor of Officer Jon D. Cook, U.S. House of Representatives, June 27, 2002. Online and available at http://www.house.gov/pelosi/flSFGayPridandCook062702.htm.

20. CNN Transcripts, "The Situation Room: Florida State Rep. Negron to Replace Foley in Midterms," October 2, 2006. Online and available at http://transcripts.cnn.com/TRANSCRIPTS/0610/02/sitroom.01.html.

21. Lord, "When Nancy Met Harry."

22. Harold Meyerson, "How Nancy Pelosi Took Control," *The American Prospect*, June 2004.

23. Rep. George Miller, "Pelosi: First Female Speaker," *NewsHour:* Report—PBS, January 2, 2007.

24. Meyerson, "How Nancy Pelosi Took Control."

25. Bresnahan, "Pelosi's Plan."

26. Grigoriadis, "Why Is Nancy Pelosi Always Smiling?"

27. Ibid.

28. Bzdek, *Woman of the House*, 161.

29. Molly Hooper and the Associated Press, "Hoyer Wins House Majority Leader Race, Giving Pelosi First Setback," FOXNews.com, November 16, 2006. Online and available at http://www.foxnews.com/story/0,2933,229819,00.html.

30. David Espo and the Associated Press, "Pelosi Says She Would Drain GOP 'Swamp,'" *The Washington Post*, October 6, 2006. Online and available at http://www.washingtonpost.com/wp-dyn/content/article/2006/10/06/AR2006100600056.html.

31. Werner and the Associated Press, "New House Speaker Shows She's Boss."

32. Hooper and the Associated Press, "Hoyer Wins House Majority Leader Race."

33. Glenn Thrush, "Pelosi's List: Who's on Her Bad Side?" Politico, March 2, 2009. Online and available at http://www.politico.com/news/stories/0309/19481.html.

34. Mark Mazzetti, "The 2006 Elections: Choice for Intelligence Panel Poses Early Test for Pelosi," *The New York Times*, November 9, 2006. Online and available at http://query.nytimes.com/gst/fullpage.html?res=9A06E3DB1F3FF933A25752C1A9609C8B63; Glenn Thrush, "Pelosi Long Aware of Harman's Wiretap," Politico, April 23, 2009. Online and available at http://www.politico.com/news/stories/0409/21614.html.

35. Thrush, "Pelosi's List: Who's on Her Bad Side?"

36. Bacon, "Don't Mess with Nancy Pelosi."

37. Ryan Grim, "Fight Club," *Washington Monthly*, January–February 2007. Online and available at http://findarticles.com/p/articles/mi_m1316/is_1_39/ai_n17216300/.

38. Speaker Nancy Pelosi, "Speaker Pelosi Remarks About Briefing on Enhanced Interrogation Techniques," Office of the Speaker—The Gavel Blog, May 14, 2009. Online and available at http://www.speaker.gov/blog/?p=1790.

39. Jed Babbin, "Richard Milhous Pelosi," *Human Events*, May 18, 2009. Online and available at http://www.humanevents.com/article.php?id=31897.

40. Porter J. Goss, "Security Before Politics," *The Washington Post*, April 25, 2009. Online and available at http://www.washingtonpost.com/wp-dyn/content/article/2009/04/24/AR2009042403339.html.

41. Charles Hurt, "Pelosi's Confession: Dem Boss Knew of Waterboarding," *New York Post*, May 15, 2009. Online and available at http://www.nypost.com/p/news/national/item_iw1NjSa6sPr61oT59lqjXN;jsessionid=F63BD8851E4AB4E5CA42BDE7F9A1C6D3.

42. Leon E. Panneta, "Message from the Director: Turning Down the Volume," CIA Press Release, May 15, 2009. Online and available at https://www.cia.gov/news-information/press-releases-statements/message-from-the-director-turning-down-the-volume.html.

43. Babbin, "Richard Milhous Pelosi."

44. Newt Gingrich, "Why Pelosi Should Step Down," *Human Events*, May 20, 2009. Online and available at http://www.humanevents.com/article.php?id=31940.

45. Glenn Thrush, "Nancy Pelosi Unable to Quell Firestorm Over Waterboarding Briefing," Politico, May 20, 2009. Online and available at http://www.politico.com/news/stories/0509/22795.html.

46. Ibid.

47. Bacon, "Don't Mess with Nancy Pelosi."

48. "Rep. Stupak: Speaker Pelosi Had Extra Health Care Votes 'In Her Pocket'," *Catholic News Agency*, March 26, 2010. Online and available at http://www.catholicnewsagency.com/news/rep._stupak_speaker_pelosi_had_extra_health_care_votes_in_her_pocket/.

Chapter Seven: The Big Power Grab: Health Care

1. Mary Lynn F. Jones, "Woman on Top: Nancy Pelosi Is the Democrats' Mid-Course Correction," *The American Prospect*, December 16, 2002.

2. Katie Connolly, "Obama Signs Health-Care Bill, Changes the Story of His Presidency," NewsweekBlog, March 23, 2010. Online and available at http://blog.newsweek.com/blogs/thegaggle/archive/2010/03/23/obama-signs-health-care-bill-f-hischanges-the-story-o-presidency.aspx.

3. Christina Bellantoni, "Pelosi Invokes Ted Kennedy in Floor Speech on Health Care," TPM LiveWire, March 22, 2010. Online and available at http://tpmlivewire.talkingpointsmemo.com/2010/03/pelosi-invokes-ted-kennedy-in-floor-speech-on-health-care.php.

4. Richard E. Cohen, "Pelosi's Bill: How She Did It," *National Journal*, November 14, 2009.

5. Huma Khan, Jonathan Karl and Z. Byron Wolf, "Health Care Bill: House Passes $938 Billion Bill, Sweeping Legislation on Its Way to Become Law," ABC News, March 21, 2010. Online and available at http://abcnews.go.com/Politics/HealthCare/health-care-bill-house-passes-sweeping-reform-legislation/story?id=10162080.

6. Patricia Murphy and Jill Lawrence, "Health Reform: What's In, What's Out and What It Will Cost," *Politics Daily*, March 26, 2010. Online and available at http://www.politicsdaily.com/2010/03/26/health-reform-whats-in-whats-out-and-what-it-will-cost.

7. "The Worst Bill Ever: Epic New Spending and Taxes, Pricier Insurance, Rationed Care, Dishonest Accounting: The Pelosi Health Bill Has It All," *The Wall*

Street Journal, November 1, 2009. Online and available at http://online.wsj.com/article/ SB10001424052748703399204574505423751140690.html.

8. Bzdek, *Woman of the House*, 50.

9. Jacobs, *A Rage for Justice*, 131.

10. Mike Allen, "Nancy Pelosi: Make Millionaires Pay for Health Care," Politico, July 20, 2009. Online and available at http://www.politico.com/news/stories/0709/25144 .html.

11. "Pelosi Remarks at the 2010 Legislative Conference for National Association of Counties," Office of Speaker Nancy Pelosi, March 9, 2010. Online and available at http://www.speaker.gov/newsroom/pressreleases?id=1576.

12. David Gratzer, *Why Obama's Government Takeover of Health Care Will Be a Disaster* (New York: Encounter Books, 2009), 3–4.

13. Shailagh Murray and Paul Kane, "Pelosi Vows Passage of Health-Care Overhaul; 'It Will Win': Confidence Grows as Democrats Plan to Resume Talks," *The Washington Post*, July 27, 2009.

14. Rogers, "Nancy Pelosi's Lesson."

15. Camille Paglia, "Pelosi's Victory for Women: Sure, Her Healthcare Bill Is a Mess, but Her Gritty Maneuvering Shows Her Mettle," Salon.com, November 10, 2009. Online and available at http:// salon.com/news/opinion/camille_paglia/2009/11/10/pelosi/index.html.

16. Faye Fiore and Richard Simon, "She Had to Leave Left Coast Behind; To Build a Majority on Healthcare Legislation, Pelosi Yielded on Liberal Touchstones Including Abortion," *Los Angeles Times*, November 9, 2009.

17. Murray and Kane, "Pelosi Vows Passage of Health-Care Overhaul."

18. Sudhin Thanawala and the Associated Press, "Pelosi Confident House Will Pass Health Care Bill," ABC News, March 13, 2010. Online and available at http://abcnews .go.com/Politics/wireStory?id=10094776.

19. Fiore and Simon, "She Had to Leave Left Coast Behind."

20. Cohen, "Pelosi's Bill: How She Did It."

21. Ibid.

22. Rich Lowry, "Another Rank Deal: Unions to Escape 'Cadillac Tax'," *New York Post*, January 15, 2010. Online and available at http://www.nypost.com/p/news/opinion/ opedcolumnists/another_rank_deal_yw10pr1eUhSAMnIn3Z8ZEI.

23. Luke Russert and Ali Weinberg, "Pelosi Denies Snowe in Control," MSNBC FirstRead, October 15, 2009. Online and available at http://firstread.msnbc.msn.com/ archive/2009/10/15/2100049.aspx.

24. Patrick O'Connor and Glenn Thrush, "Nancy Pelosi Takes Swipe at President Obama's Campaign Promises," Politico, January 5, 2010. Online and available at http:// www.politico.com/news/stories/0110/31180.html.

25. Peter Nicholas, "The Nation; Unions Object to 'Cadillac Tax' Plan; Labor Leaders Meet with Obama About the Senate's Healthcare Bill. They Favor the House Approach," *Los Angeles Times*, January 12, 2010.

26. "Nancy Pelosi: Madam Speaker/Auto Honcho," *Investor's Business Daily*, January 14, 2010. Online and available at http://www.investors.com/NewsAndAnalysis/Article .aspx?id=518189.

27. "ObamaCare's Latest Bribe," *New York Post*, January 15, 2010. Online and available at http://www.nypost.com/p/news/opinion/editorials/obamacare_latest_bribe_ yAliYQ9aPnUJDQH2zlxr9N.

28. Carl Campanile, "Unions Will Dodge O's Health Tax," *New York Post*, January 15, 2010. Online and available at http://www.nypost.com/p/news/national/unions_ get_pecial_treatment_in_health_AB053CwqPIJlIxXAm37DOM.

29. Lowry, "Another Rank Deal."

30. Alyssa Rosenberg, "Bill Ties Cadillac Tax to Feds' Health Care Costs," Government Executive.com, March 18, 2010. Online and available at http://www.govexec .com/dailyfed/0310/031810ar2.htm; Emily P. Walker, "Senate Passes Healthcare Reconciliation Bill," MedPage Today, March 25, 2010. Online and available at http://www .medpagetoday.com/Washington-Watch/Reform/19231.

31. Luke Russert, "Pelosi Blasts Health Insurance Companies," MSNBC FirstRead, July 30, 2009. Online and available at http://firstread.msnbc.msn.com/archive/2009/07/ 30/2015322.aspx.

32. Pelosi/Hearth, *Know Your Power,* 162.

33. Bellantoni, "Pelosi Invokes Ted Kennedy in Floor Speech on Health Care."

34. Sally C. Pipes, *The Top Ten Myths of American Health Care: A Citizen's Guide* (San Francisco: Pacific Research Institute, 2008), 9.

35. Pipes, *The Top Ten Myths,* 31-33, 34–36.

36. Glenn Thrush, "Nancy Pelosi: Insurers Are 'Immoral' Villains," Politico, July 31, 2009. Online and available at http://politico.com/news/stories/0709/25651.html.

37. Russert, "Pelosi Blasts Health Insurance Companies."

38. Paglia, "Pelosi's Victory for Women."

39. Vince Bzdek, "Why Did Health-Care Reform Pass? Nancy Pelosi Was in Charge." *The Washington Post,* March 28, 2010. Online and available at http://www .washingtonpost.com/wp-dyn/content/article/2010/03/26/AR2010032602225.html.

40. E. J. Dionne, "An Ebullient Pelosi: Watch Out Insurance Companies, and Rahm Is a Softie," PostPartisan, *The Washington Post,* March 23, 2010. Online and available at http://voices.washingtonpost.com/postpartisan/2010/03/an_ebullient_pelosi_watch_ out.html.

41. Allen, "Nancy Pelosi: Make Millionaires Pay for Health Care."

42. Henry I. Miller and Jeff Stier, "Stop the (Health Reform) Juggernaut: The Pelosi Bill Will Hurt Not Only Drugmakers, But Patients Too," Forbes.com, November 13, 2009. Online and available at http://www.forbes.com/2009/11/13/nancy-pelosi-health-reform-pharmaceuticals-opinions-contributors-health-care.html.

43. Ibid.

44. Allen, "Nancy Pelosi: Make Millionaires Pay for Health Care."

45. "Major Tax Provisions in U.S. Healthcare Bill," Reuters, March 22, 2010. Online and available at http://www.reuters.com/article/idUSN2220951920100322.

46. Craig Broffman and Deirdre Walsh, "Key House Committee Passes Health Care Bill," CNNPolitics.com, August 18, 2009. Online and available at http://www .cnn.com/2009/POLITICS/07/31/health.care/index.html.

47. "The Worst Bill Ever," *The Wall Street Journal,* November 1, 2009.

48. Shailagh Murray and Lori Montgomery, "House Passes Health-Care Reform Bill Without Republican Votes," *The Washington Post,* March 22, 2010. Online and available at http://www.washingtonpost.com/wp-dyn/content/article/2010/03/21/ AR2010032100943_3.html?sid=ST2010032201830.

49. David Espo and the Associated Press, "House Narrowly Passes Landmark Health Care Bill: Landmark Health Care Reform Bill Clears House in Close Vote; Senate Debate Next," ABC News, November 7, 2009. Online and available at http:// abcnews.go.com/Business/wireStory?id=9021231.

50. "Dean Claims Social Security and Medicare Were Passed Without Republican Support," Politifact.com, *St. Petersburg Times,* August 28, 2009. Available and online at http://www.politifact.com/truth-o-meter/statements/2009/aug/28/howard-dean/dean-claims-social-security-and-medicare-were-pass.

51. Carl Hulse and Robert Pear, "Sweeping Health Care Plan Passes House," *The New York Times*, November 8, 2009.

52. Fiore and Simon, "She Had to Leave Left Coast Behind."

53. Betsy Cline, "Pelosi's Giant Gavel," MSNBC FirstRead, March 21, 2010. Online and available at http://firstread.msnbc.msn.com/archive/2010/03/21/2235618.aspx; Steve Brusk, "Pelosi to Use Historic Gavel to Preside over Vote," politicalticker, CNN Politics, March 21, 2010. Online and available at http://politicalticker.blogs.cnn.com/2010/03/21/pelosi-to-use-historic-gavel-to-preside-over-reform/?fbid=etG6Z3JzC7I.

54. Murray and Montgomery, "House Passes Health-Care Reform Bill Without Republican Votes."

55. Andrea Stone, "Health Care Reform Is Moment for Nancy Pelosi," AOL News, March 21, 2010. Online and available at http://www.aolnews.com/healthcare/article/health-care-reform-is-moment-for-speaker-pelosi/19408228.

56. Dick Morris and Eileen McGann, "Pelosi Bill: Jail for No Insurance," The Hill's Pundits Blog, *The Hill*, November 8, 2009. Online an available at http://thehill.com/blogs/pundits-blog/healthcare/66879-pelosi-bill-jail-for-no-insurance.

57. James R. Copland, "Tort-Bar Treat: PelosiCare's Perks for Lawyers," *New York Post*, November 3, 2009.

58. House Republican Leader John Boehner, "Speaker Pelosi's Government-Run Health Plan Will Require a Monthly Abortion Premium," GOP Leader Blog, November 5, 2009. Online and available at http://republicanleader.house.gov/blog/?p=666.

59. Bzdek, "Why Did Health-Care Reform Pass?"

60. Brad Knickerbocker, "What Happened to Obama's 'Government Transparency' Pledge?" *Christian Science Monitor*, January 9, 2010. Online and available at http://www.csmonitor.com/USA/Politics/The-Vote/2010/0109/What-happened-to-Obama-s-government-transparency-pledge.

61. Andrew Malcolm, "C-SPAN Pleads with Reid, Pelosi to Open Final Drafting Sessions for Obama's Healthcare Bill," Top of the Ticket, *Los Angeles Times*, January 5, 2010. Online and available at http://latimesblogs.latimes.com/washington/2010/01/democrats-reid-pelosi-healthcare-cspan.html.

62. Eric Zimmermann and Michael O'Brien, "Pelosi Tells C-SPAN: 'There Has Never Been a More Open Process'," Blog Briefing Room, The Hill, January 5, 2010. Online and available at http://thehill.com/blogs/blog-briefing-room/news/74389-pelosi-resp.

63. C-SPAN's coverage of the U.S. House of Representatives, January 14, 2005; "Pelosi Says 'Absolute Outrage' Not Give Members Three Days to Read the Bill," YouTube. Online and available at http://www.youtube.com/watch?v=SgGwwzRoHao&feature=player_embedded#.

64. Allen, "Nancy Pelosi: Make Millionaires Pay for Health Care."

65. Luke Russert, "Pelosi Gets Emotional," MSNBC FirstRead, September 17, 2009. Online and available at http://firstread.msnbc.msn.com/archive/2009/09/17/2073142.aspx.

66. "25% Agree with Pelosi That Health Insurers are 'Villains,'" Rasmussen Reports, August 7, 2009. Available and online at http://rasmussenreports.com/public_content/politics/current_events/healthcare/august_2009/25_agree_with_pelosi_that_health_insurers_are_villains.

67. Cohen, "Pelosi's Bill: How She Did It."

68. Paul Kane, "Waxman Defeats Dingell," Capitol Briefing, *The Washington Post*, November 20, 2008. Online and available at http://voices.washingtonpost.com/capitol-briefing/2008/11/waxman_defeats_dingell.html.

69. David Kocieniewski, "Rangel Failed to Disclose $500,000 in Assets for '07," *The New York Times*, August 26, 2009.

70. Raymond Hernandez and Jim Rutenberg, "Under Scrutiny, Rangel Is Frayed but Defiant," *The New York Times*, November 23, 2009.

71. Jacobs, *A Rage for Justice*, 386.

72. Ibid., 253–254, 248.

73. Ibid., 261.

74. Bellantoni, "Pelosi Invokes Ted Kennedy."

75. Byron York, "Democrats Threaten Companies Hit Hard by Health Care Bill," *Washington Examiner*, March 28, 2010. Online and available at http://www.washington examiner.com/politics/Democrats-threaten-companies-hit-hard-by-health-care-bill-89347127.html.

76. Sharyl Attkisson, "No Debating Congress' Lavish Health Care: 24-Hour On-Site Care, No Coverage Limits; Congress Gets It All—But You Pay for It," CBS News, October 13, 2009. Online and available at http://cbsnews.com/stories/2009/10/13/cbsnews_investigates/main5382699.shtml.

77. Ibid.

78. "The Worst Bill Ever," *The Wall Street Journal*.

79. Shailagh Murray and Paul Kane, "Pelosi: House Won't Pass Senate Bill to Save Health-Care Reform," *The Washington Post*, January 22, 2010. Online and available at http://www.washingtonpost.com/wp-dyn/content/article/2010/01/21/AR2010012101604 .html.

80. Ronald Brownstein, "Pelosi Says Votes Are There for Reform," Health Care, *National Journal*, January 27, 2010. Online and available at http://healthtopic.national journal.com/2010/01/pelosi-says-votes-are-there-fo.php#088606.

81. Murray and Kane, "Pelosi: House Won't Pass Senate Bill to Save Health-Care Reform."

82. Bzdek, "Why Did Health-Care Reform Pass?"

83. Carolyn Lochhead, "Pelosi: Pole Vaults and Parachutes," Politics Blog, *San Francisco Chronicle*, January 28, 2010. Online and available at http://www.sfgate.com/ cgi-bin/blogs/nov05election/detail?entry_id=56238.

84. Jeffrey M. Jones, "In U.S., Majority Favors Suspending Work on Healthcare Bill," Gallup, January 22, 2010.

85. Lori Montgomery and Paul Kane, "House May Try to Pass Senate Health-Care Bill Without Voting on It," *The Washington Post*, March 16, 2010. Online and available at http:// www.washingtonpost.com/wp-dyn/content/article/2010/03/15/AR2010031503742.html.

86. David M. Herszenhorn and Robert Pear, "Democrats Consider New Moves for Health Bill," *The New York Times*, March 17, 2010.

87. Montgomery and Kane, "House May Try to Pass Senate Health-Care Bill Without Voting on It."

Chapter Eight: The Big Power Grab: Energy

1. "Pelosi: We Will Work Together to Tackle Global Warming, One of Humanity's Greatest Challenges," Office of Speaker Nancy Pelosi, February 8, 2007. Online and available at http://www.house.gov/pelosi/press/releases/Feb07/GlobalWarming.html.

2. Ibid.

3. "Pelosi Reveals Who's Who on Global Warming Panel," *The Washington Post*, March 12, 2007. Available and online at http://www.washingtonpost.com/wp-dyn/ content/article/2007/03/11/AR2007031101044.html.

4. "Pelosi: We Will Work Together."

5. Pelosi/Hearth, *Know Your Power*, 164.

6. "Pelosi on New Science Report: 'Global Warming Already Underway, but It Is Not Too Late to Slow It Down'," Office of Speaker Nancy Pelosi, April 6, 2007. Online and available at: http://www.speaker.gov/newsroom/pressreleases?id=0136.

7. Patrick O'Connor, "Waxman Dethrones Dingell as Chairman," Politico, November 20, 2008. Online and available at http://www.politico.com/news/stories/1108/15822.html.

8. "Pelosi Reveals Who's Who on Global Warming Panel," *The Washington Post*.

9. Rick Klein, "Markey Caught in Wrangling on Global Warming," *Boston Globe*, January 19, 2007. Online and available at http://www.boston.com/news/nation/washington/articles/2007/01/19/markey_caught_in_wrangling_on_global_warming/.

10. Dennis Behreandt, "Cutting Off Energy: With a Democrat-Controlled Congress, Measures Punishing 'Big Oil' and Fighting Global Warming Are Taking Center Stage, but It Is Middle-Class America That Will Lose in the End," *The New American*, March 5, 2007, Volume 23, Issue 5.

11. O'Connor, "Waxman Dethrones Dingell."

12. Werner, "New House Speaker Shows She's Boss."

13. Jenifer Joy Madden, "Greening the Capitol: The House (but Not the Senate) Cleans Up Its Act," *E*, May-June 2008, Volume 19, Issue 3.

14. Madden, "Greening the Capitol."

15. Chicago Climate Exchange, Overview. Online and available at http://www.chicagoclimatex.com.

16. James Valvo, "The Green Money Machine: Politicians, Philanthropists and Financiers Collude over 'Cap-and-Trade'," Foundation Watch, Capital Research Center, December 2009. Online and available at http://www.capitalresearch.org/pubs/pdf/v1259679999.pdf.

17. Madden, "Greening the Capitol."

18. Jordy Yager, "CAO to Push Pelosi's 'Greening' Plan," The Hill, January 10, 2010. Online and available at http://thehill.com/homenews/house/75103-cao-pushing-pelosis-greening-plan-in-house-through-the-year.

19. "Enabling a Green Workforce: Building a Culture of Sustainability in the House; A Progress Report," January 8, 2010. Online and available at http://cao.house.gov/GreenTheCapitol/static/media-lib/pdf/GreenOfficeReport-2009.pdf.

20. Zachary Coile, "Energy Bill Draft Splits House Dems: It's Pelosi Greens Against Industry Protectionists," *San Francisco Chronicle*, June 8, 2007.

21. David M. Herszenhorn, "Fuel Bill Shows House Speaker's Muscle," *The New York Times*, December 2, 2007. Online and available at http://www.nytimes.com/2007/12/02/washington/02energy.html?_r=1.

22. Ibid.

23. "Pelosi Co-sponsors Legislation to Stop Global Warming," Office of Congresswoman Nancy Pelosi, July 25, 2006. Online and available at http://www.house.gov/pelosi/press/releases/July06/GlobalWarming.html.

24. "Pelosi on New Science Report."

25. Fred Pearce, "Leaked Climate Change Emails Scientist 'Hid' Data Flaws," *Guardian*, February 1, 2010. Online and available at http://www.guardian.co.uk/environment/2010/feb/01/leaked-emails-climate-jones-chinese.

26. Behreandt, "Cutting off Energy."

27. Ian Talley, "Pelosi Investment Shows Unlikely Energy Alliance: Shares Purchased in Pickens Firm; Oil Man's New Role," *The Wall Street Journal*, August 23, 2008. Online and available at http://online.wsj.com/article/SB121944622079465097.html;

Mark Tapscott, "Pelosi Will Profit from Obama-Waxman-Markety Cap-and-Trade Energy Bill," *Washington Examiner*, June 24, 2009. Online and available at http://www.washingtonexaminer.com/opinion/blogs/beltway-confidential/Pelosi-will-profit-from-Obama-Waxman-Markety-cap-and-trade-energy-bill-49034421.html.

28. Rogers, "Pelosi: 'I'm Trying to Save the Planet'."

29. Bennett Roth, "House Approves Offshore Drilling Bill: But Skeptical Republicans Raise Objections," *Houston Chronicle*, September 16, 2008. Online and available at http://www.chron.com/disp/story.mpl/headline/biz/6006117.html.

30. Lindsay Renick Mayer, "Big Oil, Big Influence," *NOW* on PBS, August 1, 2008. Online and available at http://www.pbs.org/now/shows/347/oil-politics.html.

31. Carla Marinucci, "Pelosi Won't Limit Vote to Offshore Drilling: She Calls That Effort 'a Hoax,' Insists on Broad Energy Plan," *San Francisco Chronicle*, August 15, 2008. Online and available at http://articles.sfgate.com/2008-08-15/news/17121268_1_offshore-oil-drilling-america-s-daughters-house-speaker-nancy-pelosi.

32. Ibid.

33. Susan Page, "Pelosi Firm: No Vote on Offshore Drilling," *USA Today*, August 3, 2008. Online and available at http://www.usatoday.com/money/industries/energy/2008-08-03-offshore_N.htm.

34. Bennett Roth, "House Approves Offshore Drilling Bill: But Skeptical Republicans Raise Objections."

35. Max Schulz, "Nancy Pelosi's Drilling Smoke Screen," *New York Daily News*, August 20, 2008. Online and available at http://www.nydailynews.com/opinions/2008/08/21/2008-08-21_nancy_pelosis_drilling_smoke_screen.html.

36. Barbara Taylor, "Pelosi Cautiously Endorses Off-Shore Drilling Plan," KCBS, April 1, 2010. Online and available at http://www.kcbs.com/pages/6709118.php?contentType=4&contentId=5852413.

37. Christina Lovato, "Pelosi and Representatives Release Draft of Clean Energy Act," University of New Mexico/Talk Radio News Service, April 21, 2009. Online and available at http://talkradionews.com/2009/04/pelosi-and-representatives-release-draft-of-clean-energy-act.

38. Raymond Hernandez and Jim Rutenberg, "Under Scrutiny, Rangel Is Frayed but Defiant," *The New York Times*, November 23, 2009.

39. John M. Broder, "House Passes Bill to Address Threat of Climate Change," *The New York Times*, June 27, 2009.

40. Lisa Lerer and Patrick O'Connor, "House Passes Climate-Change Bill," Politico, June 25, 2009. Online and available at http://www.politico.com/news/stories/0609/24232.html.

41. Carolyn Lochhead, "Landmark Climate Bill Squeaks Through," *San Francisco Chronicle*, June 27, 2009. Online and available at http://articles.sfgate.com/2009-06-27/news/17210650_1_climate-change-house-democrats-tauscher/4.

42. Broder, "House Passes Bill to Address Threat of Climate Change."

43. Lerer and O'Connor, "House Passes Climate-Change Bill."

44. Ibid.

45. Audra Ang, "Pelosi Appeals for China's Help on Climate Change," The Associated Press, May 28, 2009.

46. Michael Wines, "In China, Pelosi Calls for Cooperation on Climate," *The New York Times*, May 28, 2009, A12.

47. Sharyl Attkisson, "Copenhagen Summit Turned Junket?" CBS News, January 11, 2010. Online and available at http://www.cbsnews.com/stories/2010/01/11/cbsnews_investigates/main6084364.shtml; Sharyl Attkisson, "Congress Went to Denmark, You

Got the Bill," CBS News, January 25, 2010. Online and available at http://www
.cbsnews.com/stories/2010/01/25/cbsnews_investigates/main6140406.shtml; "Rep. Johnson Seeks to End 'CODEL' Excesses," Office of Representative Timothy V. Johnson,
January 15, 2010. Online and available at http://timjohnson.house.gov/index.cfm
?sectionid=29&itemid=303.

48. Andrew Gilligan, "Copenhagen Climate Summit: 1,200 Limos, 140 Private
Planes and Caviar Wedges; Copenhagen Is Preparing for the Climate Change Summit
That Will Produce As Much Carbon Dioxide As a Town the Size of Middlesbrough,"
Telegraph, December 5, 2009. Online and available at http://www.telegraph.co.uk/earth/
copenhagen-climate-change-confe/6736517/Copenhagen-climate-summit-1200-limos-
140-private-planes-and-caviar-wedges.html.

49. Ibid.

50. Eric Zimmermann, "Pelosi: Climate Change Is a Women's Issue," Blog Briefing
Room, The Hill, December 17, 2009. Online and available at http://thehill.com/blogs/
blog-briefing-room/news/72777-pelosi-climate-change-is-a-womens-issue.

Chapter Nine: From Shoe Boxes to Corporate Stocks

1. "Text of Nancy Pelosi's Speech," *San Francisco Chronicle*, January 4, 2007.
Online and available at http://www.sfgate.com/cgi-bin/article.cgi?f=/c/a/2007/01/04/
BAG5ANCTQ27.DTL&type=politics.

2. Peter Eisler and Kathy Kiely, "Democrats: Identify Pork Sponsors," *USA
Today*, November 13, 2006. Online and available at http://www.usatoday.com/news/
washington/2006-11-12-dems-pork-sponsors_x.htm.

3. "Community Funding Requests," Office of Speaker Nancy Pelosi. Online and
available at http://www.house.gov/pelosi/CommunityFundingRequests/.

4. "Judicial Watch Announces List of Washington's 'Ten Most Wanted Corrupt
Politicians' for 2007," Judicial Watch, December 19, 2007. Online and available at http://
www.judicialwatch.org/judicial-watch-announces-list-washington-s-ten-most-wanted-
corrupt-politicians-2007.

5. "H. R. 1495." Online and available at http://frwebgate.access.gpo.gov/cgi-bin/
getdoc.cgi?dbname=110_cong_bills&docid=f:h1495enr.txt.pdf; Geoff Earle, "Her San
Fran Treat; Pelosi Water-Bill Bid Drawing Fire," *New York Post*, May 8, 2007. Online
and available at http://www.nypost.com/p/news/national/item_aZrREwNpXN5Tlp20f
EatXP;jsessionid=97E942367FA93347FF1DB5B3BA7DAF9E.

6. Erica Werner, "GOP Criticizes Pelosi's Water Project," *The Washington
Post*, May 7, 2007. Online and available at http://www.washingtonpost.com/wp-dyn/
content/article/2007/05/07/AR2007050701152.html.

7. "Judicial Watch Announces List . . . for 2007"; "Judicial Watch Announces List of
Washington's 'Ten Most Wanted Corrupt Politicians' for 2008," Judicial Watch, December 31, 2008. Online and available at http://www.judicialwatch.org/news/2008/dec/
judicial-watch-announces-list-washingtons-ten-most-wanted-corrupt-politicians-2008;
"Judicial Watch Announces List of Washington's 'Ten Most Wanted Corrupt Politicians' for 2009," Judicial Watch. Online and available at http://www.judicialwatch.org/
news/2009/dec/judicial-watch-announces-list-washingtons-ten-most-wanted-corrupt-
politicians-2009.

8. "Water Resources Development Act Authorization Requests," Office of
Speaker Nancy Pelosi, December 3, 2009. Online and available at http://www.house
.gov/pelosi/WaterResources/WaterResourcesRequest2009.html.

9. Jonathan Weisman, "In Backing Murtha, Pelosi Draws Fire; Her Ethics Vow Is Questioned," *The Washington Post*, November 14, 2006. Online and available at http:// www.washingtonpost.com/wp-dyn/content/article/2006/11/13/AR2006111300722 .html.

10. Weisman and Lois Romano, "Pelosi Splits Democrats with Push for Murtha; Speaker-to-Be Accused of Strong-Arm Tactics," *The Washington Post*, November 16, 2006. Online and available at http://www.washingtonpost.com/wp-dyn/ content/article/2006/11/15/AR2006111501521.html.

11. Jonathan Weisman, "In Backing Murtha, Pelosi Draws Fire."

12. Jim Acosta and Janet Rodriguez, "Remote Murtha Airport Lands Big Bucks from Washington," CNNPolitics.com, April 23, 2009. Online and available at http:// www.cnn.com/2009/POLITICS/04/23/murtha.airport/index.html.

13. Weisman, "In Backing Murtha, Pelosi Draws Fire."

14. "Rep. John P. Murtha (D-PA)," Crew's Most Corrupt. Online and available at http://www.crewsmostcorrupt.org/summaries/murtha.php.

15. Weisman, "In Backing Murtha, Pelosi Draws Fire."

16. Ibid.

17. Sandalow, *Madam Speaker*, 120.

18. Coile, "Pelosi Seeks Input."

19. Povich, *Nancy Pelosi*, 51.

20. "San Francisco Leaders Announce Hunters Point Naval Shipyard Agreement," Office of U.S. Senator Dianne Feinstein, March 31, 2004. Online and available at http:// feinstein.senate.gov/04Releases/r-hunters.html.

21. Ahimsa Porter Sumchai, M.D., "Singing in the Rain: Hunters Point Shipyard Enriches SF's Most Powerful Families; a Chronology of Legal, Ethical and Regulatory Oversight Violations Involving the Transfer and Development of Parcel A of the Hunters Point Shipyard with Investigatory Follow Up 2002-2009," *San Francisco BayView*, April 5, 2009. Online and available at http://www.sfbayview.com/2009/singing-in-the-rain-hunters-point-shipyard-enriches-sf%E2%80%99s-most-powerful-families/.

22. Weisman, "In Backing Murtha, Pelosi Draws Fire."

23. Paul Singer and Tory Newmyer, "Feds Treading Close to Murtha; Ties to PMA Provoke Scrutiny," *Roll Call*, February 11, 2009. Online and available at http://www .rollcall.com/issues/54_87/news/32276-1.html; "Rep. John P. Murtha (D-PA)," Crew's Most Corrupt.

24. "Editorial: Old-School Corruption; House Democrats' Ethics Problem," *Washington Times*, November 2, 2009. Online and available at http://washingtontimes.com/ news/2009/nov/02/old-school-corruption/?feat=home_editorials; Weisman, "In Backing Murtha, Pelosi Draws Fire."

25. "Rep. John P. Murtha (D-PA)," Crew's Most Corrupt.

26. Singer and Newmyer, "Feds Treading Close to Murtha."

27. Brody Mullins, "House Ethics Office Ends Probe of Murtha, 2 Others," *The Wall Street Journal*. Blogs, December 18, 2009. Online and available at http://blogs.wsj .com/washwire/2009/12/18/house-ethics-office-ends-probe-of-murtha-2-others/.

28. "Judicial Watch Announces List . . . for 2008."

29. David Kocieniewski, "Rangel Failed to Disclose More Income on Assets, Form Shows," *The New York Times;* August 29, 2009.

30. "Judicial Watch Announces List . . . for 2008."

31. Kocieniewski, "Rangel Failed to Disclose $500,000 in Assets for '07."

32. Coile, "Pelosi Seeks Input."

33. Carl Hulse, "Focus on Rangel, a Chairman Under Investigation," *The New York Times*, October 3, 2009; "Rangel Steps Down as Top Tax Writer," Reuters, March 3, 2010. Online and available at http://www.reuters.com/article/idUSTRE6220KT20100303.

34. "Text of Nancy Pelosi's Speech."

35. "Pelosi PAC Fined $21,000 by Federal Elections Officials," *USA Today*, February 11, 2004. Online and available at http://www.usatoday.com/news/politicselections/state/california/2004-02-11-pelosi-pac-fined_x.htm.

36. Mike Soraghan, "Pelosi Buys $16K Worth of Flowers," The Hill, December 12, 2007. Online and available at http://thehill.com/homenews/new/13877-pelosi-buys-16k-worth-of-flowers; Jake Sherman and Meredith Shiner, "Nancy Pelosi Spends $2,993 on Flowers," Politico, December 1, 2009. Online and available at http://www.politico.com/news/stories/1109/30013.html.

37. "Pelosi Defends Request for Jet," *Washington Times*, February 8, 2007. Online and available at http://www.washingtontimes.com/news/2007/feb/08/20070208-115704-7410r; "Pelosi's Push for Jet Remains Up in Air," Washington Times, February 7, 2007. Online and available at http://www.washingtontimes.com/news/2007/feb/07/20070207-123706-5963r.

38. "Judicial Watch Uncovers Documents Detailing Pelosi's Repeated Requests for Military Travel; House Speaker Issued Unprecedented Demands for Military Aircraft and Wasted Taxpayer Resources with Last Minute Cancellations," Judicial Watch, March 10, 2009. Online and available at http://www.judicialwatch.org/news/2009/mar/judicial-watch-uncovers-documents-detailing-pelosis-repeated-requests-military-travel.

39. "Pelosi's Push for Jet Remains Up in Air," *Washington Times*.

40. "Pelosi Defends Request for Jet," *Washington Times*.

41. "Pelosi's Push for Jet Remains Up in Air," *Washington Times*; "Pelosi Defends Request for Jet," *Washington Times*.

42. "Pelosi Airliner Tempting Target for Miffed GOP," *Washington Times*, February 10, 2007. Online and available at http://www.washingtontimes.com/news/2007/feb/10/20070210-120724-4310r/; "Pelosi Defends Request for Jet," *Washington Times*.

43. "Pelosi Defends Request for Jet," *Washington Times*.

44. Michelle Malkin, "Malkin: Fly As I Say, Not As I Fly; Pelosi Hypocrisy over Business Executive Perks, Military," *Washington Times*, March 14, 2009. Online and available at http://www.washingtontimes.com/news/2009/mar/14/fly-as-i-say-not-as-i-fly/.

45. "Judicial Watch Uncovers New Documents Detailing Pelosi's Use of Air Force Aircraft; House Speaker's Military Travel Cost the United States Air Force $2,100,744.59 over a Two-Year Period, Including $101,429 for In-Flight Expenses," Judicial Watch, January 28, 2010. Online and available at http://www.judicialwatch.org/news/2010/jan/judicial-watch-uncovers-new-documents-detailing-pelosis-use-air-force-aircraft.

46. "Judicial Watch Uncovers Documents Detailing Pelosi's Repeated Requests for Military Travel"; Malkin, "Malkin: Fly As I Say, Not As I Fly."

47. Information from http://opensecrets.org.

48. Information from http://opensecrets.org.

49. Jim Puzzanghera, "Pelosi Likely to Speak Up for Tech Industry," *Los Angeles Times*, November 13, 2006. Online and available at http://articles.latimes.com/2006/nov/13/business/fi-pelosi13; Zachary Coile, "Pelosi Seeks Input from Diverse Array of Confidants."

50. Information from http://www.opensecrets.org.

51. "Cisco Announces Carbon Reduction Initiatives," September 21, 2006. Online and available at http://newsroom.cisco.com/dlls/2006/ts_092106.html; Stephen Lawson

and PC World, "Cisco Tries to Turn Cities Green; Cisco and the City of San Francisco Host Connected Urban Development Global Conference to Focus on Climate Change," *The Washington Post*, February 21, 2008. Online and available at http://www.washingtonpost.com/wp-dyn/content/article/2008/02/21/AR2008022101486_pf.html.

52. "About Connected Urban Development." Online and available at http://www.cisco.com/web/about/ac79/ps/cud/about.html.

53. "Cisco Announces Carbon Reduction Initiatives."

54. Lawson, "Cisco Tries to Turn Cities Green"; Michael Cabanatuan, "Muni's 'Connected Bus' Is About to Go Online; Muni Cisco team on 'Connected Bus' with Wi-Fi and Touch-Screen Maps," *San Francisco Chronicle*, February 21, 2008. Online and available at http://articles.sfgate.com/2008-02-21/bay-area/17141977_1_bus-fleet-connected-information-on-arrival-times.

55. Lawson, "Cisco Tries to Turn Cities Green."

56. Peter Albert, Kylie Grenier, and San Francisco Municipal Transportation Agency, "The Connected Bus Project; a Partnership of Cisco and the City and County of San Francisco." Online and available at http://www.connectedurbandevelopment.org/pdf/toolkit/cud_connected_bus_project_plan_feb_08.pdf.

57. "Pelosi Announces Department of Transportation Funding for MUNI Bus Rehabilitation," Office of Speaker Nancy Pelosi, August 22, 2008. Online and available at http://www.house.gov/pelosi/press/releases/Aug08/bus.html; and Information from http://www.legistorm.com.

58. Albert, Grenier, and San Francisco Municipal Transportation Agency, "The Connected Bus Project."

59. Information from opensecrets.org.

60. "Environment Commission." Online and available at http://www.sfenvironment.org/our_policies/overview.html?ssi=10.

61. Lawson, "Cisco Tries to Turn Cities Green."

62. Sumchai, "Singing in the Rain."

63. Povich, *Nancy Pelosi*, 49–50; Sandalow, *Madam Speaker*, 134.

64. Povich, *Nancy Pelosi*, 50.

65. Sandalow, *Madam Speaker*, 134.

66. Povich, *Nancy Pelosi*, 50.

67. Ibid., 51.

68. Sandalow, *Madam Speaker*, 135.

69. Sandalow, *Madam Speaker*, 134; Pelosi/Hearth, *Know Your Power*, 110; Povich, *Nancy Pelosi*, 50.

70. Povich, *Nancy Pelosi*, 51–52; Sandalow, *Madam Speaker*, 135–36.

71. Pelosi/Hearth, *Know Your Power*, 110–11.

72. Alex Barnum, "Page One—Sweeping Vision for Presidio's Future; New Plan Would Create Self-Sufficient Mini-City," *San Francisco Chronicle*, April 28, 1998. Online and available at http://www.sfgate.com/cgi-bin/article.cgi?f=/c/a/1998/04/28/MN54868.DTL; Pelosi/Hearth, *Know Your Power*, 111.

73. Povich, *Nancy Pelosi*, 52.

74. Pelosi/Hearth, *Know Your Power*, 111.

75. Matt Smith, "The Pork Park: House Speaker Nancy Pelosi Is Quietly Trying to Keep the Presidio on the Public Teat. That's a Good Thing," *San Francisco Weekly*, July 23, 2008. Online and available at http://www.sfweekly.com/content/printVersion/1095403.

76. Sandalow, *Madam Speaker*, 135–38.

77. Peter Schweizer, *Do As I Say (Not As I Do): Profiles in Liberal Hypocrisy* (New York: Doubleday, 2005), 146.

78. Barnum, "Page One—Sweeping Vision for Presidio's Future."

79. Glen Martin, "Under Gun, Presidio Chief Quits/Misspending Has Long Been Alleged," *San Francisco Chronicle*, December 11, 2001. Online and available at http://articles. sfgate.com/2001-12-11/news/17629813_1_presidio-trust-toby-rosenblatt-historic-site.

80. Schweizer, *Do As I Say (Not As I Do)*, 146–47; Barnum, "Page One—Sweeping Vision for Presidio's Future."

81. Edward Epstein, "Presidio Trust Bill to Be Signed Today; Challenge Is to Make Park Pay for Itself," *San Francisco Chronicle*, November 12, 1996. Online and available at http://www.sfgate.com/cgi-bin/article.cgi?f=/c/a/1996/11/12/MN71560.DTL.

82. Sumchai, "Singing in the Rain."

83. "Pelosi, Newsom and Navy Complete First Major Transfer of Hunters Point Shipyard to San Francisco." Online and available at http://www.house.gov/pelosi/press/ releases/Jan05/HuntersPoint011205.html.

84. Dan Levy, "Anchors Aweigh/1,600 Homes, Parks, Shops Get Go-Ahead at Old Navy Yard," *San Francisco Chronicle*, November 21, 2004. Available at http://articles.sfgate .com/2004-11-21/real-estate/17453711_1_lennar-corp-hunters-point-naval-shipyard-home-construction.

85. Information from http://www.legistorm.com.

86. Sumchai, "Singing in the Rain."

87. "San Francisco Leaders Announce Hunters Point Naval Shipyard Agreement."

88. Sumchai, "Singing in the Rain."

89. Ibid.

90. "Pelosi, Newsom and Navy Complete."

91. "San Francisco Leaders Announce Hunters Point Naval Shipyard Agreement"; Sumchai, "Singing in the Rain."

92. Sumchai, "Singing in the Rain"; Sarah Phelan, "The Corporation That Ate San Francisco: Lennar's Failures at Hunters Point Shipyard Highlight the Risk of Putting the Bay Area's Prime Real Estate into the Hands of Profit-Driven Developers," *San Francisco Bay Guardian*, March 13, 2007. Online and available at http://www.sfbg .com/2007/03/14/corporation-ate-san-francisco.

93. "About Lennar." Online and available at http://www.lennar.com/about/about .aspx.

94. Phelan, "The Corporation That Ate San Francisco."

95. Sumchai, "Singing in the Rain."

96. Lance Williams and Robert Selna, "Developer Sued Over Hunters Point Toxics: Executives Say Their Firm Retaliated Against Them for Questioning Construction Dust," *San Francisco Chronicle*, March 18, 2007. Online and available at http://www .sfgate.com/cgi-bin/article.cgi?f=/c/a/2007/03/18/BAGGKOMQE129.DTL; Sumchai, "Singing in the Rain."

97. John Coté, "EPA Report: Shipyard Project Minimizing Dust," *San Francisco Chronicle*, January 5, 2010. Online and available at http://www.sfgate.com/cgi-bin/article .cgi?f=/c/a/2010/01/05/MNS91BDFIJ.DTL.

98. Sumchai, "Singing in the Rain."

99. Leslie Fulbright, "Black Population Deserting S.F., Study Says," *San Francisco Chronicle*, August 10, 2008. Online and available at http://www.sfgate.com/cgi-bin/ article.cgi?f=/c/a/2008/08/09/BA5B1272U1.DTL&tsp=1.

100. John Coté, "EPA Report: Shipyard Project Minimizing Dust."

101. Williams and Selna, "Developer Sued Over Hunters Point Toxics."

102. John Han, "Community Leaders Organize to Address Asbestos Exposure; Pelosi Called on to Intervene," FogCityJournal.com, July 19, 2007. Online and available

at http://www.fogcityjournal.com/news_in_brief/jh_asbestos_health_complaints_070719
.shtml; Phelan, "The Corporation That Ate San Francisco."

103. Coté, "EPA report: Shipyard project minimizing dust."

Chapter Ten: Holy Nancy

1. Representative Nancy Pelosi as quoted in "Nancy Pelosi Becomes First Female House Speaker," PBS transcript, originally aired January 2, 2007.

2. Michael Lerner, *The Left Hand of God: Taking Back Our Country from the Religious Right* (San Francisco: HarperSanFrancisco, 2006), 127–28.

3. Maureen Dowd, "The Red Zone," *The New York Times*, November 4, 2004. Online and available at http://www.nytimes.com/2004/11/04/opinion/04dowd.html.

4. Robert B. Reich, "The Last Word: Bush's God," *The American Prospect*, June 17, 2004. Online and available at http://www.prospect.org/cs/articles?articleId=7858.

5. Representative Nancy Pelosi as quoted in "Nancy Pelosi Becomes First Female House Speaker," PBS transcript, originally aired January 2, 2007.

6. Sally Hambrecht as quoted in "Nancy Pelosi Becomes First Female House Speaker," PBS transcript, originally aired January 2, 2007.

7. "The Gospel in a Catholic's Political Life," interview with Rep. Nancy Pelosi, *National Catholic Reporter*, January 24, 2003. Online and available at http://www.natcath
.com/NCR_Online/archives/012403/012403d.htm.

8. Eleanor Clift, "The Target: Nancy Pelosi Doesn't Care If You Like Her. All That Matters Is Getting the Job Done." Interview with Nancy Pelosi, *Newsweek*, December 21, 2009. Online and available at http://www.newsweek.com/id/227756.

9. Paul Virgo and Kevin Eckstrom, "Pope Gives Pelosi a Stern Reprimand," *Christianity Today*, February 18, 2009. Online and available at http://blog.christianitytoday
.com/ctpolitics/2009/02/pope_gives_pelo.html.

10. Ibid.

11. Ibid.

12. Ibid.

13. "The Gospel in a Catholic's Political Life."

14. Ibid.

15. "Pelosi's Archbishop Slams Her Rationale for Supporting Abortion," *Catholic News Agency*, January 13, 2010. Online and available at: http://www.catholicnewsagency
.com/news/pelosis_archbishop_slams_her_rationale_for_supporting_abortion/.

16. Clift, "The Target."

17. "The Gospel in a Catholic's Political Life."

18. Ibid.

19. Pelosi/Hearth, *Know Your Power*, 127–28.

20. Bzdek, *Woman of the House*, 52.

21. Jonah Goldberg, "Cell Mates in Full Backpedal; The Truth Emerges," National Review Online, November 30, 2007. Online and available at http://article.nationalreview
.com/print/?q=YjNkNzNlYzhmZGQzZmY5ZDdkNGUyMWNkNDg4MGU1YmQ=.

22. Hooper and the Associated Press, "Hoyer Wins House Majority Leader Race."

23. Bzdek, *Woman of the House*, 50–51.

24. Stanley Greenberg, *The Two Americas: Our Current Political Deadlock and How to Break It* (New York: Thomas Dunne Books, 2004), 98.

25. "The Gospel in a Catholic's Political Life."

26. Bzdek, *Woman of the House*, 55.

27. Clift, "The Target."
28. "The Gospel in a Catholic's Political Life."
29. "Catholic Democrats Assail Some Bishops," *The Christian Century*, June 15, 2004, Volume 121, Issue 12.
30. "The Gospel in a Catholic's Political Life."
31. Bzdek, *Woman of the House*, 18.

Chapter Eleven: Pelosi's Planet

1. "Pelosi Leads Congressional Delegation to Italy," Office of Speaker Nancy Pelosi, February 13, 2009. Online and available at http://speaker.gov/newsroom/pressreleases?id=1010; "Pelosi Remarks Before Meeting with Gianfranco Fini, President of the Italian Chamber of Deputies," Office of Speaker Nancy Pelosi, February 4, 2010. Online and available at http://www.speaker.gov/newsroom/pressreleases?id=1531.

2. Susan Cornwell, "Pelosi's Judgment Questioned over Armenia Issue," Reuters, October 21, 2007. Online and available at http://www.reuters.com/article/idUSN1932584620071021.

3. "Nancy Pelosi on Immigration; Democratic Representative (CA-8)," OnTheIssues, January 26, 2010. Online and available at http://www.ontheissues.org/CA/Nancy_Pelosi_Immigration.htm; "California House; Nancy Pelosi (Democrat, district 8) On the Issues," OnTheIssues. Online and available at http://www.ontheissues.org/CA/Nancy_Pelosi.htm#Immigration.

4. Kelly Zito, "Pelosi: End Raids Splitting Immigrant Families," *San Francisco Chronicle*, March 8, 2009. Online and available at http://articles.sfgate.com/2009-03-08/bay-area/17211696_1_nation-s-immigration-policies-immigration-reform-families.

5. "Nancy Pelosi on Immigration"; "California House; Nancy Pelosi."

6. "Pelosi: Un-American to Enforce Immigration Laws," Corruption Chronicles: A Judicial Watch Blog, March 19, 2009. Online and available at http://www.judicialwatch.org/blog/2009/mar/pelosi-enforcing-immigration-laws-un-american; William Lajeunesse, "Pelosi Tells Illegal Immigrants That Work Site Raids Are Un-American," FOXNews.com, March 18, 2009. Online and available at http://www.foxnews.com/politics/2009/03/18/pelosi-tells-illegal-immigrants-work-site-raids-american/; Zito, "Pelosi: End Raids Splitting Immigrant Families."

7. "U.S. Rep. King: Pelosi Believes Immigration Laws are 'Un-American,'" IowaPolitics.com, March 18, 2009. Online and available at http://www.iowapolitics.com/index.iml?Article=152557.

8. "U.S. House, California—8th District," *CQ Politics*. Online and available at http://www.cqpolitics.com/wmspage.cfm?docID=district-CA-08.

9. Peter Schweizer, *Do As I Say (Not As I Do)*, 148, 150, 151; information from http://www.opensecrets.org.

10. Lee Romney, "Chinese Americans Emerge as a Political Power in S.F.," *Los Angeles Times*, February 1, 2004. Online and available at http://www.latinamericanstudies.org/immigration/chinese-vote.htm.

11. "Nancy Pelosi's Record," *Washington Times*, November 18, 2002.

12. Wendy Koch and Judy Holland, "Lifelong Rights Activist Turns Guns on China: Rep. Nancy Pelosi Has Been Keeping Up the Pressure on Presidents Jiang and Clinton," *Examiner*, November 2, 1997. Online and available at http://www.sfgate.com/cgi-bin/article.cgi?f=/e/a/1997/11/02/NEWS8477.dtl.

13. Povich, *Nancy Pelosi*, 57.

14. Anthony Kuhn, "Tiananmen Mothers Press for Answers, 20 Years On," NPR, June 4, 2009. Online and available at http://www.npr.org/templates/story/story.php? storyId=104939670.

15. Randeep Ramesh, Julian Borger, Angelique Chrisafis, Graham Keeley, Elana Schor and John Hooper, "Pelosi Urges World to Condemn China Over Crackdown: US Speaker Stops Short of Olympic Boycott Call but Pressure Grows for Leaders to Stay Away from Opening Ceremony," *The Guardian*, March 22, 2008. Online and available at http://www.guardian.co.uk/world/2008/mar/22/tibet.china1; Carl Hulse, "Pelosi Suggests Bush Boycott Olympic Opening," *The New York Times*, April 2, 2008. Online and available at http://www.nytimes.com/2008/04/02/world/americas/02iht-boycott.1.11614705.html?_r=1.

16. Koch and Holland, "Lifelong Rights Activist Turns Guns on China."

17. "US Speaker Urges China to Free Political Prisoners," AFP, June 2, 2009. Online and available at http://www.google.com/hostednews/afp/article/ALeqM5hjk_oi1VmKp0_73GkjUX1WTqH9lA.

18. Tim Johnson, "An Angry China Is Lashing Out at Its Foreign Critics," McClatchy Newspapers, April 15, 2008. Online and available at http://www.mcclatchydc.com/2008/04/15/33723/an-angry-china-is-lashing-out.html.

19. Koch and Holland, "Lifelong Rights Activist Turns Guns on China."

20. Jim Lobe, "Radio, TV Martí Seen as Bust," IPS, May 4, 2010. Online and available at http://www.ipsnews.net/news.asp?idnews=51314.

21. "Nancy Pelosi's Record," *Washington Times*; "A Look at Pelosi's Voting Record," *Washington Times*, November 2, 2006. Online and available at http://www.washingtontimes.com/news/2006/nov/02/20061102-090358-9812r/.

22. "Pelosi Douses Hopes for Quick End to Cuba Travel Ban," AFP, November 19, 2009. Online and available at http://www.google.com/hostednews/afp/article/ALeqM5il-LOZAAqG3c-CGsF1iKLbZCv_yw.

23. "Nancy Pelosi's Record," *Washington Times*; "Nancy Pelosi on Foreign Policy; Democratic Representative (CA-8)," OnTheIssues, January 26, 2010. Online and available at http://www.ontheissues.org/CA/Nancy_Pelosi_Foreign_Policy.htm; Toni Marshall, "Critics of Beijing Call Normal Trade No Help on Rights," *Washington Times*, June 9, 1999.

24. Sandalow, *Madam Speaker*, 29.

25. David Stout and Hassan M. Fattah, "Bush Assails Pelosi's Trip to Syria," *The New York Times*, April 3, 2007. Online and available at http://www.nytimes.com/2007/04/03/world/americas/03iht-pelosi.4.5130701.html?_r=1; Susan Cornwell, "Cheney Accuses Pelosi of 'Bad Behavior' in Syria," Reuters, April 5, 2007. Online and available at http://www.reuters.com/article/idUSN0522207920070406.

26. Elizabeth Williamson, "Speaker's Role in Foreign Policy Is a Recent, and Sensitive, Issue," *The Washington Post*, April 5, 2007. Online and available at http://www.washingtonpost.com/wp-dyn/content/article/2007/04/04/AR2007040402752.html.

27. Stout and Fattah, "Bush Assails Pelosi's Trip to Syria."

28. Cornwell, "Cheney Accuses Pelosi of 'Bad Behavior' in Syria,"

29. Farid Ghadry, "Assad's Useful Idiot; Pelosi's Visit Had 'Hanoi Jane' Quality," *Washington Times*, April 13, 2007.

30. Sandalow, *Madam Speaker*, 230.

31. Bzdek, *Woman of the House*, 207; Paul Kane, "Top Pelosi Aide Learned of Waterboarding in 2003," *The Washington Post*, May 9, 2009. Online and available at http://

www.washingtonpost.com/wp-dyn/content/article/2009/05/08/AR2009050803967.html.

32. "Justice Department Memos on Interrogation Techniques," *The New York Times*. Online and available at http://documents.nytimes.com/justice-department-memos-on-interrogation-techniques#p=85.

33. Kane, "Top Pelosi Aide Learned of Waterboarding in 2003." Carl Hulse, "Pelosi Says She Knew of Waterboarding by 2003," *The New York Times*, May 14, 2009. Online and available at http://www.nytimes.com/2009/05/15/us/politics/15cong.html; Joby Warrick and Dan Eggen, "Hill Briefed on Waterboarding in 2002; In Meetings, Spy Panels' Chiefs Did Not Protest, Officials Say," *The Washington Post*, December 9, 2007. Online and available at http://www.washingtonpost.com/wp-dyn/content/article/2007/12/08/AR2007120801664.html; "Pelosi News Conference on Waterboarding Disclosure," CQ Transcriptwire, *The Washington Post*, May 14, 2009. Online and available at http://www.washingtonpost.com/wp-dyn/content/article/2009/05/14/AR2009051402100.html.

34. Kane, "Top Pelosi Aide Learned of Waterboarding in 2003."

35. Pamela Hess, "House Dems Seek Deal on Intelligence Briefings," *San Francisco Chronicle*, July 10, 2009. Online and available at http://articles.sfgate.com/2009-07-10/news/17216626_1_cia-director-leon-panetta-interrogation-program-white-housez.

36. Hulse, "Pelosi Says She Knew of Waterboarding by 2003."

37. Dan Gifford, "Tommy and Nancy: Like Father, Like Daughter?" *BigHollywood*, May 26, 2009. Online and available at http://bighollywood.breitbart.com/dgifford/2009/05/26/like-father-like-daughter/.

38. "Pelosi Shrugs Off Alcatraz as Possible Terror Detention Facility," FOX News.com, January 25, 2009. Online and available at http://www.foxnews.com/politics/2009/01/25/pelosi-shrugs-alcatraz-possible-terror-detention-facility/.

39. "Pelosi Shrugs Off Alcatraz as Possible Terror Detention Facility" Sam Stein, "GOP Officials Push Alcatraz as the New Guantanamo," Huffington Post, January 25, 2009. Online and available at http://www.huffingtonpost.com/2009/01/25/gop-officials-push-alcatr_n_160675.html.

40. "Pelosi Shrugs Off Alcatraz As Possible Terror Detention Facility."

Chapter Twelve: Incivility and Hypocrisy Unleashed

1. Sandalow and McCormick, "Pelosi's Goal: Democrats Back on Top."

2. Juliet Eilperin, "Nancy Pelosi Set to Be First Female Speaker: Democrats' Majority Puts Her at Helm in January," *The Washington Post*, November 8, 2006. Online and available at http://www.washingtonpost.com/wp-dyn/content/article/2006/11/07/AR2006110701726.html.

3. Schorn, "Nancy Pelosi: Two Heartbeats Away."

4. Sandalow, *Madam Speaker*, 26.

5. Bzdek, *Woman of the House*, 28.

6. Michael Olesker, "She Was a Power, a Democrat, and She Was Loyal," *Baltimore Sun*, April 9, 1995.

7. Pelosi/Hearth, *Know Your Power*, 21.

8. Marc Sandalow, "Pelosi to Be Put to Test: The Vocal and Adamant Democrat Must Now Lead the Two-Party House in Passing Legislation," *San Francisco Chronicle*, January 2, 2007. Online and available at http://www.sfgate.com/cgi-bin/article.cgi?f=/c/a/2007/01/02/MNG8QNBFOD1.DTL.

9. Sandalow, *Madam Speaker*, 238.

10. Ibid., 237–39.

11. Ibid., 234.

12. Ibid., 238.

13. Schorn, "Nancy Pelosi: Two Heartbeats Away."

14. Pelosi/Hearth, *Know Your Power*, 150.

15. Marc Sandalow, "Can Pelosi and Bush Get Along? They Will Need Each Other's Help If Dems Win House, Analysts Say," *San Francisco Chronicle*, October 16, 2006. Online and available at http://www.sfgate.com/cgi-bin/article.cgi?f=/c/a/2006/10/16/MNG7FLQ5OR1.DTL.

16. Zachary Coile, "Pelosi, Bush Make Nice Over White House Lunch/President and Future Speaker of House, Longtime Foes, Say They'll Work Together," *San Francisco Chronicle*, November 10, 2006. Online and available at http://articles.sfgate.com/2006-11-10/news/17319094_1_white-house-democratic-whip-steny-hoyer-senate-democratic-leaders.

17. Sandalow, "Can Pelosi and Bush Get Along?"

18. Sandalow, *Madam Speaker*, 286.

19. "President Bush Delivers State of the Union Address," White House Archives. Online and available at http://georgewbush-whitehouse.archives.gov/news/releases/2007/01/20070123-2.html.

20. Pelosi and Hearth, *Know Your Power*, 156–57.

21. Ibid., 148.

22. Seth Colter Walls, "Pelosi Hammers Palin, Compares Her to Bush," Huffington Post, September 16, 2008. Online and available at http://www.huffingtonpost.com/2008/09/16/pelosi-hammers-palin-comp_n_126896.html.

23. John Bresnahan, "Rangel Ruling Puts Pelosi in a Jam," Politico, February 25, 2010. Online and available at http://www.politico.com/news/stories/0210/33564.html.

24. "Rangel Refuses to Step Aside After Ethics Report: Report Says Aides Tried to Show Him Trips Violated Congressional Gift Rules," MSNBC, February 26, 2010. Online and available at http://www.msnbc.msn.com/id/35602415/ns/politics-capitol_hill/.

25. "Pelosi: Matter of Making a Decision," NECN, September 27, 2008. Online and available at http://www.necn.com/Boston/Politics/Pelosi-matter-of-making-a-decision/1222556313.html.

26. "Pelosi: 'America's National Security Is Seriously Jeopardized by This Republican Budget'," Office of Congresswoman Nancy Pelosi, May 18, 2006. Online and available at http://www.house.gov/pelosi/press/releases/May06/budgetsecurity.html.

27. Nancy Pelosi and Steny Hoyer, "'Un-American' Attacks Can't Derail Health Care Debate," USA Today Blogs, August 10, 2009. Online and available at http://blogs.usatoday.com/oped/2009/08/unamerican-attacks-cant-derail-health-care-debate-.html.

28. Pelosi/Hearth, *Know Your Power*, 133–34.

29. Russert, "Pelosi Gets Emotional."

30. Jacobs, *A Rage for Justice*, 403–5.

31. Erin McCormick, "San Francisco: Anti-War Activists Take Pelosi to Task: Minority Leader Negotiates with Lawmakers to Her Right," *San Francisco Chronicle*, January 15, 2006. Online and available at http://www.sfgate.com/cgi-bin/article.cgi?f=/c/a/2006/01/15/PELOSI.TMP.

32. Nikki Schwab and U.S. News & World Report, "Antiwar Liberals Heckle House Speaker Pelosi," CBS News Politics, June 22, 2007. Online and available at http://www.cbsnews.com/stories/2007/06/22/usnews/whispers/main2969866.shtml.

33. Pelosi and Hearth, *Know Your Power*, 9.

34. Ibid., 164.

35. "Keith Ellison: 9-11 Was a Setup," YouTube.com. Online and available at http://www.youtube.com/watch?v=fsjw_51Lfw4.

36. Audrey Hudson, "Pelosi Urged to Reprimand Ellison; Speech Compared Bush's 9/11 Reaction to Hitler's after Reichstag," *Washington Times*, July 19, 2007.

37. Michael Andersen, "Fearing 'Ambush' from Foes, Baird Opts for 'Telephone Town Halls'," *The Columbian*, TDN.com, August 6, 2009. Online and available at http://www.tdn.com/news/article_ad1f434e-3aef-5c67-9d28-4b6e3d619043.html.

38. Peter Slevin, "Key Democrat Feels the Heat After Voting for House Plan," *The Washington Post*, August 10, 2009.

39. The Ed Show, "Interview with Rep. John Dingell," Real Clear Politics, August 10, 2009. Online and available at http://www.realclearpolitics.com/articles/2009/08/10/interview_with_rep_john_dingell_97849.html.

40. Glenn Thrush, "Pete Stark Won't Pee on Your Leg," Politico, September 15, 2009. Online and available at http://www.politico.com/blogs/glennthrush/0909/Pete_Stark_wont_pee_on_your_leg.html.

41. Zachary Coile, "Pelosi Backs Away from Rep. Stark's Criticism of Bush: He Denounces Bush for Funding War but Not Kids' Health Care," *San Francisco Chronicle*, October 20, 2007. Online and available at http://articles.sfgate.com/2007-10-20/news/17267055_1_war-or-children-health-bill-children-s-health.

42. Patricia Murphy, "Nancy Pelosi: No Apology Needed for Grayson's 'Die Quickly' Floor Speech," Politics Daily, October 1, 2009. Online and available at http://www.politicsdaily.com/2009/10/01/nancy-pelosi-no-apology-needed-for-graysons-die-quickly-floor.

43. Sandalow, "Can Pelosi and Bush Get Along?"

44. Russert, "Pelosi Gets Emotional."

45. Grigoriadis, "Why Is Nancy Pelosi Always Smiling?"

Epilogue

1. Jones, "Woman on Top."

2. Paglia, "Pelosi's Victory for Women."

3. Bowden, "Bossin' Around."

4. Bzdek, *Woman of the House*, 81.

5. Jacobs, *A Rage for Justice*, 496.

6. Ronald Reagan, "A Time for Choosing (aka 'The Speech')," October 27, 1964. Online and available at http://www.americanrhetoric.com/speeches/ronaldreaganatimeforchoosing.htm.

7. Glenn Thrush, "Newt: GOP Would Be 'Clever' to Work with Pelosi," Politico, January 21, 2010. Online and available at http://www.politico.com/blogs/glenn-thrush/0110/Newt_GOP_would_be_clever_to_work_with_Pelosi.html.

8. Tumulty, "Person of the Year 2009."

9. John Bresnahan and Jonathan Allen, "Nancy Pelosi's Brutal Reality Check," Politico, March 1, 2010. Online and available at http://www.politico.com/news/stories/0210/33670.html.

10. Mary Lynn F. Jones, "Woman on Top."

11. Bzdek, *Woman of the House*, 239.

12. Bresnahan and Allen, "Nancy Pelosi's Brutal Reality Check."

13. Sandalow, *Madam Speaker*, 299–300.

INDEX